HOW TO
START A
BUSINESS
IN
ILLINOIS

HOW TO START A BUSINESS IN ILLINOIS

Third Edition

Edwin T. Gania
Mark Warda
Attorneys at Law

SPHINX® PUBLISHING
AN IMPRINT OF SOURCEBOOKS, INC.®
NAPERVILLE, ILLINOIS
www.SphinxLegal.com

Sphinx® Publishing, a imprint of Sourcebooks, Inc.®

<u>Naperville Office</u>
P.O. Box 4410
Naperville, Illinois 60567-4410
630-961-3900
Fax: 630-961-2168
www.sourcebooks.com
www.SphinxLegal.com

This publication is designed to provide accurate and authoritative information in regard to the subject matter covered. It is sold with the understanding that the publisher is not engaged in rendering legal, accounting, or other professional service. If legal advice or other expert assistance is required, the services of a competent professional person should be sought.

From a Declaration of Principles Jointly Adopted by a Committee of the
American Bar Association and a Committee of Publishers and Associations

This product is not a substitute for legal advice.

Disclaimer required by Texas statutes.

Library of Congress Cataloging-in-Publication Data
Gania, Edwin T.
  How to start a business in Illinois / Edwin T. Gania, Mark Warda.-- 3rd ed.
    p. cm. -- (Legal survival guides)
  Includes index.
  ISBN 1-57248-247-8
  1. Business enterprises--Law and legislation--Illinois--Popular works. 2. Business
law--Illinois. I. Title. II. Series

KFI1405.Z9 G36 2002
346.773'065--dc21

                                                            2002030294

Printed and bound in the United States of America.
VHG Paperback — 10 9 8 7 6 5 4 3 2 1

CONTENTS

USING SELF-HELP LAW BOOKS

Before using a self-help law book, you should realize the advantages and disadvantages of doing your own legal work and understand the challenges and diligence that this requires.

THE GROWING TREND

Rest assured that you won't be the first or only person handling your own legal matter. For example, in some states, more than seventy-five percent of divorces and other cases have at least one party representing him or herself. Because of the high cost of legal services, this is a major trend and many courts are struggling to make it easier for people to represent themselves. However, some courts are not happy with people who do not use attorneys and refuse to help them in any way. For some, the attitude is, "Go to the law library and figure it out for yourself."

We at Sphinx write and publish self-help law books to give people an alternative to the often complicated and confusing legal books found in most law libraries. We have made the explanations of the law as simple and easy to understand as possible. Of course, unlike an attorney advising an individual client, we cannot cover every conceivable possibility.

COST/VALUE ANALYSIS

Whenever you shop for a product or service, you are faced with various levels of quality and price. In deciding what product or service to buy, you make a cost/value analysis on the basis of your willingness to pay and the quality you desire.

When buying a car, you decide whether you want transportation, comfort, status, or sex appeal. Accordingly, you decide among such choices as a Neon, a Lincoln, a Rolls Royce, or a Porsche. Before making a decision, you usually weigh the merits of each option against the cost.

When you get a headache, you can take a pain reliever (such as aspirin) or visit a medical specialist for a neurological examination. Given this choice, most people, of course, take a pain reliever, since it costs only pennies; whereas a medical examination costs hundreds of dollars and takes a lot of time. This is usually a logical choice because it is rare to need anything more than a pain reliever for a headache. But in some cases, a headache may indicate a brain tumor and failing to see a specialist right away can result in complications. Should everyone with a headache go to a specialist? Of course not, but people treating their own illnesses must realize that they are betting on the basis of their cost/value analysis of the situation. They are taking the most logical option.

The same cost/value analysis must be made when deciding to do one's own legal work. Many legal situations are very straight forward, requiring a simple form and no complicated analysis. Anyone with a little intelligence and a book of instructions can handle the matter without outside help.

But there is always the chance that complications are involved that only an attorney would notice. To simplify the law into a book like this, several legal cases often must be condensed into a single sentence or paragraph. Otherwise, the book would be several hundred pages long and too complicated for most people. However, this simplification necessarily leaves out many details and nuances that would apply to special or unusual situations. Also, there are many ways to interpret most legal questions. Your case may come before a judge who disagrees with the analysis of our authors.

Therefore, in deciding to use a self-help law book and to do your own legal work, you must realize that you are making a cost/value analysis. You have decided that the money you will save in doing it yourself outweighs the chance that your case will not turn out to your satisfaction. Most people handling their own simple legal matters never have a problem, but occasionally people find that it ended up costing them more to have an attorney straighten out the situation than it would have if they had hired an attorney in the beginning. Keep this in mind if you decide to handle your own case, and be sure to consult an attorney if you feel you might need further guidance.

LOCAL RULES   The next thing to remember is that a book that covers the law for the entire nation, or even for an entire state, cannot possibly include every procedural difference of every county court. Whenever possible, we provide the exact form needed; however, in some areas, each county, or even each judge, may require unique forms and procedures. In our *state* books, our forms usually cover the majority of counties in the state, or provide examples of the type of form that will be required. In our *national* books, our forms are sometimes even more general in nature but are designed to give a good idea of the type of form that will be needed in most locations. Nonetheless, keep in mind that your *state*, county, or judge may have a requirement, or use a form, that is not included in this book.

You should not necessarily expect to be able to get all of the information and resources you need solely from within the pages of this book. This book will serve as your guide, giving you specific information whenever possible and helping you to find out what else you will need to know. This is just like if you decided to build your own backyard deck. You might purchase a book on how to build decks. However, such a book would not include the building codes and permit requirements of every city, town, county, and township in the nation; nor would it include the lumber, nails, saws, hammers, and other materials and tools you would need to actually build the deck. You would use the book as your guide, and then do some work and research involving such matters as whether you need a permit of some kind, what type and grade of wood are available in your area, whether to use hand tools or power tools, and how to use those tools.

Before using the forms in a book like this, you should check with your court clerk to see if there are any local rules of which you should be aware, or local forms you will need to use. Often, such forms will require the same information as the forms in the book but are merely laid out differently, use slightly different language, or use different color paper so the clerks can easily find them. They will sometimes require additional information.

CHANGES IN
THE LAW
Besides being subject to state and local rules and practices, the law is subject to change at any time. The courts and the legislatures of all fifty states are constantly revising the laws. It is possible that while you are reading this book, some aspect of the law is being changed or a court is interpreting a law in a different way. You should always check the most recent statutes, rules and regulations to see what, if any changes have been made.

In most cases, the change will be of minimal significance. A form will be redesigned, additional information will be required, or a waiting period will be extended. As a result, you might need to revise a form, file an extra form, or wait out a longer time period; these types of changes will not usually affect the outcome of your case. On the other hand, sometimes a major part of the law is changed, the entire law in a particular area is rewritten, or a case that was the basis of a central legal point is overruled. In such instances, your entire ability to pursue your case may be impaired.

Again, you should weigh the value of your case against the cost of an attorney and make a decision as to what you believe is in your best interest.

INTRODUCTION

Each year tens of thousands of new corporations are registered in Illinois, and thousands more partnerships and proprietorships open for business. The demand for new businesses keeps growing, and Illinois continues to be a desirable place to start a business.

Be your own boss and be as successful as you dare. But if you do not follow the laws of the state, your progress can be slowed or stopped by government fines, civil judgments, or criminal penalties.

This book is intended to give you the framework for legally opening and operating a business in Illinois. It also includes information on where to find special rules for each type of business. If you have problems that are not covered by this book, you should seek out an attorney who can be available for your ongoing needs.

In order to cover all of the aspects of any business you are thinking of starting, you should read through this entire book, rather than skipping to the parts that look most important. There are many laws that may not sound like they apply to you but do have provisions that will affect your business.

The forms included in this book were the most recent available at the time of publication. It is possible that some may be revised by the time you read this book, but in most cases they will be similar and require the same information.

DECIDING TO START A BUSINESS 1

If you are reading this book, then you have probably made a serious decision to take the plunge and start your own business. You need to know why some succeed while others fail. Knowledge can only help your chances of success. Some of what follows may seem obvious, but to someone wrapped up in a new business idea, some of this information is occasionally overlooked.

KNOW YOUR STRENGTHS

You should consider all of the skills and knowledge that running a successful business needs and decide if you have what it takes. If you do not, it does not necessarily mean you are doomed to be an employee all your life. Perhaps you just need a partner who has the skills you lack, or you can hire the skills you need, or you can structure your business to avoid areas where you are weak. If those suggestions do not work, maybe you can learn the skills you are lacking.

For example, if you are not good at dealing with employees (either you are too passive and get taken advantage of or too tough and scare them off) you can:

- handle product development yourself and have a partner or manager deal with employees;

- take seminars in employee management; or,

- structure your business so that you do not need employees. Either use independent contractors or set yourself up as an independent contractor.

Here are some of the factors to consider when planning your business:

- If it takes months or years before your business turns a profit, do you have the resources to hold out? (Businesses have gone under or been sold just before they were about to take off.)

- Are you willing to put in a lot of overtime to make your business a success? (Owners of businesses do not set their own hours, the businesses set the hours for the owners. Many business owners work long hours seven days a week, but they enjoy running their business more than family picnics or fishing.)

- Are you willing to do the dirtiest or most unpleasant work of the business? (Emergencies come up and employees are not always dependable. You might need to mop up a flooded room, spend a weekend stuffing ten thousand envelopes, or work Christmas if someone calls in sick.)

- Do you know enough about the product or service? Are you aware of the trends in the industry and what changes new technology might bring?

- Do you know enough about accounting and inventory to manage the business? Do you have a good "head for business?" (Some people naturally know how to save money and do things profitably, while others are in the habit of buying the best and the most expensive of everything. The latter can be fatal to a struggling new business.)

- Are you good at managing employees?

- Do you know how to sell your product or service? (You can have the best product on the market but people *do not* beat a path to your door. If you are a wholesaler, shelf space in major stores is hard to get—especially for a new company without a track record, a large line of products, or a large advertising budget.)

● Do you know enough about getting publicity? (The media receive thousands of press releases and announcements each day and most are thrown away. Do not count on free publicity to put your name in front of the public.)

Know Your Business

You need the experience of working in a business as well as the concept of a business. Maybe you always dreamed of running a bed and breakfast or having your own pizza place, and now that you are laid off, you think it is time to use your savings to fulfill your dream. Have you ever worked in such a business? If not, you may have no idea of the day-to-day headaches and problems of the business. Do you really know how much to allow for theft, spoilage, and unhappy customers?

You might feel silly taking an entry level job at a pizza place when you would rather start your own, but it might be the most valuable preparation you could have. A few weeks of seeing how a business operates could mean the difference between success and failure in your new business.

Working in a business as an employee is one of the best ways to be a success at running such a business. New people with new ideas who work in older industries have been known to revolutionize them with obvious improvements that no one before dared to try.

Do the Math

Conventional wisdom says you need a business plan before committing yourself to a new venture, but many businesses are started successfully without one. The owner has a great concept, puts it on the market and it takes off. But you at least need to do some basic calculations to see if the business can make a profit. Here are some examples:

- If you want to start a retail shop, figure out how many people are close enough to become customers, and how many other stores will be competing for those customers. Visit some of those other shops and see how busy they are. Without giving away your plans to compete, ask some general questions like "How is business?" Maybe they will share their frustrations or successes.

- Whether you sell a good or a service, find out how much profit is possible. For example, if you plan to start a house painting company, find out what you will have to pay to hire painters; what it will cost you for all of the insurance, bonding and licensing you will need; and, what the advertising will cost. Figure out how many jobs you can do per month and what other painters are charging.

- Find out if there is a demand for your product or service. Suppose you have designed a beautiful new kind of candle and your friends all say you should open a shop because "everyone will want them." Before making a hundred of them and renting a store, bring a few to craft shows or flea markets and see what happens.

- Figure out what the income and expenses would be for a typical month of your new business. List monthly expenses such as rent, salaries, utilities, insurance, taxes, supplies, advertising, services, and other overhead. Then figure out how much profit you will average from each sale. Next, figure out how many sales you will need to cover your overhead and then divide by the number of business days in the month. Can you reasonably expect that many sales? How will you get those sales?

Most types of businesses have trade associations, which often have figures on the profitability of its members. Some even have start-up kits for people wanting to start businesses. One good source of information on such organizations is the *Encyclopedia of Associations* published by Gale Research Inc., which is available in many library reference sections. Producers of products to the trade often give assistance to small companies getting started to win their loyalty. Contact the largest suppliers of the products your business will be using and see if they can be of help. The Illinois Department of Commerce has useful startup profiles for common businesses on its website. The web address is:

http://www.commerce.state.il.us/doingbusiness/first_stop/thefirst.htm.

SOURCES OF FURTHER GUIDANCE

The following offices offer free or low cost guidance to new businesses.

SCORE Service Corps of Retired Executives is a nonprofit group of retired people who volunteer to give guidance to businesses.

Chicago SCORE
Citicorp Center
500 W. Madison Street, #1250
Chicago, IL   60661
Phone: (312) 353-7724
Fax: (312) 886-5688

Greater Alton SCORE
5800 Godfrey Road
Alden Hall
Godfrey, IL   62035
Phone: (618) 467-2280
Fax: (618) 466-8289

Peoria SCORE
c/o Peoria Chamber of Commerce
124 SW Adams, Suite 300
Peoria, IL   61602
Phone: (309) 676-0755
Fax: (309) 676-7534

Quad Cities SCORE
c/o Chamber of Commerce
622 19th Street
Moline, IL   61265
Phone: (309) 797-0082
Fax: (309) 757-5435

Fox Valley SCORE
1444 N. Farnsworth, Room 504
Aurora IL   60505
Phone: 630-692-1162
Fax: (630) 897-7002

Quincy Tri-State SCORE
c/o Chamber of Commerce
300 Civic Center Plaza, Suite 245
Quincy, IL   62301
Phone: (217) 222-8093
Fax: (217) 222-3033

Decatur SCORE
Milliken University
1184 W. Main Street
Decatur, IL   62522
Phone: (217) 424-6297
Fax: (217) 424-3993

Springfield SCORE
511 West Capitol Avenue
Suite 302
Springfield, IL   62704
Phone: (217) 492-4359
Fax: (217) 492-4867

Southern Illinois SCORE 0374
150 E. Pleasant Hill Road
Box 1
Carbondale, IL   62901
Phone: (618) 453-6654
Fax: (618) 453-5040

Northern Illinois SCORE
515 North Court Street
Rockford, IL   61103
Phone: (815) 962-0122
Fax: (815) 962-0122

SMALL BUSINESS DEVELOPMENT CENTERS

Educational programs for small businesses are offered through the Small Business Development Centers at many Illinois colleges and universities. For further details see:

http://www.commerce.state.il.us/bus/sba.html

Check their programs for courses in any areas in which you are weak. (The development centers are listed in alphabetical order by city.)

Waubonsee Community College
Small Business Development Center
Aurora Campus, 5 East Galena Blvd.
Aurora, IL 60506
Phone: (630) 906-4179
Fax: (630) 892-4668

Southern Illinois University at Carbondale
Small Business Development Center
150 E. Pleasant Hill Road
Carbondale, IL 62901-6702
Phone: (618) 536-2424
Fax: (618) 453-5040

Kaskaskia College
Small Business Development Center
27210 College Road
Centralia, IL 62801
Phone: (618) 545-3380
Fax: (618) 532-4983

Latin American Chamber of Commerce
Small Business Development Center
3512 W. Fullerton
Chicago, IL 60647
Phone: (773) 252-5211
Fax: (773) 252-7065

Greater North Pulaski
Development Corporation
Small Business Development Center
4054 West North Avenue
Chicago, IL 60639
Phone: (773) 384-2262
Fax: (773) 384-3850

Asian American Alliance
Small Business Development Center
222W. Cermak Road, Suite 303
Chicago, IL 60616-1986
Phone: 312-326-2200
Fax: 312-326-0399

Back of the Yards Neighborhood Council
Small Business Development Center
1751 West 47th Street
Chicago, IL 60609
Phone: (773) 523-4419
Fax: (773) 254-3525

Department of Commerce and Community
Affairs - James R. Thompson Center
Small Business Development Center
100 West Randolph, Suite 3-400
Chicago, IL 60601
Phone: (312) 814-6111
Fax: (312) 814-2807

Eighteenth St. Development Corporation
Small Business Development Center
1839 South Carpenter
Chicago, IL 60608
Phone: (312) 733-2270
Fax: (312) 733-7315

Industrial Council of NW Chicago
Small Business Development Center
2023 West Carroll
Chicago, IL 60612
Phone: (312) 421-3941
Fax: (312) 421-1871

North Business and Industrial Council
Small Business Development Center
2500 West Bradley Place
Chicago, IL 60618
Phone: (773) 588-5855
Fax: (773) 588-0734

Women's Business Development Center
Small Business Development Center
8 South Michigan, Suite 400
Chicago, IL 60603
Phone: (312) 853-3477
Fax: (312) 853-0145

Apparel Industry Board
Small Business Development Center
350 N. Orleans, Suite 1047
Chicago, IL 60654
Phone: (312) 836-1041

Midwest Chicago Avenue
Business Association
Small Business Development Center
3709 West Chicago Avenue
Chicago, IL 60651
Phone: (773) 826-4055
Fax: (773) 826-7375

University of Illinois at Chicago
Small Business Development Center
CUB 601 S. Morgan
2231 UH M/C 075
Chicago, IL 60607
Phone: (773) 996-4057
Fax: (773) 996-4567

McHenry County College
Small Business Development Center
8900 U.S. Highway 14
Crystal Lake, IL 60012-2761
Phone: (815) 455-6098
Fax: (815) 455-9319

Danville Area Community College
Small Business Development Center
28 West North Street
Danville, IL 61832
Phone: (217) 442-7232
Fax: (217) 442-6228

University of Illinois Extension
Small Business Development Center
2525 Federal Drive, Suite #1105
Decatur, IL 62526
Phone: (217) 875-8284
Fax: (217) 875-8288

Sauk Valley Community College
Small Business Development Center
173 Illinois Route #2
Dixon, IL 61021-9110
Phone: (815) 288-5511
Fax: (815) 288-5958

Black Hawk College
Small Business Development Center
301 42nd Avenue
East Moline, IL 61244
Phone: (309) 755-2200, Ext. 211
Fax: (309) 755-9847

Department of Commerce and Community
Affairs - State Office Building
Small Business Development Center
10 Collinsville
East St. Louis, IL 62201
Phone: (618) 583-2270
Fax: (618) 583-2274

Southern Illinois University at Edwardsville
Small Business Development Center
Campus Box 1107:
Edwardsville, IL 62026
Phone: (618) 692-2929
Fax: (618) 692-2647

Elgin Community College
Small Business Development Center
1700 Spartan Drive
Elgin, IL 60123
Phone: (847) 888-7488
Fax: (847) 931-3911

Evanston Business and Technology Center
Small Business Development Center
1840 Oak Avenue
Evanston, IL 60201-3670
Phone: (847) 866-1817
Fax: (847) 866-1808

College of DuPage
Small Business Development Center
425 22nd Street
Glen Ellyn, IL 61832
Phone: (630) 942-2771
Fax: (630) 942-3789

Lewis and Clark Community College
Small Business Development Center
5800 Godfrey Road
Godfrey, IL 62035
Phone: (618) 466-3411
Fax: (618) 466-0810

College of Lake County
Small Business Development Center
19351 West Washington Street
Grayslake, IL 60030
Phone: (847) 543-2033
Fax: (847) 223-9371

Southeastern Illinois College
Small Business Development Center
303 S. Commercial Street
Harrisburg, IL 62946-2125
Phone: (618) 252-5001
Fax: (618) 252-0210

Rend Lake College
Small Business Development Center
Route #1
Ina, IL 62846
Phone: (618) 437-5321, ext. 335
Fax: (618) 437-5677, ext. 385

Joliet Junior College
Small Business Development Center
Renaissance Center, Room 312
214 North Ottawa Street
Joliet, IL 60431
Phone: (815) 727-6544, Ext. 1321
Fax: (815) 722-1895

Kankakee Community College
Small Business Development Center
P.O. Box 888
River Road
Kankakee, IL 60901
Phone: (815) 933-0376
Fax: (815) 933-0217

Western Illinois University
Small Business Development Center
214 Seal Hall
Macomb, IL 61455
Phone: (309) 298-2211
Fax: (309) 298-2520

Maple City Business & Technology Center
Small Business Development Center
620 South Main Street
Monmouth, IL 61462-2688
Phone: (309) 734-4664
Fax: (309) 734-8579

Illinois Valley Community College
Small Business Development Center
815 North Orlando Smith Ave., Bldg. 11
Oglesby, IL 61348
Phone: (815) 223-1740
Fax: (815) 224-3033

Illinois Eastern Community College
Small Business Development Center
401 East Main Street
Olney, IL 62450
Phone: (618) 395-3011
Fax: (618) 395-1922

Moraine Valley College
Small Business Development Center
10900 South 88th Avenue
Palos Hills, IL 60465
Phone: (708) 974-5469
Fax: (708) 974-0078

Bradley University
Small Business Development Center
141 North Jobst Hall, First Floor
Peoria, IL 61625
Phone: (309) 677-3075
Fax: (309) 677-3386

Triton College
Small Business Development Center
2000 Fifth Avenue
River Grove, IL 60171
Phone: (708) 456-0300, Ext. 246
Fax: (708) 583-3118

Rock Valley College
Small Business Development Center
1220 Rock Street
Rockford, IL 61110-1437
Phone: (815) 968-4087
Fax: (815) 968-4157

Illinois Small Business Development Center
Department of Commerce
and Community Affairs
620 East Adams Street, Third Floor
Springfield, IL 62701
Phone: (217) 524-0171
Fax: (217) 785-6328

Illinois Easter Seal Society
Small Business Development Center
2715 South 4th Street
Springfield, IL 62703
Phone: (217) 525-0398
Fax: (217) 525-0442

Lincoln Land Community College
Small Business Development Center
100 North Eleventh Street
Springfield, IL 62703
Phone: (217) 789-1017
Fax: (217) 789-0958

Shawnee Community College
Small Business Development Center
Shawnee College Road
Ullin, IL 62992
Phone: (618) 634-9618
Fax: (618) 634-9028

Governors State University
Small Business Development Center
College of Business, Room C-3305
University Park, IL 60466
Phone: (708) 534-4929
Fax: (708) 534-8457

Choosing the Form of Your Business 2

Basic Forms of Doing Business

An important decision you will need to make at the outset is the choice of legal structure for your business. There are numerous factors that will need to be considered to make the correct decision for your particular business. The most important consideration is that the corporate form will limit your liability for business debts and adverse judgments solely to the corporate assets as opposed to your own personal assets.

The four most popular forms for a business in Illinois are sole proprietorship, partnership, corporation, and limited liability company. However, bear in mind that limited liability will only hold up if the corporate entity is maintained separate and apart from the owner. If there is an intermingling of monies between the corporate and the owner's individual accounts, then the owner may become personally liable for business debts, despite the corporate form. The characteristics, advantages and disadvantages of each form of business are as follows:

SOLE PROPRIETORSHIP

Characteristics. A sole proprietorship is one person doing business in his or her own name or under a fictitious name.

Advantages. A sole proprietorship has simplicity. Plus, there is no organizational expense and no extra tax forms or reports.

Disadvantages. The proprietor is personally liable for all debts and obligations. Also, there is no continuation of the business after death. All profits are directly taxable, certainly a disadvantage for the proprietor, and business affairs are easily mixed with personal affairs.

PARTNERSHIP

Characteristics. A general partnership involves two or more people carrying on a business together, normally pursuant to a partnership agreement, and sharing the profits and losses.

Advantages. Partners can combine expertise and assets. A general partnership also allows liability to be spread among more people. The business can be continued after the death of a partner if bought out by surviving partner.

Disadvantages. Each partner is liable for acts of other partners within the scope of the business. This means that if your partner harms a customer or signs a million-dollar credit line in the partnership name, you can be personally liable. Even if left in the business, all profits are taxable. There are two more disadvantages: control is shared by all parties and the death of a partner may result in liquidation. In a general partnership, it is often difficult to get rid of a bad partner.

CORPORATION

Characteristics. A corporation is an artificial, legal "person" that conducts the business through its officers for its shareholders. (In Illinois, one person may form a corporation and be the sole shareholder and officer). Laws governing corporations are contained in Illinois Compiled Statutes (Ill. Comp. Stat.) Title 805, Section 5.

An *S corporation* is a corporation that has filed IRS Form 2553 choosing to have all profits taxed to the shareholders, rather than to the corporation. An S corporation files a tax return but pays no federal or state tax. The profit shown on the S corporation tax return is reported on each owner's tax returns.

A C *corporation* is any corporation that has not elected to be taxed as an S corporation. A C corporation pays income tax on its profits. The effect of this is when dividends are paid to shareholders they are taxed twice, once by the corporation and once when they are paid to the shareholders. In Illinois, a C corporation must also pay corporate income tax.

A *professional service corporation* is a corporation formed by a professional such as a doctor or accountant. Illinois has special rules for professional service corporations which differ slightly from those of other corporations. These are included in Ill. Comp. Stat. Title 805, Section 10. There are also special tax rules for professional service corporations.

A *nonprofit corporation* is usually used for organizations such as churches and condominium associations. However, with careful planning, some types of businesses can be set up as nonprofit corporations and save a fortune in taxes. While a nonprofit corporation cannot pay dividends, it can pay its officers and employees fair salaries. Some of the major American nonprofit organizations pay their officers well over $100,000 a year. Illinois' special rules for nonprofit corporations are included in Ill. Comp. Stat. Title 805 Section 105.

Advantages. If properly organized, shareholders have no liability for corporate debts and lawsuits, and officers usually have no personal liability for their corporate actions. The existence of a corporation may be perpetual. There are tax advantages allowed only to corporations. There is prestige in owning a corporation. There are two excellent advantages: capital may be raised by issuing stock and it is easy to transfer ownership upon death. A small corporation can be set up as an S corporation to avoid corporate taxes but still retain corporate advantages. Some types of businesses can be set up as nonprofit corporations, which provide significant tax savings.

Disadvantages. The start-up costs for forming a corporation are certainly a disadvantage; plus, there are certain formalities such as annual meetings, separate bank accounts, and tax forms. Unless a corporation registers as an S corporation, it must pay federal income tax separate from the tax paid by the owners, and must pay Illinois income tax.

LIMITED
PARTNERSHIP

Characteristics. A limited partnership has characteristics similar to both a corporation and a partnership. There are *general partners* who have the control and liability, and there are *limited partners* who only put up money and whose liability is limited to what they paid for their share of the partnership (like corporate stock).

Advantages. Capital can be contributed by limited partners who have no control of the business or liability for its debts.

Disadvantages. High start-up costs are a great disadvantage. Also, an extensive partnership agreement is required because general partners are personally liable for partnership debts and for each other's acts. (One solution to this problem is to use a corporation as the general partner.)

LIMITED
LIABILITY
COMPANY
(LLC)

Characteristics. Illinois was the eighteenth state in the United States to allow a limited liability company. This relatively new invention is like a limited partnership without general partners. It has characteristics of both a corporation and a partnership. It is fast becoming the first choice of small business owners. None of the partners have liability and all can have some control.

Advantages. The limited liability company offers the tax benefits of a partnership with the protection from liability of a corporation. It offers more tax benefits than an S corporation because it may pass through more depreciation and deductions, it may have different classes of ownership, an unlimited number of members, and may have aliens as members.

Disadvantages. Start-up and annual fees are higher than for a corporation. LLCs pay social security tax on all profits (up to a limit), whereas S corporation profits are exempt from social security tax. LLCs must also pay Illinois corporate income tax. Because a limited liability company is a new invention, there are not a lot of answers to legal questions that may arise. (However, the courts will probably rely on corporation and limited partnership law.)

LIMITED
LIABILITY
PARTNERSHIP
(LLP)

Characteristics. The limited liability partnership is like a general partnership without personal liability. It was devised to allow partnerships of lawyers and other professionals to limit their personal liability without losing their partnership structure. This was important because converting to an LLC could have tax consequences, and some states do not allow professionals to operate as LLCs. Both general and limited partnerships can register as LLPs.

Advantages. The limited liability partnership offers the flexibility and tax benefits of a partnership with the protection from liability of a - corporation.

Disadvantages. Start-up and annual fees are higher for LLPs than for corporations. Also, the law requires the partnership to maintain certain minimum insurance.

The selection of a form of doing business is best made with the advice of an accountant and an attorney. If you were selling harmless objects by mail, a sole proprietorship would be the easiest way to get started. But if you own a taxi service, it would be important to incorporate to avoid losing your personal assets if one of your drivers were to injure someone in an accident where the damages could exceed your insurance. If you can expect a high cash buildup the first year, then a corporation may be the best way to keep taxes low. If you expect the usual start-up losses, then a proprietorship, partnership, or S corporation would probably be best.

While the above list may seem overwhelming at first, as a practical matter the majority of Illinois' nearly seven hundred thousand businesses are either a sole proprietorship or corporation. Keep in mind that you can change the structure of your business at any time if needed. It is best to keep things simple at first and wait for a clear need to develop before adopting a more complex business structure.

START-UP PROCEDURES

PROPRIETORSHIP

In a proprietorship, all accounts, property, and licenses are taken in the name of the owner. (See Chapter 3 for information about using an assumed name.

PARTNERSHIP

To form a partnership, a written agreement should be prepared to spell out the rights and obligations of the parties. (See Chapter 3 for using an assumed name.) In most cases, licenses can be in either the name of the partnership or in the names of the partners.

CORPORATION	Articles of Incorporation must be filed with the Secretary of State in Springfield along with $75 in filing fees and an additional amount for the franchise tax. An organizational meeting is then held. At the meeting, officers are elected, stock issued, and other formalities are complied with to avoid the corporate entity being set aside later. It is very important to maintain the corporation as a separate entity from its owners in order to preserve limited liability. Licenses and accounts are titled in the name of the corporation.
LIMITED PARTNERSHIP	A written limited partnership agreement must be drawn up and registered with the Secretary of State in Springfield, and a lengthy disclosure document given to all prospective limited partners. Because of the complexity of securities laws and the criminal penalties for violation, it is advantageous to have an attorney organize a limited partnership.
LIMITED LIABILITY COMPANY	One or more persons may form a limited liability company by filing articles of organization with the Secretary of State in Springfield. Licenses and accounts are in the name of the company.
LIMITED LIABILITY PARTNERSHIP	Two or more persons may form a limited liability partnership by filing a Statement of Registration of Illinois Registered Limited Liability Partnership with the Secretary of State in Springfield. Licenses and accounts are in the name of the company.

BUSINESS COMPARISON CHART

	Sole Proprietorship	General Partnership	Limited Partnership	Limited Liability Co.	Corporation C or S	Nonprofit Corporation
Liability Protection	No	No	For limited partners	For all members	For all shareholders	For all members
Taxes	Pass through	Pass through	Pass through	Pass through	S corps. pass through C corps. pay tax	None on income Employees pay on wages
Minimum # of members	1	2	2	1	1	3
Startup fee	None	None	$75	$400	$75 plus 0.15% (min. $25)	$50
Annual fee	None	None	$75	$400 or $500	$25 plus of paid-in capital	$5
Diff. classes of ownership	No	Yes	Yes	Yes	S corps. No C corps. Yes	No ownership Diff. classes of membership
Survives after Death	No	No	Yes	Yes	Yes	Yes
Best for	1 person low-risk business or no assets	low-risk business	low-risk business with silent partners	All types of businesses	All types of businesses	Educational Charitable

Registering the Name of Your Business 3

Preliminary Considerations

Before deciding upon a name for your business, you should be sure that it is not already being used by someone else. Many business owners have spent thousands of dollars on publicity and printing only to throw it all away because another company owned the name. A company that owns a name can take you to court and force you to stop using that name. It can also sue you for damages if it thinks your use of the name cost it a financial loss.

If you will be running a small local shop with no plans for expansion you should at least check if the name has been trademarked. If someone else is using the same name anywhere in the country and has registered it as a federal trademark, they can sue you. If you plan to expand or to deal nationally you should do a thorough search of the name.

The first places to look are the local phone books and official records of your county. Next, you should check with the Secretary of State's office in Springfield to see if someone has registered a fictitious name or corporate name the same as, or confusingly similar to, the one you have chosen. This can be done either by calling them or by visiting their Internet site:

http://www.sos.state.il.us/departments/business_services/corpnames.html

To do a national search, you should check trade directories and phone books of major cities. These can be found at many libraries and are usually reference books which cannot be checked out. The *Trade Names Directory*, published by Gale Research Co., is a two volume set of names compiled from many sources.

If you have a computer with internet access you can use it to search all of the yellow page listings in the U.S. for no charge at a number of sites. One website, **http://www.infoseek.com**, offers free searches of yellow pages for all states at once.

To be sure that your use of the name does not violate someone else's trademark rights you should have a trademark search done in the United States Patent and Trademark Office. In the past, this required a visit to their offices or the hiring of a search which can cost over a hundred dollars. But in 1999, the USPTO put its trademark records online and you can now search them at:

http://www.uspto.gov/main/trademarks.htm

If you do not have access to the internet you might be able to do it at a public library or to have one of their employees order an online search for you for a small fee. If this is not available to you, you can have the search done through a firm. One such firm is Government Liaison Services, Inc., P.O. Box 10648, Arlington, VA 22210. The firm can be reached at 800-642-6564. It also offers searches of one hundred trade directories and 4800 phone books.

No matter how thorough your search is, there is no guarantee that there is not a local user somewhere with rights to the mark. If, for example, you register a name for a new chain of restaurants and later find out that someone in Tucumcari, New Mexico has been using the name longer than you, that person will still have the right to use the name, but just in his or her local area. If you do not want his or her restaurant to cause confusion with your chain, you can try to buy him or her out. Similarly, if you are operating a small business under a unique name and a law firm in New York writes and offers to buy the right to your name, you can assume that some large corporation wants to start a major expansion under that name.

The best way to make sure a name you are using is not already owned by someone else is to make up a name. Such names as Xerox, Kodak, and Exxon were made up and didn't have any meaning prior to their use. Remember that there are millions of businesses and even something you make up may already be in use. It is safer to do a search anyway.

ASSUMED NAMES

In Illinois as in most states, unless you do business in your own legal name, you must register the name you are using. The name must be registered in each county where you intend to conduct business. The registration costs only $5 and does not have to be renewed.

It is a misdemeanor to fail to register an assumed name, and you may not sue anyone unless you are registered. If someone sues you and you are not registered, they may be entitled to attorney's fees and court costs.

If your name is *John Doe* and you are operating a masonry business, you may operate your business as *John Doe, Mason* without registering it. But any other use of a name should be registered, such as:

Doe Masonry	Doe Masonry Company
Doe Company	Illinois Masonry

You cannot use the words, "Corporation," "Incorporated," "Corp.," or "Inc." unless you are a corporation. However, corporations do not have to register the name they are using unless it is different from their registered corporate name.

Professionals licensed by the Department of Professional Regulation do not have to register the names under which they practice their profession.

When you use a fictitious name you are "doing business as" (d/b/a) whatever name you are using. Legally, you would use the name "John Doe d/b/a Doe Masonry."

To register an assumed name, you must first file an application with the county clerk. (See Appendix D for the blank form.) Unlike corporate names and trademarks, which are carefully screened by the Secretary of State to avoid duplication, fictitious name registrations are accepted without regard to who else is using the name. If you apply for registration of a trademark or corporate name, the Secretary of State will check all other registrations and refuse registration if the name or a similar name is already registered. However, the registration of a fictitious name does not bestow any rights to the name upon the registrant; it is merely notice to the world of who is behind the business. So the county clerk will allow anyone to register any name, even if one hundred others have already registered that name.

As discussed in Chapter 1, you should do some research to see if the name you intend to use is already being used by anyone else. Even persons who have not registered a name can acquire some legal rights to the name simply through use.

Some businesses have special requirements for registration of their fictitious names. For example, a private investigative agency must obtain permission from the Department of Business and Professional Regulation for the use of its proposed name prior to obtaining its license from the state. Other businesses may have similar requirements. (See Chapter 6 for a list of state regulated professions with references to the laws which apply to them.)

Fictitious name instructions and a sample filled-in form are included Appendix C. A blank form is included in Appendix D. (see form 2, p.189.)

Next, you must place an ad in a newspaper of general circulation in the county in which you will be maintaining your principal place of business, announcing your intent to use the name. The ad only has to be run once a week for three consecutive weeks, and would usually be placed in the classified section under "Legal Notices." It could be worded as follows:

> Notice is hereby given, pursuant to "An Act in relation to the use of an Assumed Business Name in the conduct or transaction of Business in the State," as amended, that a certification was filed by the undersigned with the Recorder of Deeds, Cook County.
>
> Under the Assumed Name of <u>DOE COMPANY</u> with the business located at <u>1234 W. Main Street, Chicago, IL 60601</u>.
>
> The true name(s) and residence address of the owner(s) are:
>
> <u>JOHN DOE</u>   <u>1234 W. Main Street, Chicago, IL 60601</u>
>
> <u>JIM DOE</u>   <u>2550 W. Maple Street, Chicago, IL 60601</u>

You should compare rates before placing the ad. Many counties have weekly newspapers that specialize in legal ads and charge a third of what the large newspapers charge. In Chicago, or anywhere in Cook County, you may place an ad in the *Chicago Law Bulletin*. To do so, call 312-644-7800.

CORPORATE NAMES

A corporation does not have to register a fictitious name because it already has a legal name. The name of a corporation must contain one of the following words:

Incorporated	Inc.
Company	Co.
Corporation	Corp.
Limited	Ltd.

It is not advisable to use only the word "Company" or "Co." because unincorporated businesses also use these words; a person dealing with you might not realize you are incorporated. If this happens, you might end up with personal liability for corporate debts. Instead, you can use a combination of two of the words, such as ABC Co., Inc.

If the name of the corporation does not contain one of the above words, it will be rejected by the Secretary of State. It will also be rejected if the name is already taken, is similar to the name of another corporation, or it uses a forbidden word such as "Bank" or "Trust." To check on a name, you may call the corporate name information number in Springfield, 217-782-9520, or you can also check their website listed on page 19.

If a name you pick is taken by another company, you may be able to change it slightly and have it accepted. For example, if there is already a Tri-City Upholstery, Inc., and it is in a different county, you may be allowed to use Tri-City Upholstery of Cook County, Inc. However, even if this is approved by the Secretary of State, you might get sued by the other company if your business is close to theirs or there is a likelihood of confusion.

Also, don't have anything printed until your corporate papers are returned to you. Sometimes a name is approved over the phone and rejected when submitted. Once you have chosen a corporate name and know it is available, you should immediately register your corporation. A name can be reserved for ninety days for $20, nonetheless, it is easier to register the corporation than to waste time on the name reservation.

If a corporation wants to do business under a name other than its corporate name, it can register a fictitious name such as "Doe Corporation d/b/a Doe Industries." But if the name used leads people to believe that the business is not a corporation, the right to limited liability may be lost. If such a name is used it should always be accompanied by the corporate name.

PROFESSIONAL SERVICE CORPORATIONS

Professional service corporations are corporations formed by professionals such as attorneys, doctors, dentists and architects. Under Illinois law, a professional corporation cannot use the usual corporate designations, Inc., Corp., or Co., but must use one of the following words or abbreviations: "Chartered," "Limited," "Ltd.," "Professional Corporation," "Prof. Corp.," or "P.C."

DOMAIN NAMES

With the Internet changing so rapidly, all of the rules for Internet names have not yet been worked out. Originally, the first person to reserve a name owned it, and enterprising souls bought up the names of most of the fortune 500 corporations. Then a few of the corporations went to court and the rule was developed that if a company had a trademark for a name, that company could stop someone else from using it if the other person did not have a trademark. More recently, Congress made it illegal for "cybersquatters" to register the names of famous persons and companies.

You cannot yet get a trademark merely for using a domain name. Trademarks are granted for the use of a name in commerce. Once you have a valid trademark, you will be safe using it for your domain name.

If you wish to protect your domain name, the best thing to do at this point is to get a trademark for it. To do this, you would have to use it on your goods or services. The following section gives some basic information about trademarks.

To find out if a domain name is available, go to:
http://www.whois.net

TRADEMARKS

As your business builds goodwill, its name will become more valuable and you will want to protect it from others who may wish to copy it. To protect a name used to describe your goods or services, you can register it as a trademark (for goods) or a service mark (for services) with either the Illinois Secretary of State or with the United States Patent and Trademark Office.

You cannot obtain a trademark for the name of your business, but you can trademark the name you use on your goods and services. In most cases, you use your company name on your goods as your trademark. In effect, it protects your company name. Another way to protect your company name is to incorporate, because particular corporate name can only be registered by one company in Illinois.

State registration would be useful if you only expect to use your trademark within the state of Illinois. Federal registration would protect your mark anywhere in the country. The registration of a mark gives you exclusive use of the mark for the types of goods it is registered. The only exception is those who have already been using the mark. You cannot stop people who have been using the mark prior to your registration. (It is much cheaper to register with the Secretary of State and the protection provided is adequate within the state.)

ILLINOIS
REGISTRATION

The procedure for state registration is simple and costs only $10. First, you should write to the Secretary of State's Office, Department of Business Services Trademarks, Room 328 Howlett Building, Springfield, IL 62756, or call 217-524-0400 to ask them to search your name and tell you if it is available.

Before a mark can be registered, it must be used in Illinois. For goods this means it must be used on the goods themselves, or on containers, tags, labels or displays of the goods. For services it must be used in the sale or advertising of the services. The use must be in an actual transaction with a customer. A sample mailed to a friend is not considered an acceptable use.

The $10 fee will register the mark in only one "class of goods." If the mark is used on more than one class of goods a separate registration must be filed. The registration is good for ten years. Six months prior to its expiration it must be renewed. The renewal fee is $5 for each class of goods.

Many of the forms you may need are included in this book. Be sure to check Appendices C and D. You can also get information and forms from the Illinois Secretary of State's office. Their web site is: **http://www.sos.state.il.us/depts/bus_serv/trademark.html** and their addresses are:

Springfield Office:
Room 328 Howlett Bldg.
Springfield, IL 62756
Hours: M-F 8 A.M. - 4:30 P.M.

Chicago Office:
17 North State Street, Suite 1137
Chicago, IL 60602
Hours: M-F 8:30 A.M. - 5 P.M.

FEDERAL REGISTRATION

For federal registration, the procedure is a little more complicated. There are two types of applications, depending on whether you have already made actual use of the mark or whether you merely have an intention to use the mark in the future.

For a trademark that has been in use, you must file an application form along with specimens showing actual use and a drawing of the mark that complies with all of the rules of the United States Patent and Trademark Office.

For an intent to use application, you must file two separate forms, one when you make the initial application and the other after you have made actual use of the mark, as well as the specimens and drawing.

Before a mark can be entitled to federal registration the use of the mark must be in "interstate commerce," or in commerce with another country. The fee for registration is $245, but if you file an intent to use application, there is a second fee of $100 for the filing after actual use.

FINANCING YOUR BUSINESS 4

The way to finance your business is determined by how fast you want your business to grow and how much risk of failure you are able to handle. Letting the business grow with its own income is the slowest but safest way to grow. Taking out a personal loan against your house to expand quickly is the fastest but riskiest route.

GROWING WITH PROFITS

Many successful businesses have started out with little money and used the profits to grow bigger. If you have another source of income to live on (such as a job or a spouse) you can plow all the income of your fledgling business into growth.

Some businesses start as hobbies or part time ventures on the weekend while the entrepreneur holds down a full time job. Many types of goods or services businesses can start this way. Even some multi-million dollar corporations, such as Apple Computer, began this way.

This way you have no risk. If you find you are not good at running that type of business, or the time or location was not right for your idea, all you are out is the time you spent and your start-up capital.

However, a business can only grow so big from its own income. In many cases as a business grows, the orders become so big that money must be borrowed to fill them. With this kind of order there is the risk that if the customer cannot pay or goes bankrupt, the business will also fail. At such a point a business owner should investigate the credit worthiness of the customer and weigh the risks. Some businesses have grown rapidly, some have gone under, and others have decided not to take the risk and stayed small. You can worry about that down the road.

Using Your Savings

When possible, the best source to get your business started is savings. If you have savings you can tap to get your business started, that is the best source. You won't have to pay high interest rates and you will not have to worry about paying someone back, such as relatives.

HOME EQUITY

If you have owned your home for several years, it is possible that the equity has grown substantially and you can get a second mortgage to finance your business. Some lenders will make second mortgages that exceed the equity if you have been in the home for many years and have a good record of paying your bills. Just remember, if your business fails you may lose your house.

RETIREMENT ACCOUNTS

Be careful about borrowing from your retirement savings. There are tax penalties for borrowing from or against certain types of retirement accounts. Also, your future financial security may be lost if your business does not succeed.

HAVING TOO MUCH MONEY

It probably does not seem possible to have too much money to start a business with, but many businesses have failed for that reason. With plenty of start-up capital available, a business owner does not need to watch expenses and can become wasteful. Employees get used to lavish spending. Once the money runs out and the business must rely on its own earnings, it fails.

Starting with the bare minimum forces a business to watch its expenses and be frugal. It necessitates finding the least expensive solutions to problems that crop up and creative ways to be productive.

Borrowing Money

It is extremely tempting to look to others to get the money to start a business. The risk of failure is less worrisome and the pressure is lower, but that is a problem with borrowing. If it is other people's money, you do not have quite the same incentive to succeed as when everything you own is on the line.

Actually, you should be even more concerned when using the money of others. Your reputation should be more valuable than the money itself, which can always be replaced. Yet that is not always the case. How many people borrow again and again from their parents for failed business ventures?

FAMILY Depending on how much money your family can spare, it may be the most comfortable or most uncomfortable source of funds for you. If you have been assured a large inheritance and your parents have more funds than they need to live, you may be able to borrow against your inheritance without worry. It will be your money anyway and you need it much more now than you will in ten or twenty or more years. If you lose it all, it is your own loss anyway.

However, if you are borrowing your widowed mother's source of income, asking her to cash in a CD she lives on to finance your get-rich-quick scheme, you should have second thoughts. Stop and consider all the real reasons your business might not take off and what your mother would do without the income.

FRIENDS Borrowing from friends is like borrowing from family members. If you know they have the funds available and could survive a loss, you may want to risk it; if they would be loaning you their only resources, do not chance it.

Financial problems can be the worst thing for a relationship, whether it is a casual friendship or a long term romantic involvement. Before you borrow from a friend, try to imagine what would happen if you could not pay it back and how you would feel if it caused the end of your relationship.

The ideal situation is for your friend to be a co-venturer in your business. Then the burden would not be entirely on you to see how the funds were spent. Still, realize that such a venture will put extra strain on the relationship.

BANKS

In a way, a bank can be a more comfortable party to borrow from because you do not have a personal relationship with them as you do with a friend or family member. If you fail, they will write off your loan rather than disown you. But a bank can be the least comfortable party to borrow from because they will demand realistic projections and be on top of you to perform. If you do not meet their expectations, they may call your loan just when you need it most.

The best thing about a bank loan is that they will require you to do your homework: you must have plans that make sense to a banker. If they approve your loan, you know that your plans are at least reasonable.

Bank loans are not cheap or easy. You will be paying a good interest rate, and you will have to put up collateral. If your business does not have equipment or receivables, they may require you to put up your house and other personal property to guarantee the loan.

Banks are a little easier to deal with when you get a Small Business Administration (SBA) loan. That is because the SBA guarantees that it will pay the bank if you default on the loan. SBA loans are obtained through local bank branches.

CREDIT CARDS

Borrowing against a credit card is one of the fastest growing ways of financing a business, but it can be one of the most expensive ways. The rates can go higher than twenty percent, but many cards offer lower rates and some people are able to get numerous cards. Some successful businesses have used the partners' credit cards to get off the ground or to weather through a cash crunch, but if the business does not begin to generate the cash to make the payments, you could soon end up in bankruptcy. A good strategy is only to use credit cards for a long term asset, like a computer, or for something that will quickly generate cash, like buying inventory to fill an order. Do not use credit cards to pay expenses that are not generating revenue.

A Rich Partner

One of the best business combinations is a young entrepreneur with ideas and ambition and a retired investor with business experience and money. Together they can supply everything the business needs.

How to find such a partner? Be creative. You should have investigated the business you are starting and know others who have been in such businesses. Have any of them had partners retire over the last few years? Are any of them planning to phase out of the business?

Selling Shares of Your Business

Silent investors are the best source of capital for your business. You retain full control of the business and if it happens to fail, you have no obligation to them. Unfortunately, few silent investors are interested in a new business. It is only after you have proved your concept to be successful and built up a rather large enterprise that you will be able to attract such investors.

The most common way to obtain money from investors is to issue stock to them. For this, the best type of business entity is the corporation. It gives you almost unlimited flexibility in the number and kinds of shares of stock you can issue.

Securities Laws

There is one major problem with selling stock in your business: complying with all of the federal and state regulations There are also hundreds of court cases attempting to explain what these laws mean. Obviously, a thorough explanation of this area of law is beyond the scope of this book.

Basically, securities have been held to exist in any case in which a person provides money to someone with the expectation that he or she will get a profit through the efforts of that person. This can apply to any situation where someone buys stock in, or makes a loan to, your business. What the laws require is disclosure of the risks involved, and in some cases, registration of the securities with the government. There are some exemptions, such as for small amounts of money and for limited numbers of investors.

Penalties for violation of securities laws are severe, including triple damages and prison terms. You should consult a specialist in securities laws before issuing any security. You can often get an introductory consultation at a reasonable rate to explain your options.

USING THE INTERNET TO FIND CAPITAL

In 1995, the owners of Wit Beer made headlines in all the business magazines by successfully raising $1.6 million for their business on the Internet. It seemed so easy, every business wanted to try. What was not made clear in most of the stories was that the owner was a corporate securities lawyer, and he did all of the necessary legal work to prepare a prospectus and properly register the stock, something which would have cost anyone else over $100,000 in legal fees. Also, most of the interest in the stock came from the articles, not from the Internet promotion. Today, a similar effort would probably not be nearly as successful.

Before attempting to market your company's shares on the Internet, be sure to get an opinion from a securities lawyer or do some serious research into securities laws. The lawyer who marketed Wit Beer's shares on the Internet has started a business to advise others on raising capital. It is Wit SoundView Corporation located at 826 Broadway, 7th Floor, New York, NY 10003.

http://www.witcapital.com/home/index.jsp

The Internet does have some sources of capital listed; however, the following sites may be helpful.

America's Business Funding Directory:
http://www.businessfinance.com

Angel Capital Electronic Network (SBA): http://www.sba.gov

Inc. Magazine: http://mothra.inc.com/finance

NVST: http://www.nvst.com

The Capital Network: http://www.thecapitalnetwork.com

LOCATING YOUR BUSINESS 5

The right location for your business will be determined by what type of business it is and how fast you expect to grow. For some types of businesses, the location will not be important to your success or failure; in others, it will be crucial.

WORKING OUT OF YOUR HOME

Many small businesses get started out of the home. Chapter 6 discusses the *legalities* of home businesses. This section discusses the *practicalities*.

Starting a business out of your home can save you the rent, electricity, insurance, and other costs of setting up at another location. For some people this is ideal, and they can combine their home and work duties easily and efficiently. However, for other people it is a disaster. A spouse, children, neighbors, television, and household chores can be so distracting that no other work gets done.

Since residential rates are usually lower than business lines, many people use their residential telephone line or add a second residential line to conduct business. However, if you wish to be listed in the yellow pages, you will need to have a business line in your home. If you are running two or more types of businesses, you can probably add their names as additional listings on the original number and avoid paying for another business line.

You also should consider whether the type of business you are starting is compatible with a home office. For example, if your business mostly consists of making phone calls or calling clients, then the home may be an ideal place. If your clients need to visit you or you will need daily pickups and deliveries by truck, the home may not be a good location. This is discussed in more detail in the next chapter.

CHOOSING A RETAIL SITE

For most types of retail stores the location is of prime importance. Such things to consider are: how close it is to your potential customers, how visible it is to the public, and how easily accessible it is to both autos and pedestrians. The attractiveness and safety should also be considered.

Location would be less important for a business that is the only one of its kind in the area. For example, if there was only one moped parts dealer or Armenian restaurant in a metropolitan area, people would have to come to wherever you are if they want your products or services. However, even with such businesses, keep in mind that there is competition. People who want moped parts can order them by mail and restaurant customers can choose another type of cuisine.

You should look up all the businesses like the one you are planning in the phone book and mark them on a map. For some businesses, like a cleaners, you would want to be far from the others. But for other businesses, like antique stores, you would want to be near the others. Since antique stores usually do not carry the same things, they do not compete and people like to go to an "antique district" and visit all the shops.

Choosing Office, Manufacturing, or Warehouse Space

If your business will be the type where customers will not come to you, then of course locating it near customers is not as much of a concern. You can probably save money by locating away from the high traffic, central business districts. However, you should consider the convenience for employees, and not locate in an area that would be unattractive to them or too far from where they would likely live.

For manufacturing or warehouse operations, you should consider your proximity to a post office, trucking company, or rail line. Where several sites are available, you might consider which one has the earliest or most convenient pick-up schedule for the carriers you plan to use.

Leasing a Site

A lease of space can be one of the biggest expenses of a small business, so you should do a lot of homework before signing one. There are a lot of terms in a commercial lease which can make or break your business. These are the most critical:

ZONING

Before signing a lease, you should be sure everything your business will need to do is allowed by the zoning of the property.

RESTRICTIONS

In some shopping centers, existing tenants have guarantees that other tenants do not compete with them. For example, if you plan to open a restaurant and bakery, you may be forbidden to sell carry-out baked goods if the supermarket has a bakery and a noncompete clause.

SIGNS

Business signs are regulated by zoning laws, sign laws, and property restrictions. If you rent a hidden location with no possibility for adequate signage, your business will have a much smaller chance of success than with a more visible site or a much larger sign.

ADA COMPLIANCE — The Americans with Disabilities Act requires that reasonable accommodations be made so businesses are accessible to the handicapped. When a business is remodeled, many more changes are required than if no remodeling is done. When renting space, you should be sure that it complies with the law, or that the landlord will be responsible for compliance, or be aware of the full costs you will bear.

EXPANSION — As your business grows, you may need to expand your space. The time to find out about your options is before you sign the lease. Perhaps you you can take over adjoining units when those leases expire.

RENEWAL — For some businesses, location is a key to success. If you spend five years building up clientele, you do not want someone to take over the locale at the end of your lease. Therefore, you should have a renewal clause in your lease. Usually this allows for an increase in rent based on inflation.

GUARANTEE — Most landlords of commercial space will not rent to a small corporation without a personal guarantee of the lease. This is a very risky thing for a new business owner. The lifetime rent on a long term commercial lease can be hundreds of thousands of dollars, and if your business fails the last thing you want to be is personally responsible for five years of rent.

Where space is scarce or a location is hot, a landlord can get the guarantees he or she demands and there is nothing you can do about it (except perhaps set up an asset protection plan ahead of time). But where several units are vacant or the commercial rental market is soft, you can often negotiate out of the personal guarantee. If the lease is five years, maybe you can get away with a guarantee of just the first year.

DUTY TO OPEN — Some shopping centers have rules requiring all shops to be open certain hours. If you can't afford to staff it the whole time required, or if you have religious or other reasons that make this a problem, you should negotiate it out of the lease or find another location.

SUBLEASE — At some point you may decide to sell your business, and in many cases is most valuable aspect is the location. For this reason, you should be sure you have the right to either assign your lease or to sublease the property. If this is impossible, one way around a prohibition is to incorporate your business before signing the lease, and when you sell the business, also sell the stock. Nonetheless, some lease clauses prohibit transfer of "any interest" in the business, so read the lease carefully.

BUYING A SITE

If you are experienced with owning rental property, you will probably be more inclined to buy a site for your business. If you have no experience with real estate, you should probably rent and not take on the extra cost and responsibility of buying.

One reason to buy your site is to build up equity. Rather than pay rent to a landlord, you can pay off a mortgage and eventually own the property.

SEPARATING THE OWNERSHIP

One risk in buying a business site is if the business gets into financial trouble, the creditors may go after the building as well. For this reason, most people who buy a site for their business keep the ownership out of the business. For example, the business will be a corporation and the real estate will be owned personally by the owner or by a trust unrelated to the business.

EXPANSION

Before buying a site, you should consider the growth potential of your business. If it grows quickly will you be able to expand at that site or will you have to move? Might the property next door be available for sale in the future if you need it? Can you get an option on it?

If the site is a good investment whether or not you have your business then by all means, buy it. But if its main use is for your business, think twice.

ZONING

Some of the concerns when buying a site are the same as when renting. You will want to make sure the zoning permits the type of business you wish to start, or you can get a variance without a large expense or delay. Be aware that just because a business is now using the site does not mean you can expand or remodel the business at that site. Some zoning laws allow businesses to be grandfathered in, but not to expand. Check with the zoning department and find out exactly what is allowed.

SIGNS   Signs are another concern. Some cities have regulated signs and do not allow new ones, or require them to be smaller. Some businesses have used these laws to get publicity. A car dealer who was told to take down a large number of American flags on his lot filed a federal lawsuit and rallied the community behind him.

ADA   ADA compliance is another concern when buying a commercial build-
COMPLIANCE   ing. Find out from the building department if the building is in compliance, or what needs to be done to put it in compliance. If you remodel, the requirements may be more strict.

NOTE: *When dealing with public officials, always keep in mind that they do not always know, or honestly tell you, what the law is. They are often overzealous and try to intimidate people into doing things which are not required by law. Read the requirements yourself and question them if they seem to be interpreting it wrong. Seek legal advice if they refuse to budge from a clearly erroneous position. But also consider that keeping them happy may be worth the price. If you are already getting away with something they have overlooked, do not make a big deal over a little thing they want changed, or they may subject you to a full inspection or audit.*

CHECK GOVERNMENTAL REGULATIONS

When looking for a site for your business, you should investigate the differences in governmental regulations in your area. For example, a location just outside the city or county limits might have a lower licensing fee, lower sales tax rate, and less strict sign requirements.

LICENSING YOUR BUSINESS **6**

OCCUPATIONAL LICENSES AND ZONING

Before opening your business you are supposed to obtain a county occupational license. If you are working in a city, you will need a city occupational license. Businesses that do work in several cities, such as builders, must obtain a license from each city in which they work. This does not have to be done until you actually begin a job in a particular city.

County occupational licenses can be obtained from the tax collector in the county courthouse. City licenses are usually available at city hall. Be sure to find out if zoning allows your type of business before buying or leasing property, because the licensing departments will check the zoning before issuing your license.

If you will be preparing or serving food, you will need to check with the local health department to be sure the premises complies with their regulations. In some areas, if food has been served on the premises in the past, there is no problem getting a license. If food has never been served on the premises, the property must comply with all the newest regulations. These can be very costly.

HOME
BUSINESSES

Problems occasionally arise when people attempt to start a business in their home. A small new business cannot afford to pay rent for commercial space and cities often try to forbid businesses in residential areas. Getting a county occupational license or advertising a fictitious name often gives notice to the city that a business is being conducted in a residential area.

Some people avoid the problem by starting their businesses without occupational licenses, figuring that the penalties are less expensive than the cost of office space. Others get the county license and ignore the city rules. If a person has commercial trucks and equipment all over his property, there will probably be complaints from neighbors, and the city may take legal action. But if a person's business consists merely of making phone calls out of the home and keeping supplies there, the problem may never become an issue.

If a problem does arise regarding a home business that does not disturb the neighbors, a good argument can be made that the zoning law which prohibits the business is unconstitutional. When zoning laws were first instituted, they were not meant to stop people from doing things in a residence which had historically been part of the life in a residence. Consider an artist. Should a zoning law prohibit a person from sitting in his home and painting pictures? If he sells them for a living is there a difference? Can the government force him to rent commercial space just because he decides to sell the paintings he paints?

Similar arguments can be made for many home businesses. For hundreds of years people performed income-producing activities in their homes. But court battles with a city are expensive and probably not worth the effort for a small business. The best course of action is to keep a low profile. Using a post office box is sometimes helpful in diverting attention away from the residence.

STATE REGULATED PROFESSIONS

Many professionals require special state licenses. You will probably be called upon to produce such a license when applying for an - occupational license.

If you are in a regulated profession you should be aware of the laws that apply to your profession. The following pages contain a list of professions and the state laws and regulations covering them. You can make copies of these laws at your local public library or court law library. If you do not think your profession is regulated, you should read through the list anyway. Some of those included may surprise you.

The following citations are to the Illinois Compiled Statutes (Ill. Comp. Stat.) and the Illinois Administrative Code (Ill. Admin. Code).

Accountancy	Ill. Comp. Stat. Title 225, Section 450; Ill. Admin. Code Title 68, Section 1420.10
Aircraft, Pilots and Airports	Ill. Comp. Stat. Title 620, Section 5
Architecture and Landscape Arch.	Ill. Comp. Stat. Title 225, Section 305, 340
Attorneys	Ill. Comp. Stat. Title 705, Section 205
Art Auction House	Ill. Comp. Stat. Title 225, Section 405
Auctioneers	Ill. Comp. Stat. Title 225, Section 405
Barbering	Ill. Comp. Stat. Title 225, Section 410; Ill. Admin. Code Title 68, Section 1175.100
Cemeteries	Ill. Comp. Stat. Title 760, Section 100/8
Chiropractic	Ill. Comp. Stat. Title 225, Section 60
Clinical Social Workers	Ill. Comp. Stat. Title 225, Section 20; Ill. Admin. Code Title 68, Section 1470.5
Cosmetology	Ill. Comp. Stat. Title 225, Section 410; Ill. Admin. Code Title 68, Section 1175.100
Counseling and Psychotherapy	Ill. Comp. Stat. Title 225, Section 15, 107; Ill. Admin. Code Title 68 , Section 1400.10
Day Care	Ill. Comp. Stat. Title 225, Section 10/4; Ill. Admin. Code Title 89, Section 377.1
Dentistry	Ill. Comp. Stat. Title 225, Section 25; Ill. Admin. Code Title 68 , Section 1220.110

Detective Agencies	Ill. Comp. Stat. Title 225, Section 446
Driving Schools	Ill. Comp. Stat. Title 625, Section 5/6-401
Electrical Contracting	Ill. Comp. Stat. Title 65, Section 5/11-33-1
Employment Agencies	Ill. Comp. Stat. Title 225, Section 515; 68 Ill. Admin. Code Title , Section 680.100
Engineering	Ill. Comp. Stat. Title 225, Section 325; Ill. Admin. Code Title 68, Section 1380.210
Financial Planning	Ill. Comp. Stat. Title 205, Section 665
Funeral Directing and Embalming	Ill. Comp. Stat. Title 225, Section 41
Health Testing Services	Ill. Comp. Stat. Title 210, Section 25
Hearing Aid Sales	Ill. Comp. Stat. Title 225, Section 50; 77 Ill. Admin. Code Title , Section 3000.10
Interior Design	Ill. Comp. Stat. Title 225, Section 310
Investigative Services	Ill. Comp. Stat. Title 225, Section 445; Ill. Admin. Code Title 68, Section 1240.5
Land Surveying	Ill. Comp. Stat. Title 225, Section 330; Ill. Admin. Code Title 68, Section 1270.10
Landscape Architects	Ill. Comp. Stat. Title 225, Section 315; Ill. Admin. Code Title 68, Section 750.1000
Massage Practice	Ill. Comp. Stat. Title 55, Section 515
Mortgage Brokers	Ill. Comp. Stat. Title 205, Section 635
Nursing	Ill. Comp. Stat. Title 225, Section 65; Ill. Admin. Code Title 68, Section 1300.10
Nursing Homes	Ill. Comp. Stat. Title 225, Section 70; Ill. Admin. Code Title 68, Section 1310.20
Occupational Therapists	Ill. Comp. Stat. Title 225, Section 70; Ill. Admin. Code Title 68, Section 1315.90
Optometry	Ill. Comp. Stat. Title 225, Section 80; Ill. Admin. Code Title 68, Section 1320.20
Osteopathy	Ill. Comp. Stat. Title 225, Section 60
Outdoor Advertising	Ill. Comp. Stat. Title 225, Section 440
Pest Control	Ill. Comp. Stat. Title 415, Section 60/10
Pharmacy	Ill. Comp. Stat. Title 225, Section 85, 120; Ill. Admin. Code Title 68, Section 1330.10
Physical Therapy	Ill. Comp. Stat. Title 225, Section 90; Ill. Admin. Code Title 68, Section 1340.20

Physicians	Ill. Comp. Stat. Title 225, Section 60; Ill. Admin. Code Title 68, Section 1285.20
Plumbing	Ill. Comp. Stat. Title 225, Section 320
Podiatry	Ill. Comp. Stat. Title 225, Section 100; Ill. Admin. Code Title 68, Section 1360.10
Radiologic Technologists	Ill. Comp. Stat. Title 420, Section 40/6
Real Estate Brokerage, Sales and Schools	Ill. Comp. Stat. Title 225, Section 455; Ill. Admin. Code Title 68, Section 1450.10
Roofing	Ill. Comp. Stat. Title 225, Section 335; Ill. Admin. Code Title 68, Section 1460.10
Speech Pathology and Audiology	Ill. Comp. Stat. Title 225, Section 110; Ill. Admin. Code Title 68, Section 1465.10
Vendors	Ill. Comp. Stat. Title 225, Section 465
Veterinary Medicine	Ill. Comp. Stat. Title 225, Section 115; Ill. Admin. Code Title 68, Section 1500.5

FEDERAL LICENSES

So far there are few businesses which require federal registration. If you are in any of the types of businesses listed below you should check with the federal agency below it.

Radio or television stations or manufacturers of equipment emitting radio waves:

Federal Communications Commission
1919 M Street, NW
Washington, DC 20550

Manufacturers of alcohol, tobacco or fire arms:

Bureau of Alcohol, Tobacco and Firearms,
Treasury Department
1200 Pennsylvania Ave., NW
Washington, DC 20226

Securities brokers and providers of investment advice:

>Securities and Exchange Commission
>450 - 5th Street NW
>Washington, DC 20549

Manufacturers of drugs and processors of meat:

>Food and Drug Administration
>5600 Fishers Lane
>Rockville, MD 28057

Interstate carriers:

>Interstate Commerce Commission
>12th St. & Constitution Ave.
>Washington, DC 20423

Exporting:

>Bureau of Export Administration
>Department of Commerce
>14th St. & Constitution Ave., NW
>Washington, DC 20220

Contract Laws 7

As a business owner you will need to know the basics of forming a simple contract for your transactions with both customers and vendors. There is a lot of misunderstanding about the law, and people may give you erroneous information. Relying on this information can cost you money. This chapter will give you a quick overview of the principles that apply to your transactions and pitfalls to avoid. If you face more complicated contract questions, you should consult a law library or an attorney familiar with small business law.

Traditional Contract Law

One of the first things taught in law school is that a contract is not legal unless three elements are present: offer, acceptance, and consideration. For your purposes, the important things to remember are:

- If you make an offer to someone it may result in a binding contract, even if you change your mind or find out it was a bad deal for you.

- Unless an offer is accepted and both parties agree to the same contract, there is no contract.

- A contract does not always have to be in writing. Some laws require certain contracts to be in writing, but as a general rule an oral contract is legal. The problem is proving that the contract actually existed.

- Without *consideration*, or the exchange of something of value or mutual promises there is not a valid contract.

The most important rules for the business owner are:

- An advertisement is not an offer. Suppose you put an ad in the newspaper offering "New IBM computers only $999!" but there is a typo in the ad and it says $9.99? Can people come in and say "I accept, here's my $9.99" creating a legal contract? Fortunately, no. Courts have ruled that the ad is not an offer that a person can accept. It is an invitation to come in and make offers which the business can accept or reject.

- The same rule applies to the price tag on an item. If someone switches price tags on your merchandise, or if you accidentally put the wrong price on it, you are not required by law to sell it at that price. If you intentionally put the wrong price you may be liable under the "bait and switch" law. Many merchants honor a mistaken price because refusing to would constitute bad will and possibly lose a customer.

- When a person makes an offer, several things may happen. It may be accepted, creating a legal contract, or it may be rejected. It may expire before it has been accepted, or it may be withdrawn before acceptance. A contract may expire either by a date made in the offer (For example, "This offer remains open until noon on October 1, 2002") or after a reasonable amount of time. What is reasonable is a legal question that a court must decide. If someone makes you an offer to sell goods, clearly you cannot come back five years later and accept. Depending on the type of goods and the circumstances, you may be able to accept a week or a month later and create a legal contract.

- A person accepting an offer cannot add any terms to it. If you offer to sell a car for $1,000, and the other party accepts as long as you put new tires on it, there is no contract. An acceptance with changed terms is considered a rejection and a counteroffer.

- When someone rejects your offer and makes a counteroffer, a contract can be created by your acceptance of the counteroffer.

These rules can affect your business on a daily basis. Suppose you offer to sell something to one customer over the phone and five minutes later another customer walks in and offers you more. To protect yourself, you should call the first customer and withdraw your offer before accepting the offer of the second customer. If the first customer accepts before you have withdrawn your offer, you may be sued if you have sold the item to the second customer.

There are a few exceptions to the basic rules of contracts that you should be aware of. These are:

- Consent to a contract must be voluntary. If it is made under a threat, the contract is not valid. If a business refuses to give a person's car back unless they pay $200 for changing the oil, the customer could probably sue and get the $200 back.

- Contracts to do illegal acts or acts against public policy are not enforceable. If an electrician signs a contract to put some wiring in a house that is not legal, the customer could probably not force him to do it because the court would refuse to require an illegal act.

- If either party to an offer dies, the offer expires and cannot be accepted by the heirs. If a painter is hired to paint a portrait, and dies before completing it, his wife cannot finish it and require payment. However, a corporation does not die, even if its owners die. If a corporation is hired to build a house and the owner dies, his heirs may take over the corporation and finish the job and require payment.

- Contracts made under misrepresentation are not enforceable. For example, if someone tells you a car has 35,000 miles on it and you later discover it has 135,000 miles, you may be able to rescind the contract for fraud and misrepresentation.

- If there was a mutual mistake a contract may be rescinded. For example, if both you and the seller thought the car had 35,000 miles on it and both relied on that assumption, the contract could be rescinded. However, if the seller knew the car has 135,000 miles on it, and you assumed it had 35,000 but did not ask, you probably could not rescind the contract.

STATUTORY CONTRACT LAW

The previous section discussed the basics of contract law. These are not stated in the statutes, but are the principles decided by judges hundreds of years ago. In recent times, the legislatures have made numerous exceptions to these principles, and in most cases, these laws have been passed when the legislature felt that traditional law was not fair. The important laws that affect contracts follow.

STATUTES OF FRAUD
Statutes of fraud state when a contract must be in writing to be valid. Some people believe a contract is not valid unless it is in writing, but that is not true. Only those types of contracts mentioned in the statutes of fraud must be in writing. Of course, an oral contract is much harder to prove in court than one in writing. In Illinois, some of the contracts that must be in writing are:

- agreements which take over one year to complete (Ill. Comp. Stat. Title 740, Section 80/1)

- sales of any interest in real estate (Ill. Comp. Stat. Title 740, Section 80/2)

- leases of real estate over one year (Ill. Comp. Stat. Title 740, Section 80/2)

- guarantees of debts of another person (Ill. Comp. Stat. Title 740, Section 80/1)

- sales of goods of over $500 (Ill. Comp. Stat. Title 810, Section 5/2 - 201/1)

- sales of securities (Ill. Comp. Stat. Title 740, Section 80/1)

CONSUMER PROTECTION LAWS
Due to alleged unfair practices by some types of businesses, laws have been passed controlling the types of contracts they may use. Most notable among these are health clubs and door-to-door solicitations. The laws covering these businesses usually give the consumer a certain time to cancel the contract. These laws are described in Chapter 11 on Advertising and Promotion Laws.

PREPARING YOUR CONTRACTS

Before you open your business, you should obtain or prepare the contracts or policies you will use in your business. In some businesses such as a restaurant, you will not need much. Perhaps you will want a sign near the entrance stating "Shirt and shoes required," or "Diners must be seated by 10:30 P.M."

However, if you are a building contractor or a similar business, you will need detailed contracts to use with your customers. If you do not clearly spell out your rights and obligations, you may end up in court and lose thousands of dollars in profits.

Of course the best way to have an effective contract is to have an - attorney, who is experienced in the subject, prepare a contract to meet the needs of your business. However, since this may be too expensive for your new operation, you may want to go elsewhere. Three sources for the contracts you will need are other business like yours, trade associations, and legal form books. You should obtain as many different contracts as possible, compare them, and decide what terms are most useful to you.

Insurance Laws 8

There are few laws requiring you to have insurance, but if you do not have insurance, you may face liability that would ruin your business. You should be aware of the types of insurance available and weigh the risks of a loss against the cost of a policy.

Be aware that there can be a wide range of prices and coverage in insurance policies. You should get at least three quotes from different insurance agents and ask each one to explain the benefits of his or her policy.

Workers' Compensation

Workers' compensation is a system of benefits provided by law to most workers who have job-related injuries or diseases. The amount of benefits are limited by law and are paid without regard to fault. Almost every employee in Illinois is covered under this system.

The employer is responsible for providing benefits and does so either directly or through an insurance company that administers the program for the employer. This insurance can be obtained from most insurance companies, and in many cases is not expensive. If you have such coverage, you are protected against suits by employees or their heirs in case of accidents and against potentially ruinous claims.

There are other requirements of the workers' compensation law, such as reporting any on-the-job deaths of a worker within twenty-four hours. Also, it is unlawful to deduct the amount of the premiums from the employee's wages.

This law has been subject to frequent change so you should check with the Industrial Commission of Illinois for the latest requirements, or ask for the booklet *Handbook on Workers' Compensation and Occupational Diseases*. Call 217-785-7084 or write:

Illinois Industrial Commission
701 S. Second Street
Springfield, IL 62704

You can also visit their website at:

http://www.state.il.us/agency/iic

LIABILITY INSURANCE

In most cases, you are not required to carry liability insurance. Liability insurance can be divided into two main areas: coverage for injuries on your premises and by your employees, and coverage for injuries caused by your products.

Coverage for the first type of injury is usually very reasonably priced. Injuries in your business or by your employees (such as in an auto accident) are covered by standard premises or auto policies. But coverage for injuries by products may be harder to find and more expensive.

ASSET
PROTECTION
If insurance is unavailable or unaffordable, you can go without and use a corporation and other asset protection devices to protect yourself from liability.

The best way to find out if insurance is available for your type of business is to check with other businesses. If there is a trade group for your industry, their newsletter or magazine may contain ads for insurers.

UMBRELLA
POLICY

As a business owner, you will be more visible as a target for lawsuits, even if there is little merit to them. Lawyers know that a *nuisance suit* is often settled for thousands of dollars. Because of your greater exposure, you should consider getting a personal umbrella policy. This is a policy which covers you for claims of up to a million dollars (possibly even two or five million) and is very reasonably priced.

HAZARD INSURANCE

One of the worst things that can happen to your business is a fire, flood, or other disaster. Due to lost customer lists, inventory, and equipment, many businesses have been forced to close after such a disaster.

The premium for this insurance is usually reasonable and could protect you from loss of your business. You can even get business interruption insurance, which will cover your losses while your business is getting back on its feet.

HOME BUSINESS INSURANCE

There is a special insurance problem for home businesses. Most homeowner and tenant insurance policies do not cover business activities. In fact, under some policies you may be denied coverage if you use your home for a business.

You probably will not have a problem and will not need extra coverage if you merely use your home to make business phone calls and send letters. If you own equipment or have dedicated a portion of your home exclusively to the business, you could have a problem. Check with your insurance agent for the options that are available to you.

If your business is a sole proprietorship and you have a computer that you use both personally and for your business, it would probably be covered under your homeowners policy. But if you incorporate your business and bought the computer in the name of the corporation, coverage might be denied. It is possible to get a special insurance policy in the company name covering just the computer if it is your main business asset. One company that offers such a policy is Safeware at 800-723-9273 or 1-800-800-1492.

AUTOMOBILE INSURANCE

If you or any of your employees will be using an automobile for business purposes, be sure to have this use covered. Sometimes a policy may contain an exclusion for business use. Check to be sure your liability policy covers you if one of your employees causes an accident while running a business errand.

HEALTH INSURANCE

While new businesses can rarely afford health insurance for their employees, the sooner they can obtain it, the better chance they will have to find and keep good employees. Those starting a business usually need insurance for themselves, and they can sometimes receive a better rate if they obtain a small business package.

EMPLOYEE THEFT

If you fear employees may be able to steal from your business, you may want to have them bonded. This means that you pay an insurance company a premium to guarantee employees' honesty and if they cheat you the insurance company pays you damages. This can cover all existing and new employees.

YOUR BUSINESS AND THE INTERNET 9

The Internet has opened up a world of opportunities for businesses. A few years ago, getting national visibility cost a fortune. Today a business can set up a Web page for a few hundred dollars and, with some clever publicity and a little luck, millions of people around the world will see it.

But this new world has new legal issues and new liabilities. Not all of them have been addressed by laws or by the courts. Before you begin doing business on the Internet, you should know the existing rules and the areas where legal issues exist.

DOMAIN NAMES

A *domain name* is the address of your website. For example, www.apple.com is the domain name of Apple Computer Company. The last part of the domain name, the ".com" (or "dot com") is the *top level domain*, or TLD. Dot com is the most popular, but others are currently available in the United States, including .net and .org. (Originally .net was only available to network service providers and .org only to nonprofit organizations, but regulations have eliminated those requirements.) Due to an overwhelming number of people registering ".com," ".net," and ".org" addresses, regulations have recently started assigning people new names, such as ".biz."

It may seem like most words have been taken as a dot-com name, but if you combine two or three short words or abbreviations, a nearly unlimited number of possibilities are available. For example, if you have a business dealing with automobiles, most likely someone has already registered automobile.com and auto.com. But you can come up with all kinds of variations, using adjectives or your name, depending on your type of business:

autos4u.com	joesauto.com	autobob.com
myauto.com	yourauto.com	onlyautos.com
greatauto.com	autosfirst.com	usautos.com
greatautos.com	firstautoworld.com	4autos.com

When the Internet first began, some individuals realized that major corporations would soon want to register their names. Since the registration was easy and cheap, people registered names they thought would ultimately be used by someone else.

At first, some companies paid high fees to buy their names from the registrants. But one company, Intermatic, filed a lawsuit instead of paying. The owner of the name they wanted had registered numerous trademarks, such as britishairways.com and ussteel.com. The court ruled that since Intermatic owned a trademark on the name, the registration of their name by someone else violated that trademark and that Intermatic was entitled to it.

Since then people have registered names that are not trademarks, such as CalRipkin.com, and have attempted to charge the individuals with those names to buy their domain. In 1998, Congress stepped in and passed the Anti-Cybersquatting Consumer Protection Act. This law makes it illegal to register a domain with no legitimate need to use it.

This law helped a lot of companies protect their names, but then some companies started abusing it and tried to stop legitimate users of similar names. This is especially likely against small companies. Two organizations have been set up to help small companies protect their domains: the Domain Defense Advocate and the Domain Name Rights Coalition. Their websites are:

www.ajax.org/dda

www.domain-name.org

Registering a domain name for your own business is a simple process. There are many companies that offer registration services. For a list of those companies, visit the site of the Internet Corporation for Assigned Names and Numbers (ICANN) at **http://www.icann.org**. You can link directly to any member's site and compare the costs and registration procedures required for the different top-level domains.

WEB PAGES

There are many new companies eager to help you set up a website. Some offer turnkey sites for a low flat rate. Custom sites can cost tens of thousands of dollars. If you have plenty of capital you may want to have your site handled by one of these professionals. However, setting up a website is a fairly simple process, and once you learn the basics you can handle most of it in-house.

If you are new to the Web, you may want to look at the following sites, which will familiarize you with the Internet jargon and give you a basic introduction to the Web:

http://www.learnthenet.com   http://www.webopedia.com

SITE SETUP   There are seven steps to setting up a website: site purpose, design, content, structure, programming, testing, and publicity. Whether you do it yourself, hire a professional site designer, or use a college student, the steps toward creating an effective site are the same.

Before beginning your own site you should look at other sites, including those of major corporations and of small businesses. Look at the sites of all the companies that compete with you. Look at hundreds of sites and click through them to see how they work (or do not work).

Site purpose. To know what to include on your site, you must decide what its purpose will be. Do you want to take orders for your products or services, attract new employees, give away samples, or show off your company headquarters? You might want to do several of these things.

Site design. After looking at other sites you can see that there are numerous ways to design a site. It can be crowded, or open and airy; it can have several windows (frames) open at once or just one, and it can allow long scrolling or just click-throughs.

You will have to decide whether the site will have text only; text plus photographs and graphics; or text plus photos, graphics, and other design elements such as animation or Java script. Additionally, you will begin to make decisions about colors, fonts, and the basic graphic appearance of the site.

Site content. You must create the content for your site. For this, you can use your existing promotional materials, you can write new material just for the website, or you can use a combination of the two. Whatever you choose, remember that the written material should be concise, free of errors, and easy for your target audience to read. Any graphics, including photographs, and written materials not created by you require permission. You should obtain such permission from the lawful copyright holder in order to use any copyrighted material. Once you know your site's purpose, look, and content, you can begin to piece the site together.

Site structure. You must decide how the content (text plus photographs, graphics, animation, etc.) will be structured (what content will be on which page), and how a user will link from one part of the site to another. For example, your first page may have the business name and then choices to click on, such as "about us," "opportunities," "product catalog," etc. Have those choices connect to another page containing the detailed information so that a user will see the catalog when they click on "product catalog." Or your site could have a choice to click on a link to another website related to yours.

Site programming and setup. When you know nothing about setting up a website, it can seem like a daunting task that will require an expert. However, *programming* here means merely putting a site together. There are inexpensive computer programs available that make it very simple.

Commercial programs such as Microsoft FrontPage, Dreamweaver, Pagemaker, Photoshop, MS Publisher, and PageMill allow you to set up Web pages as easily as laying out a print publication. These programs will convert the text and graphics you create into HTML, the programming language of the Web. Before you choose Web design software and design your site, you should determine which Web hosting service you will use. Make sure that the design software you use is compatible with the host server's system. The Web host will be the provider who will give you space on their server and who may provide other services to you, such as secure order processing and analysis of your site to see who is visiting and linking to it.

If you have an America Online account, you can download design software and a tutorial for free. AOL has recently collaborated with a Web hosting service at **http://www.verioprimehost.com** and offers a number of different hosting packages for the consumer and e-business. You do not have to use AOL's design software in order to use this service. You are eligible to use this site whether you design your own pages, have someone else do the design work for you, or use AOL's templates. This service allows you to use your own domain name and choose the package that is appropriate for your business.

If you have used a page layout program, you can usually get a simple Web page up and running within a day or two. If you do not have much experience with a computer, you might consider hiring a college student to set up a Web page for you.

Site testing. Some of the website setup programs allow you to thoroughly check your new site to see if all the pictures are included and all the links are proper. There are also websites you can go to that will check out your site. Some even allow you to improve your site, such as by reducing the size of your graphics so they download faster. Use a major search engine listed on page 64 to look for companies that can test your site before you launch it on the Web.

Site publicity. Once you set up your website, you will want to get people to look at it. *Publicity* means getting your site noticed as much as possible by drawing people to it.

The first thing to do to get noticed is to be sure your site is registered with as many *search engines* as possible. These are pages that people use to find things on the Internet, such as Yahoo and Excite. They do not automatically know about you just because you created a website. You must tell them about your site, and they must examine and catalog it.

For a fee, there are services that will register your site with numerous search engines. If you are starting out on a shoestring, you can easily do it yourself. While there are hundreds of search engines, most people use a dozen or so of the bigger ones. If your site is in a niche area, such as geneology services, then you would want to be listed on any specific geneology search engines. Most businesses should be mainly concerned with getting on the biggest ones. The biggest search engines at this time are:

search.msn.com	www.hotbot.com
www.about.com	www.infoseek.com
www.askjeeves.com	www.looksmart.com
www.altavista.com	www.lycos.com
www.excite.com	www.metacrawler.com
www.fastsearch.com	www.webcrawler.com
www.google.com	www.yahoo.com

Most of these sites have a place to click to "add your site" to their system. There are sites that rate the search engines, help you list on the search engines, or check to see if you are listed. One site is:

http://www.searchiq.com

A *meta tag* is an invisible subject word added to your site that can be found by a search engine. For example, if you are a pest control company, you may want to list all of the scientific names of the pests you control and all of the treatments you have available; but you may not need them to be part of the visual design of your site. List these words as meta tags when you set up your page so people searching for those words will find your site.

Some companies thought that a clever way to get viewers would be to use commonly searched names, or names of major competitors, as meta tags to attract people looking for those big companies. For example, a small delivery service that has nothing to do with UPS or Federal Express might use those company names as meta tags so people looking for them would find the smaller company. While it may sound like a good idea, it has been declared illegal trademark infringement. Today many companies have computer programs scanning the Internet for improper use of their trademarks.

Once you have made sure that your site is passively listed in all the search engines, you may want to actively promote your site. However, self-promotion is seen as a bad thing on the Internet, especially if its purpose is to make money.

Newsgroups are places on the Internet where people interested in a specific topic can exchange information. For example, expectant mothers have a group where they can trade advice and experiences. If you have a product that would be great for expectant mothers, that would be a good place for it to be discussed. However, if you log into the group and merely announce your product, suggesting people order it from your Web site, you will probably be *flamed* (sent a lot of hate mail).

If you join the group, however, and become a regular, and in answer to someone's problem, mention that you "saw this product that might help," your information will be better received. It may seem unethical to plug your product without disclosing your interest, but this is a procedure used by many large companies. They hire people to plug their product (or rock star) all over the Internet. So, perhaps it has become an acceptable marketing method and consumers know to take plugs with a grain of salt. Let your conscience be your guide.

Keep in mind that Internet publicity works both ways. If you have a great product and people love it, you will get a lot of business. If you sell a shoddy product, give poor service, and do not keep your customers happy, bad publicity on the Internet can kill your business. Besides being an equalizer between large and small companies, the Internet can be a filtering mechanism between good and bad products.

There is no worse breach of Internet etiquette ("netiquette") than to send advertising by e-mail to strangers. It is called *spamming*, and doing it can have serious consequences. There is anti-spamming legislation currently pending at the federal level. Many states, including California, Colorado, Connecticut, Delaware, Idaho, Illinois, Iowa, Louisiana, Missouri, Nevada, North Carolina, Oklahoma, Pennsylvania, Rhode Island, Tennessee, Virginia, Washington, and West Virginia, have enacted anti-spamming legislation. This legislation sets specific requirements for unsolicited bulk e-mail and makes certain practices illegal. You should check with an attorney to see if your business practices fall within the legal limits of these laws. Additionally, many Internet Service Providers (ISPs) have restrictions on unsolicited bulk e-mail (spam); you should check with your ISP to make sure you do not violate its policies.

ADVERTISING

Banner ads are the small rectangular ads on many Web pages that usually blink or move. Although most computer users seem to have become immune to them, there is still a big market in the sale and exchange of them.

If your site gets enough viewers, people may pay you to place their ads there. Another possibility is to trade ads with another site. In fact there are companies that broker ad trades among Web sites. Such trades used to be taxable transactions, but after January 5, 2000, such trades are no longer taxable under IRS Notice 2000-6.

LEGAL ISSUES

Before you set up a Web page, you should consider the legal issues described below.

JURISDICTION

Jurisdiction is the power of a court in a particular location to decide a particular case. Usually you have to have been physically present in a jurisdiction or have done business there before you can be sued there. Since the Internet extends your business's ability to reach people in far-away places, there may be instances when you could be subject to legal jurisdiction far from your own state (or country). There are a number of cases that have been decided in this country regarding the Internet and jurisdiction, but very few cases have been decided on this issue outside of the United States.

In most instances, U.S. courts use the pre-Internet test—whether you have been present in another jurisdiction or have had enough contact with someone in the other jurisdiction. The fact that the Internet itself is not a "place" will not shield you from being sued in another state when you have shipped you company's product there, have entered into a contract with a resident of that state, or have defamed a foreign resident with content on your website.

According to the Court, there is a spectrum of contact required between you, your website, and consumers or audiences. (*Zippo Manufacturing Co. v. Zippo Dot Com, Inc.*, 952 F. Supp. 1119 (W.D. Pa 1997)) It is *clear* that the one end of the spectrum includes the shipping, contracting, and defamation mentioned above as sufficient to establish jurisdiction. The more interactive your site is with consumers, the more you target an audience for your goods in a particular location, and the farther you reach to send your goods out into the world; the more it becomes possible for someone to sue you outside of your own jurisdiction—possibly even in another country.

The law is not even remotely final on these issues. The American Bar Association, among other groups, is studying this topic in detail. At present, no final, global solution or agreement about jurisdictional issues exists.

One way to protect yourself from the possibility of being sued in a faraway jurisdiction would be to have a statement on your website stating that those using the site or doing business with you agree that "jurisdiction for any actions regarding this site" or your company will be in your home county.

For extra protection you can have a preliminary page that must be clicked before entering your website. However, this may be overkill for a small business with little risk of lawsuits. If you are in any business for which you could have serious liability, you should review some competitors' sites and see how they handle the liability issue. They often have a place to click for "legal notice" or "disclaimer" on their first page.

You may want to consult with an attorney to discuss the specific disclaimer you will use on your website, where it should appear, and whether you will have users of your site actively agree to this disclaimer or just passively read it. However, these disclaimers are not enforceable everywhere in the world. Until there is global agreement on jurisdictional issues, this may remain an area of uncertainty for some time to come.

LIBEL

Libel is any publication that injures the reputation of another. This can occur in print, writing, pictures, or signs. All that is required for *publication* is that you transmit the material to at least one other person. When putting together your website you must keep in mind that it is visible to millions of people all over the planet and that if you libel a person or company you may have to pay damages. Many countries do not have the freedom of speech that we do and a statement that is not libel in the United States may be libelous elsewhere.

COPYRIGHT INFRINGEMENT

It is so easy to copy and borrow information on the Internet that it is easy to infringe copyrights without even knowing it. A *copyright* exists for a work as soon as the creator creates it. There is no need to register the copyright or to put a copyright notice on it. So, practically everything on the Internet belongs to someone. Some people freely give their works away. For example, many people have created web artwork (*gifs* and *animated gifs)* that they freely allow people to copy. There are numerous sites that provide hundreds or thousands of free gifs that you can add to your Web pages. Some require you to acknowledge the source; some do not. You should always be sure that the works are free for the taking before using them.

LINKING AND FRAMING

One way to violate copyright laws is to improperly link other sites to yours either directly or with framing. *Linking* is when you provide a place on your site to click, which takes someone to another site. *Framing* occurs when you set up your site so that when you link to another site, your site is still viewable as a frame around the linked-to site.

While many sites are glad to be linked to others, some, especially providers of valuable information, object. Courts have ruled that linking and framing can be a copyright violation. One rule that has developed is that it is usually okay to link to the first page of a site, but not to link to some valuable information deeper within the site. The rationale for this is that the owner of the site wants visitors to go through the various levels of his or her site (viewing all the ads) before getting the information. By linking directly to the information, you are giving away their product without the ads.

The problem with linking to the first page of a site is that it may be a tedious or difficult task to find the needed page from there. Many sites are poorly designed and make it nearly impossible to find anything.

The best solution, if you wish to link to another page, is to ask permission. Email the Webmaster or other person in charge of the site, if one is given, and explain what you want to do. If they grant permission, be sure to print out a copy of their e-mail for your records.

PRIVACY   Since the Internet is such an easy way to share information, there are many concerns that it will cause a loss of individual privacy. The two main concerns arise when you post information that others consider private, and when you gather information from customers and use it in a way that violates their privacy.

While public actions of politicians and celebrities are fair game, details about their private lives are sometimes protected by law, and details about persons who are not public figures are often protected. The laws in each state are different, and what might be allowable in one state could be illegal in another. If your site will provide any personal information about individuals, you should discuss the possibility of liability with an attorney.

Several well-known companies have been in the news lately for violations of their customers' privacy. They either shared what the customer was buying or downloading, or looked for additional information on the customer's computer. To let customers know that you do not violate certain standards of privacy, you can subscribe to one of the privacy codes that has been promulgated for the Internet. These allow you to put a symbol on your site guaranteeing to your customers that you follow the code.

The websites of two of the organizations that offer this service, and their fees at the time of this publication are:

www.privacybot.com	$100
www.bbbonline.com	$200 to $6,000

PROTECTING YOURSELF
The easiest way to protect yourself personally from the various possible types of liability is to set up a corporation or limited liability company to own the website. This is not foolproof protection since, in some cases, you could be sued personally as well, but it is one level of protection.

COPPA
If your website is aimed at children under the age of thirteen, or if it attracts children of that age, then you are covered by the federal Children Online Privacy Protection Act of 1998 (COPPA). This law requires such Web sites to:

- give notice on the site of what information is being collected;

- obtain verifiable parental consent to collect the information;

- allow the parent to review the information collected;

- allow the parent to delete the child's information or to refuse to allow the use of the information;

- limit the information collected to only that necessary to participate on the site; and,

- protect the security and confidentiality of the information.

FINANCIAL TRANSACTIONS

In the future, there will be easy ways to exchange money on the Internet. Some companies have already been started that promote their own kinds of electronic money. Whether any of these become universal is yet to be seen.

For now, the easiest way to exchange money on the Internet is through traditional credit cards. Because of concerns that email can be abducted in transit and read by others, most companies use a *secure* site in which customers are guaranteed that their card data is encrypted before being sent.

When setting up your website, you should ask the provider if you can be set up with a secure site for transmitting credit card data. If they cannot provide it, you will need to contract with another software provider. Use a major search engine listed on page 64 to look for companies that provide credit card services to businesses on the web.

As a practical matter, there is very little to worry about when sending credit card data by email. If you do not have a secure site, another option is to allow purchasers to fax or phone in their credit card data. However, keep in mind that this extra step will lose some business unless your products are unique and your buyers are very motivated.

The least effective option is to provide an order form on the site, which can be printed out and mailed in with a check. Again, your customers must be really motivated or they will lose interest after finding out this extra work is involved.

FTC Rules

Because the Internet is an instrument of interstate commerce, it is a legitimate subject for federal regulation. The Federal Trade Commission (FTC) first said that all of its consumer protection rules applied to the Internet, but lately it has been adding specific rules and issuing publications. The following publications are available from the FTC website at **http://www.ftc.gov/bcp/menu-internet.htm** or by mail from Consumer Response Center, Federal Trade Commission, 600 Pennsylvania, NW, Room H-130, Washington, DC 20580-0001.

- *Advertising and Marketing on the Internet: The Rules of the Road*

- *BBB-Online: Code of Online Business Practices*

- *Electronic Commerce: Selling Internationally. A Guide for Business*

- *How to Comply With The Children's Online Privacy Protection Rule*

- *Internet Auctions: A Guide for Buyer and Sellers*

- *Selling on the Internet: Prompt Delivery Rules*

- *Website Woes: Avoiding Web Service Scams*

FRAUD

Because the Internet is somewhat anonymous, it is a tempting place for those with fraudulent schemes to look for victims. As a business consumer, you should exercise caution when dealing with unknown or anonymous parties on the Internet.

Recently, the U.S. Department of Justice, the Federal Bureau of Investigation (FBI) and the National White Collar Crime Center launched the Internet Fraud Complaint Center (IFCC). If you suspect that you are the victim of fraud online, whether as a consumer or a business, you can report incidents to the IFCC on their website, **http://www.ifccfbi.gov**. The IFCC is currently staffed by FBI agents and representatives of the National White Collar Crime Center and will work with state and local law enforcement officials to prevent, investigate, and prosecute high-tech and economic crime online.

HEALTH AND SAFETY LAWS 10

FEDERAL LAWS

OSHA The Occupational Safety and Health Administration (OSHA) is a good example of government regulation so severe it strangles businesses out of existence. Robert D. Moran, a former chairman of the committee that hears appeals from OSHA rulings once said that "there isn't a person on earth who can be certain he is in full compliance with the requirements of this standard at any point in time." The point of the law is to place the duty on the employer to keep the workplace free from recognized hazards that are likely to cause death or serious bodily injury to workers.

For example, OSHA decided to analyze repetitive-strain injuries, or "RSI," such as carpal tunnel syndrome. The Bureau of Labor Statistics estimated that 7% of workplace illnesses are RSI and the National Safety Council estimated 4%. OSHA, however, determined that 60% is a more accurate figure and came out with a 600 page list of proposed regulations, guidelines, and suggestions. These regulations would have affected over one-half of all businesses in America and cost billions of dollars. Fortunately, these regulations were shot down by Congress in 1995, after an outcry from businesses. Shortly thereafter, OSHA officials ignored Congress' sentiment and promised to launch a new effort.

Fortunately, for small businesses the regulations are not as cumbersome as for larger enterprises. If you have ten or fewer employees or if you are in certain types of businesses, you do not have to keep a record of illnesses, injuries, and exposure to hazardous substances of employees. If you have eleven or more employees, you do have to keep this record, which is called *Log 200*. All employers are required to display a poster that you can get from OSHA.

Within forty-eight hours of an on-the-job death of an employee or injury of five or more employees on the job, the area director of OSHA must be contacted.

For more information, you should write or call the following regional OSHA office:

OSHA Regional Office
230 South Dearborn Street
Room 3244
Chicago, IL   60604
312-353-2220
312-353-7774 (fax)

or visit their website: **http://www.osha.gov** and obtain copies of their publications, *OSHA Handbook for Small Business* (OSHA 2209), and *OSHA Publications and Audiovisual Programs Catalog* (OSHA 2019). They also have a poster that is required to be posted in the workplace. Find it at:

http://www.osha.gov/oshpubs/poster.html

The Hazard Communication Standard requires that employees be made aware of the hazards in the workplace. (Code of Federal Regulations (C.F.R., Title 29, Section (Sec.) 1910.1200.) It is especially applicable to those working with chemicals but this can even include offices that use copy machines. Businesses using hazardous chemicals must have a comprehensive program for informing employees of the hazards and for protecting them from contamination.

For more information, you can contact OSHA at the previously-mentioned addresses, phone numbers, or websites. They can supply a copy of the regulation and a booklet called *OSHA 3084*, which explains the law.

EPA   The Worker Protection Standard for Agricultural Pesticides requires safety training, decontamination sites and, of course, posters. The Environmental Protection Agency will provide information on compliance with this law. They can be reached at 800-490-9198, or their website at:

http://www.epa.gov

They can be reached by mail at:

> Environmental Protection Agency
> 1200 Pennsylvania Ave. N.W.
> Washington, DC 20460

FDA   The Pure Food and Drug Act of 1906 prohibits the misbranding or adulteration of food and drugs. It also created the Food and Drug Administration (FDA), which has promulgated tons of regulations and which must give permission before a new drug can be introduced into the market. If you will be dealing with any food or drugs you should keep abreast of their policies. Their website is: **http://www.fda.gov**, their small business site is: **http://www.fda.gov/ora/fed_state/small_business/ sb_guide/default.htm** and their local small business representative is:

> FDA, Central Region
> Small Business Representative, Marie T. Falcone
> U.S. Customhouse
> 2nd and Chestnut Streets
> Room 900
> Philadelphia, PA   19106
> Phone: 215-597-2120, ext. 4003
> Fax: 215-597-5798
> Email: mfalcone@ora.fda.gov

HAZARDOUS MATERIALS TRANSPORTATION   There are regulations that control the shipping and packing of hazardous materials. For more information contact:

> Office of Hazardous Materials Transportation
> 400 Seventh St.
> S.W., Washington, DC 20590
> 202-366-8553.
> http://hazmat.dot.gov

CPSC   The Consumer Product Safety Commission has a set of rules that cover the safety of products. The commission feels that because its rules cover products, rather than people or companies, they apply to everyone producing such products. However, federal laws do not apply to small businesses that do not affect interstate commerce. Whether a small business would fall under a CPSC rule would depend on the size and nature of your business.

The CPSC rules are contained in CFR Title 16 in the following parts. These can be found at most law libraries, some public libraries, and on the internet at:

http://www.access.gpo.gov/nara/cfr/cfr-table-search.html.

The CPSC's site is at:

http://cpsc.gov/index.html.

PRODUCT	PART
Antennas, CB and TV	1402
Architectural Glazing Material	1201
Articles Hazardous to Children Under 3	1501
Baby Cribs-Full Size	1508
Baby Cribs-Non-Full Size	1509
Bicycle Helmets	1203
Bicycles	1512
Carpets and Rugs	1630, 1631
Cellulose Insulation	1209, 1404
Cigarette Lighters	1210
Citizens Band Base Station Antennas	1204
Coal and Wood Burning Appliances	1406
Consumer Products Containing Chlorofluorocarbons	1401
Electrically Operated Toys	1505
Emberizing Materials Containing Asbestos (banned)	1305
Extremely Flammable Contact Adhesives (banned)	1302
Fireworks	1507
Garage Door Openers	1211
Hazardous Lawn Darts (banned)	1306

Hazardous Substances	1500
Human Subjects	1028
Lawn Mowers, Walk-Behind	1205
Lead-Containing Paint (banned)	1303
Matchbooks	1202
Mattresses	1632
Pacifiers	1511
Patching Compounds Containing Asbestos (banned)	1304
Poisons	1700
Rattles	1510
Self-Pressurized Consumer Products	1401
Sleepwear-Childrens	1615, 1616
Swimming Pool Slides	1207
Toys, Electrical	1505
Unstable Refuse Bins (banned)	1301

ADDITIONAL REGULATIONS

Every day there are proposals for new laws and regulations. To be up to date on the laws that affect your type of business, you should belong to a trade association for your industry and subscribe to newsletters that cover your industry. Attending industry conventions is a good way to learn more and to discover new ways to increase your profits.

ILLINOIS LAWS

SMOKING

The Illinois Clean Indoor Air Act (Ill. Comp. Stat. Title 410, Section 80) passed in 1990 contains the following rules regarding smoking in public places and at public meetings.

Public places means any enclosed indoor area used by the public or serving as a place of work including, but not limited to, hospitals, restaurants, retail stores, offices, commercial establishments, elevators, indoor theatres, libraries, art museums, concert halls, public conveyances, educational facilities, nursing homes, auditoriums, arenas, and meeting rooms. There are also excluded locations, these include: bowling establishments; places whose primary business is the sale of alcoholic beverages for consumption on the premises; rooms rented for the purpose of living quarters, sleeping, or housekeeping accommodations from a hotel, and private, enclosed offices occupied exclusively by smokers even though such offices may be visited by non-smokers.

- No person may smoke in a public place except in designated smoking areas, and in private social functions where the seating is controlled by the sponsor.

- Smoking areas of reasonable size may be designated. Smoke in adjacent non-smoking areas must be minimized, but no physical modification of the area is required.

- No more than half the rooms in a health care facility may be designated as smoking areas.

- No more than half the square footage of an enclosed area used for common purposes in a public place shall be designated for smoking except restaurants, which cannot have more than sixty-five percent of their dining room seats located in a designated smoking area.

- Designated smoking areas must be conspicuously posted with letters of reasonable size that can be easily read. "NO SMOKING EXCEPT IN DESIGNATED AREAS." Signs may also be posted when appropriate.

- Employers of smoking and non-smoking employees are required to institute and post policies regarding designation of smoking and non-smoking areas.

Employment and Labor Laws

11

Hiring and Firing Laws

For small businesses, there are not many rules regarding whom you may hire or fire. Fortunately, the ancient law that an employee can be fired at any time, or may quit at any time, still prevails for small businesses. But in certain situations, and as you grow, you will come under a number of laws that affect your hiring and firing practices.

One of the most important things to consider when hiring people is that if you fire them, they may be entitled to unemployment compensation. If so, your unemployment compensation taxes will go up and it can cost you a lot of money. Therefore, you should only hire people you are sure you will keep, and you should avoid situations where your former employees can collect compensation.

One way this can be done is by hiring only part time employees. The drawback to this is you may not be able to attract the best employees. When hiring dish washers or busboys this may not be an issue, but when hiring someone to develop a software product, you do not want them to leave halfway through the development.

A better solution is to screen applicants initially and only hire those whom you feel certain will work out. Of course, this is easier said than done. Some people interview well but turn out to be incompetent at the job.

The best record to look for is someone who has stayed a long time at each of their previous jobs. Next best is someone who has not stayed as long (for good reasons), but has always been employed. The worst type of hire would be someone who is or has been collecting unemployment compensation.

The reason those who have collected compensation are a bad risk is that if they collect in the future, even if it is not your fault, your employment of them could make you chargeable for their claim. For example, you hire someone who has been on unemployment compensation and he works out well for a year. He or she then quits to take another job, but is fired after a few weeks. In this situation, you would be chargeable for most of his claim because his last five quarters of work is analyzed. Look for a steady job history.

In some cases, the intelligence of an employee is more important than his or her experience. An employee with years of typing experience may be fast but unable to figure out how to use your new computer, whereas an intelligent employee can learn the equipment quickly and eventually gain speed. Of course, common sense is important in all situations.

The bottom line is that you cannot know if an employee will be able to fill your needs from a resume and interview. Once you have found someone whom you think will work out, offer them a job with a ninety day probationary period. If you are not completely satisfied with them after the ninety days, offer to extend the probationary period for ninety additional days rather than end the relationship immediately. Of course, all of this should be in writing.

BACKGROUND
CHECKS

Checking references is important, but beware that a former boss may be a good friend or even a relative. It has always been considered acceptable to exaggerate on resumes, but in recent years some applicants have been found to be completely fabricating sections of their education and experience.

POLYGRAPH
TESTS

Under the Federal Employee Polygraph Protection Act you cannot require an employee or prospective employee to take a polygraph test unless you are in the armored car, guard, or pharmaceutical business.

DRUG TESTS

Under the Americans with Disabilities Act, drug testing can only be required of applicants who have been offered jobs conditioned upon passing the drug test. Unlike some states, Illinois does not have drug-testing laws that regulate the private sector. Therefore, you are free to implement a reasonable drug-testing program on applicants or employees.

FIRING

In most cases, unless you have a contract with an employee for a set time period, you can fire him or her at any time. This is only fair since the employee can quit at any time. However, an employer may not terminate an employee based on race, color, religion, sex, national origin, ancestry, citizenship status, age, marital status, physical or mental handicap, or military service. Also, an employee may not be terminated for filing some sort of health or safety complaint (see Chapter 10), or for refusing your sexual advances (see page 89).

EMPLOYMENT AGREEMENTS

To avoid misunderstanding with employees you should use an employment agreement or an employee handbook. These can spell out in detail the policies of your company and the rights of your employees. They can protect your trade secrets and spell out clearly that employment can be terminated at any time by either party.

While it may be difficult or awkward to ask an existing employee to sign such an agreement, an applicant hoping to be hired will usually sign whatever is necessary to obtain the job. However, because of the unequal bargaining position, you should not use an agreement that would make you look bad if the matter ever went to court.

If having an employee sign an agreement is awkward, you can usually obtain the same rights by putting the company policies in an employee manual. Each existing and new employee should be given a copy along with a letter stating that the rules apply to all employees and that by accepting or continuing employment at your company they agree to abide by the rules. Having an employee sign a receipt for the letter and manual is proof that he or she received it.

One danger of an employment agreement or handbook is that it may be interpreted as a long term employment contract. To avoid this, be sure that you clearly state in the agreement or handbook that the employment is "at will," and can be terminated at any time by either party.

Some other things to consider in an employment agreement or handbook are:

- what the salary and other compensation will be;
- what the hours of employment will be;
- what the probationary period will be;
- that the employee cannot sign any contracts binding the employer; and,
- that the employee agrees to arbitration rather than filing a lawsuit.

USING INDEPENDENT CONTRACTORS

One way to avoid problems with employees, and taxes at the same time, is to have all of your work done through independent contractors. This can relieve you of most of the burdens of employment laws and the obligation to pay social security and medicare taxes for the workers.

Independent contractors are, in effect, a separate business that you pay to do a job. You pay them just as you pay any company from which you buy products or services. If, at the end of the year, the amount paid exceeds $600, you will issue a 1099 instead of a W-2.

This may seem too good to be true, and in some situations it is. The IRS does not like independent contractor arrangements because it is too easy for the independent contractors to cheat on their taxes. To limit the use of independent contractors, the IRS has strict regulations on who may or may not be classified an independent contractor. Also, companies who do not appear to pay enough in wages for their field of business are audited.

The highest at-risk jobs are those that are not traditionally done by independent contractors. For example, you could not get away with hiring a secretary as an independent contractor. One of the most important factors considered in determining if a worker can be an independent contractor is the amount of control the company has over his or her work. If you need people to paint your building and you agree to pay them a certain price to do it according to their own methods and schedule, you can pay them as an independent contractor. But if you tell them when to work, how to do the job, and provide them with the tools and materials, they would be classified as an employee.

If you just need some typing done and you take it to a typing service and pick it up when it is ready, you will be safe in treating them as independent contractors. But, if you need someone to come into your office to type on your machine at your schedule, you will probably be required to treat that person as an employee for tax purposes.

The IRS has a form you can use in determining if a person is an employee or an independent contractor. It is form SS-8 and can be obtained by calling the IRS at 1-800-829-3676.

INDEPENDENT CONTRACTORS v. EMPLOYEES

In deciding whether to make use of independent contractors or employees, you should weigh the following advantages and disadvantages.

Advantages of independent contractors.

- Lower taxes. You do not have to pay social security, medicare, unemployment, or other employee taxes.

- Less paperwork. You do not have to handle federal withholding deposits or the monthly employer returns to the state or federal government.

- Less insurance. You do not have to pay workers' compensation insurance, and since the workers are not your employees, you do not have to insure against their possible liabilities.

- More flexibility. You can use independent contractors when you need them and not pay them when business is slow.

Disadvantages.

- The IRS and state tax offices are strict about when workers may be qualified as independent contractors. They will audit companies whose use of independent contractors does not appear to be legitimate.

- If your use of independent contractors is found to be improper you may have to pay back taxes and penalties and have problems with your pension plan.

- While employees usually cannot sue you for their injuries (if you have covered them with workers' compensation), independent contractors can sue you if their injuries were your fault.

- If you are paying someone to produce a creative work (writing, photography, artwork) you receive less rights to the work of an independent contractor.

- You have less control over the work of an independent contractor and less flexibility in terminating them if you are not satisfied that the job is being done the way you require.

- You have less loyalty from an independent contractor who works sporadically for you and possibly others than from your own full time employees.

Consider your business plans and the consequences from each type of arrangement. Keep in mind that it will be easier to start with independent contractors and switch to employees than to hire employees and have to fire them to hire independent contractors.

TEMPORARY WORKERS

Another way to avoid the hassles of hiring employees is to get workers from a temporary agency. In this arrangement you may pay a higher amount per hour for the work, but the agency will take care of all of the tax and insurance requirements. Since these can be expensive and time-consuming, the extra cost may be worth while.

Whether or not temporary workers will work for you depends upon the type of business you are in and tasks you need performed. For such jobs as sales management, you would probably want someone who will stay with you long term and develop relationships with the buyers. For order fulfillment, temporary workers might work out well.

Another advantage of temporary workers is that you can easily stop using those who do not work out well for you, but if you find one who is ideal, you may be able to hire him or her on a full time basis.

In recent years a new wrinkle has developed in the temporary worker area. Many large companies are beginning to use them because they are so much cheaper than paying the benefits demanded by full time employees. For example, Microsoft Corp. has had as many as six thousand temporary workers, some of whom have worked there for years. Some of the temporary workers recently won a lawsuit declaring that they are really employees and are entitled to the same benefits as other employees (such as pension plans).

The law is not yet settled in this area as to what arrangements will result in a temporary worker being declared an employee. That will take several more court cases, some of which have already been filed. A few things you can do to protect yourself are:

- be sure that any of your benefit plans make it clear that they do not apply to workers obtained through temporary agencies;

- do not keep the same temporary workers for longer than a year;

- do not list temporary workers in any employee directories or hold them out to the public as your employees; and,

- do not allow them to use your business cards or stationery.

DISCRIMINATION LAWS

FEDERAL LAWS   There are numerous federal laws forbidding discrimination based upon race, sex, pregnancy, color, religion, national origin, age, or disability. The laws apply to both hiring and firing, and to employment practices such as salaries, promotions and benefits. Most of these laws only apply to an employer who has fifteen or more employees for twenty weeks of a calendar year or has federal contracts or subcontracts. Therefore, you most likely will not be required to comply with the law immediately upon opening your business. However, there are similar state laws that may apply to your business.

One exception is the Equal Pay Act that applies to employers with two or more employees and requires that women be paid the same as men in the same type of job.

Employers with fifteen or more employees are required to display a poster regarding discrimination. This poster is available from the Equal Employment Opportunity Commission, 2401 E. Street, N.W., Washington, DC 20506. Employers with 100 or more employees are required to file an annual report with the EEOC.

When hiring employees, some questions are illegal or inadvisable to ask. The following questions should not be included on your employment application, or in your interviews, unless the information is somehow directly tied to the duties of the job:

- Do not ask about an applicant's citizenship or place of birth. But after hiring an employee you must ask about his or her right to work in this country.

- Do not ask a female applicant her maiden name. In order to do a background check, you may ask if she has been known by any other name.

- Do not ask if applicants have children, plan to have them, or have child care. You can ask if an applicant will be able to work the required hours.

- Do not ask if the applicant has religious objections for working Saturday or Sunday. You can mention if the job requires such hours and ask whether the applicant can meet this job requirement.

- Do not ask an applicant's age. You can ask if an applicant is eighteen or over, or in regards to a liquor-related job, if they are twenty-one or over.

- Do not ask an applicant's weight.

- Do not ask if an applicant has AIDS or is HIV positive.

- Do not ask if the applicant has filed a workers' compensation claim.

- Do not ask about the applicant's previous health problems.

- Do not ask if the applicant is married or whether their spouse would object to the job, hours, or duties.

- Do not ask if the applicant owns a home, furniture, car, as it is considered racially discriminatory.

- Do not ask if the applicant was ever arrested. You can ask if the applicant was ever convicted of a crime.

The most recent applicable law is the Americans with Disabilities Act (ADA) of 1990. Under this law employers who do not make "reasonable accommodations for disabled employees" will face fines of up to $100,000, as well as other civil penalties and civil damage awards.

While the goal of creating more opportunities for people with disabilities is a good one, the result of this law is to place all of the costs of achieving this goal on businesses that are faced with disabled applicants. For example, it has been suggested that the requirement of "reasonable accommodation" will require some companies to hire blind applicants for jobs which require reading and then to hire second employees to read to the blind employees.

A study released by two MIT economists in late 1998 indicated that since the ADA was passed, employers have hired less rather than more disabled people. It is theorized that this may be due the the expense of the "reasonable accommodations," or the fear of lawsuits by disabled employees.

The ADA currently applies to employers with fifteen or more employees. Employers who need more than fifteen employees might want to consider independent contractors to avoid problems with this law, particularly if the number of employees is only slightly larger than fifteen.

To find out how this law affects your business, you might want to pay the government $25 for their *ADA Technical Assistance Manual.* You can order it from The Superintendent of Documents, P. O. Box 371954, Pittsburgh, PA 15250-7954, or you can fax your credit card order to 202-512-2233.

Tax benefits. There are three types of tax credits to help small businesses with the burden of these laws.

- Businesses can deduct up to $15,000 a year for making their premises accessible to the disabled and can depreciate the rest. (Internal Revenue Code (IRC) Section 190)

- Small businesses (under $1,000,000 in revenue and under 30 employees) can get a tax credit each year for 50% of the cost of making their premises accessible to the disabled, but this only applies to the amount between $250 and $10,500.

- Small businesses can get a credit of up to 40% of the first $6,000 of wages paid to certain new employees who qualify. See **Pre-screening Notice and Certification Request (IRS form 8850)** and its instructions (see form 14, p.226.)

ILLINOIS LAWS *Discrimination.* Illinois has its own laws regarding discrimination in employment practices, although they are not much different from federal laws. The Illinois Human Rights Act (Ill. Comp. Stat. Title 775, Section 5) prohibits discrimination or classification based upon race, color, religion, sex, national origin, age (over forty), handicap, marital status, or unfavorable discharge from military service. This law applies to employers with fifteen or more employees. An employer who violates this law can be sued and required to pay back pay, damages, and punitive damages. For more information, write to: Department of Human Rights, 222 S. College, Rm. 101A, Springfield, IL 62704.

Equal Pay. The Equal Wage Act (Ill. Comp. Stat. Title 820, Section 110) is Illinois' counterpart to the federal law providing for equal pay for the same job to both sexes. This statute applies only to employers engaged in manufacturing with six or more employees.

Sexual Harassment

FEDERAL LAWS

In the 1980s, the Equal Employment Opportunity Commission interpreted the Title VII of the Civil Rights Act of 1964 to forbid sexual harassment. After that, the courts took over and reviewed all types of conduct in the workplace. The numerous lawsuits that followed began a trend toward expanding the definition of sexual harassment.

Some of the actions that have been considered harassment are:

- displaying sexually explicit posters in the workplace;
- requiring female employees to wear revealing uniforms;
- rating of sexual attractiveness of female employees as they passed male employees' desks; and,
- continued sexual jokes and innuendos.

In 1993, the United States Supreme Court ruled that an employee can make a claim for sexual harassment even without proof of a specific injury. However, lower federal courts in more recent cases (such as the Paula Jones case against President Clinton) have dismissed cases where no specific injury was shown (although these cases may be overruled by a higher court).

On the other hand, another recent case ruled that an employer can be liable for the harassment of an employee by a supervisor, even if the employer was unaware of the supervisor's conduct, if the employer did not have a system in place to allow complaints against harassment. This area of law is still developing, and to avoid a possible lawsuit you should be aware of the things that could potentially cause liability.

Some things a business can do to protect against claims of sexual harassment are:

- distribute a written policy against all kinds of sexual harassment to all employees;

- encourage employees to report all incidents of sexual harassment; or,

- insure there is no retaliation against those who complain.

ILLINOIS LAWS Although the federal civil rights laws only apply to businesses with fifteen or more employees, it is possible for an employee to sue for sexual harassment in civil court. However, this is difficult and expensive and would only be worthwhile if there were substantial damages.

WAGE AND HOUR LAWS

FEDERAL LAWS **Businesses covered.** The Fair Labor Standards Act (FLSA) applies to all employers who are engaged in *interstate commerce* (anything which will cross the state line), or in the production of goods for interstate commerce and all employees of hospitals, schools, residential facilities for the disabled or aged, or public agencies. It also applies to all employees of enterprises that gross $500,000 or more per year.

While many small businesses might not think they are engaged in interstate commerce, the laws have been interpreted broadly so that nearly any use of the mails, interstate telephone service, or other interstate services, is enough to bring a business under the law.

Minimum wage. The federal wage and hour laws are contained in the federal Fair Labor Standards Act (FLSA). In 1996, Congress passed and President Clinton signed legislation raising the minimum wage to $5.15 an hour beginning September 1, 1997. Those under 18 years of age may be paid $4.65 per hour.

For employees who regularly receive more than $30 a month in tips, the minimum wage is $3.09 per hour. But if the employee's tips do not bring him or her up to the full $5.15 minimum wage, the employer must make up the difference.

Overtime. Workers who work over forty hours in a week must be paid time-and-a-half for the time worked over forty hours.

Exempt employees. While nearly all businesses are covered, certain employees are exempt from the FLSA. Exempt employees include employees that are considered executives, administrative and managerial, professionals, computer professionals, and outside salespeople.

Whether or not one of these exceptions applies to a particular employee is a complicated legal question. Thousands of court cases have been decided on this issue, but they have given no clear answers. In one case a person could be determined to be exempt because of his duties, but in another, a person with the same duties could be found not exempt.

One thing is clear: the determination is made on the employee's function, not just the job title. You cannot make a secretary exempt by calling her a manager if most of her duties are clerical.

For more information contact:

> Wage and Hour Division
> U. S. Department of Labor
> 200 Constitution Ave., N.W. Room S-3325
> Washington, DC 20210

Or call the closest office:

> Chicago 312-353-8145
> Springfield 217-492-4060

On the internet you can obtain information on the Department of Labor's *Employment Law Guide* at:

http://www.dol.gov/dol/asp/public/programs/handbook/contents.htm

ILLINOIS LAWS   Illinois has adopted the federal minimum wage, $5.15 per hour for employers of four or more workers. Workers under the age of eighteen may be paid up to 50¢ less per hour. Employers with fewer than four employees (not counting the employer's close relatives) are not subject to the minimum wage rate.

For more information, contact:

> Department of Labor
> #1 W. Old State Capitol Plaza
> Springfield, IL 62701

or visit their website at:

> http://www.state.il.us/agency/idol.

PENSION AND BENEFIT LAWS

There are no laws requiring small businesses to provide any types of special benefits to employees. Such benefits are given to attract and keep good employees. The main concern with pension plans is that if you do start one, it must comply with federal tax laws.

There are no federal or Illinois laws that require that employees be given holidays off. You can require them to work Thanksgiving and Christmas, and dock their pay or fire them for failing to show. Of course you will not have much luck keeping employees with such a policy.

HOLIDAYS   Most companies give full-time employees a certain number of paid holidays, such as New Year's Day (January 1), Memorial Day (last Monday in May), Fourth of July, Labor Day (first Monday in September), Thanksgiving (fourth Thursday in November), and Christmas (December 25). Some employers include other holidays such as Martin Luther King, Jr.'s birthday (January 15), President's Day, and Columbus Day. If one of the holidays falls on a Saturday or Sunday, many employers give the preceding Friday or following Monday off.

SICK DAYS   There is no federal or Illinois law mandating that an employee be paid for time he or she is home sick. The situation seems to be that the larger the company, the more paid sick leave is allowed. Part-time workers rarely get sick leave, and small business sick leave is usually limited because they cannot afford to pay for time that employees do not work.

Some small companies have an official policy of no paid sick leave, but when an important employee misses a day because he or she is clearly sick, it is paid.

BREAKS
There are no federal or Illinois laws requiring coffee breaks or lunch breaks. However, it is common sense that employees will be more productive if they have reasonable breaks.

PENSION PLANS
Few small new businesses can afford to provide pension plans for their employees. The first concern of a small business is usually how the owner can shelter income in a pension plan without having to set up a pension plan for an employee. Under most pension plans this is not allowed.

IRA. Anyone with $2,000 of earnings can put up to that amount in an Individual Retirement Account. Unless the person (or his or her spouse) is covered by a company pension plan and has income over a certain amount, the amount put into the account is fully tax deductible.

ROTH IRA. Contributions to a Roth IRA are not tax deductible, but when the money is taken out, it is not taxable. People who expect to still have taxable income when they withdraw from their IRA can benefit from these.

SEP IRA, SAR-SEP IRA, SIMPLE IRA. With these types of retirement accounts, a person can put a much greater amount into a retirement plan and deduct it from their taxable income. Employees must also be covered by such plans, but because certain employees are exempt, it is sometimes possible to use these for the owners alone. The best source for more information is a mutual fund company (such as Vanguard, Fidelity, Dreyfus, etc.), or a local bank. Either can set up the plan and provide you with all of the rules. These have an advantage over qualified plans (discussed below) because they do not have the high annual fees. One Internet site that contains useful information on these accounts is:

http://www.retirement-information.com/iraaccts.htm.

Qualified Retirement Plans. Qualified retirement plans are 401(k) plans, Keough plans, and corporate retirement plans. These are covered by ERISA (the Employee Retirement Income Security Act), which is a complicated law meant to protect employee pension plans in situations where the plan goes bankrupt. Many banks and mutual funds have created "canned plans," which can be used instead of drafting a new one from scratch. Still, the fees for administering them are steep. Check with a bank or mutual fund for details.

Family and Medical Leave Law

FEDERAL LAWS — Congress passed the Family and Medical Leave Act of 1993, which requires an employee to be given up to twelve weeks of unpaid leave when:

- the employee or employee's spouse has a child;
- the employee adopts a child or takes in a foster child;
- the employee needs to care for an ill spouse, child or parent; or,
- the employee becomes seriously ill.

The law only applies to employers with fifty or more employees. Also, the top ten percent of an employer's salaried employees can be denied this leave because of the disruption to business their loss could cause.

ILLINOIS LAW — Illinois statutes require that employers must give each employee up to eight hours off to attend a child's school activities or conferences that cannot be held during other hours (Ill. Comp. Stat. Title 820, Section 145/15). The employee must first use up all other vacation and other time off and must give the employer seven days notice, unless it is an emergency.

Child Labor Laws

FEDERAL LAW — The Federal Fair Labor Standards Act also contains rules regarding the hiring of children. The basic rules state that children under sixteen years old may not be hired, except in a few jobs such as acting and newspaper delivery. Also, those under eighteen may not be hired for dangerous jobs. Children may not work more than three hours a day (eighteen hours a week) in a school week, or more than eight hours a day (forty hours a week) in a non-school week. If you plan to hire children, you should check the Federal Fair Labor Standards Act, which is in Chapter 29, United States Code (USC Ch. 29), as well as the related regulations that are in Chapter 29 of the Code of Federal Regulations (CFR Ch. 29).

IMMIGRATION LAWS

In 1986, a law was passed by Congress that imposed stiff penalties for any business that hires aliens who are not eligible to work. Under this law you must verify both the identity and the employment eligibility of anyone you hire by using the EMPLOYMENT ELIGIBILITY VERIFICATION (IRS FORM I-9). (see form 4, p.194.) Both you and the employee must fill out the form, and you must check an employee's identification cards or papers. Fines for hiring illegal aliens range from $250 to $2,000 for the first offense and up to $10,000 for the third offense. Failure to maintain the proper paperwork may result in a fine of up to $1,000. The law does not apply to independent contractors with whom you may contract, and it does not penalize you if the employee used fake identification.

There are also penalties that apply to employers of four or more persons for discriminating against eligible applicants because they appear foreign or because of their national origin or citizenship status.

In Appendix C, there is a sample filled-in **IRS FORM I-9**, and instructions. A blank form is in Appendix D. (see form 4, p.194.) The blank form can also be downloaded from the following web site:

http://www.ins.gov/graphics/FormsFee/Forms/index.htm

For more information call 800-870-3676 for the *Handbook for Employers and Instructions for Completing Form I-9,* or check the INS website:

http://www.ins.usdoj.gov

For specific questions, call the INS office of Business Liaison hotline at 800-357-2099.

Hiring "Off the Books"

Because of the taxes, insurance, and red tape involved with hiring employees, some new businesses hire people off the books. The employers pay them in cash and never admit they are employees. While the cash paid in wages would not be deductible, they consider this a smaller cost than compliance. Some even use off the books receipts to cover it.

Except when your spouse or child is giving you some temporary help this is a terrible idea. Hiring people off the books can result in civil fines, loss of insurance coverage, and even criminal penalties. When engaged in dangerous work, like roofing or using power tools, you are risking millions of dollars in potential damages if a worker is seriously injured or killed.

It may be more costly and time consuming to comply with the employment laws, but if you are focused on long term growth with less risk, it is the wiser way to go.

Federal Contracts

Companies that do work for the federal government are subject to several laws such as those listed below.

DAVIS-BACON ACT

The Davis-Bacon Act requires contractors engaged in U.S. government construction projects to pay wages and benefits that are equal to or better than the prevailing wages in the area.

McNamara-O'Hara Service Contract Act

The McNamara-O'Hara Service Contract Act sets wages and other labor standards for contractors furnishing services to agencies of the U.S. government.

Walsh-Healey Public Contracts Act

The Walsh-Healey Public Contracts Act requires the Department of Labor to settle disputes regarding manufacturers supplying products to the U.S. government.

Miscellaneous Laws

Affirmative action. In most cases, the federal government does not yet tell employers who they must hire, especially small new businesses. The only situation in which a small business would need to comply with affirmative action requirements would be if it accepted federal contracts or subcontracts. These requirements could include the hiring of minorities or of Vietnam veterans.

Layoffs. Companies with one hundred or more full-time employees at one location are subject to the Worker Adjustment and Retraining Notification Act. This law requires a sixty day notification prior to certain lay-offs, and has other strict provisions.

Unions. The National Labor Relations Act of 1935 (U.S.C. Chapter 29 Section151 and following) gives employees the right to organize or join a union. There are things employers can do to protect themselves, but you should consult a labor attorney or a book on the subject before taking action that might be illegal and could result in fines.

Poster laws. There are laws regarding what posters you may or may not display in the workplace. A federal judge in 1991 ruled that Playboy posters in a workplace were sexual harassment. This ruling is being appealed by the American Civil Liberties Union (ACLU). In addition, there are other poster laws that require certain posters to be displayed to inform employees of their rights. Not all businesses are required to display all posters. The following list should be of help:

- All employers must display the wage and hour poster available from:

> U. S. Department of Labor
>
> 200 Constitution Ave., NW, Room 5-3325
>
> Washington, DC 20210

- Employers with fifteen or more employees for twenty weeks of the year must display the sex, race, religion, and ethnic discrimination poster, as well as the age discrimination poster, available from:

> EEOC
>
> 2401 E Street NW
>
> Washington, DC 20506

- Employers with federal contracts or subcontracts of $10,000 or more must display the sex, race, etc. discrimination poster mentioned above, plus a poster regarding Vietnam Era veterans available from the local federal contracting office.

- Employers with government contracts subject to the Service Contract Act or the Public Contracts Act must display a notice to employees working on government contracts, which is available from:

> Employment Standards Division
>
> U. S. Department of Labor
>
> 200 Constitution Ave., NW
>
> Washington, DC 20210

ILLINOIS LAWS
Termination of employee due to wage assignments or wage deduction orders. It is illegal in Illinois to fire or suspend an employee because of wage assignments. The quantity of these wage assignments is unimportant. However, it is legal to fire an employee if he or she is subject to two or more wage deduction orders based on more than one debt.

AIDS testing. No employer may require an employee to undergo an AIDS test unless the test subject gives written consent (Ill. Comp. Stat. Title 410, Section 305/14). No employer may disclose the identity of the subject of an AIDS test, or disclose the test results (except to the test subject or legally authorized representative (Ill. Comp. Stat. Title 410, Section 305/9).

Records access (Ill. Comp. Stat. Title 820, Section 40). There are restrictions concerning the type of records an employer may keep on an employee. An employee has the right to inspect his own personnel records, excluding items such as letters of reference, test documents, or staff planning materials.

Payment by mail. An employer must pay wages to an absent employee by mail if the employee so requests in writing.

Health and physical fitness requirements (Ill. Admin. Code Title 56, Section 2500.60(b)). Employers may require job applicants to submit to a pre-employment physical or a psychological examination to determine his or her capability to adequately perform the job requirements. One limitation on the use of such tests is that an employer may not use such tests to deny employment to an applicant on the basis of future risk of injury. The results of these tests must be made available if requested by an applicant.

Required poster. The Illinois Department of Labor requires employers to display the poster entitled "Notice to Employers and Employees." Request the poster by calling 312-793-2800 or 217-782-6206.

U.S. Department of Justice
Immigration and Naturalization Service

OMB No. 1115-0136

Employment Eligibility Verification

Please read instructions carefully before completing this form. The instructions must be available during completion of this form. **ANTI-DISCRIMINATION NOTICE.** It is illegal to discriminate against work eligible individuals. Employers **CANNOT** specify which document(s) they will accept from an employee. The refusal to hire an individual because of a future expiration date may also constitute illegal discrimination.

Section 1. Employee Information and Verification. To be completed and signed by employee at the time employment begins

Print Name: Last REDDENBACHER	First MARY	Middle Initial J.	Maiden Name HASSENFUSS

Address (Street Name and Number) 1234 LIBERTY LANE	Apt. #	Date of Birth (month/day/year) 1/26/69

City CHICAGO	State IL	Zip Code 60606	Social Security # 123-45-6789

I am aware that federal law provides for imprisonment and/or fines for false statements or use of false documents in connection with the completion of this form.

I attest, under penalty of perjury, that I am (check one of the following):
- ☒ A citizen or national of the United States
- ☐ A Lawful Permanent Resident (Alien # A _____)
- ☐ An alien authorized to work until ___/___/___
  (Alien # or Admission # _____)

Employee's Signature *Mary J. Reddenbacher*	Date (month/day/year) 1/29/00

Preparer and/or Translator Certification. *(To be completed and signed if Section 1 is prepared by a person other than the employee.)* I attest, under penalty of perjury, that I have assisted in the completion of this form and that to the best of my knowledge the information is true and correct.

Preparer's/Translator's Signature	Print Name

Address (Street Name and Number, City, State, Zip Code)	Date (month/day/year)

Section 2. Employer Review and Verification. To be completed and signed by employer. **Examine one document from List A OR examine one document from List B and one from List C** as listed on the reverse of this form and record the title, number and expiration date, if any, of the document(s)

List A	OR	List B	AND	List C
Document title: PASSPORT				
Issuing authority: PASSPORT AGENCY CHGO				
Document #: 123456789				
Expiration Date (if any): 10/5/06		___/___/___		___/___/___
Document #:				
Expiration Date (if any): ___/___/___				

CERTIFICATION - I attest, under penalty of perjury, that I have examined the document(s) presented by the above-named employee, that the above-listed document(s) appear to be genuine and to relate to the employee named, that the employee began employment on *(month/day/year)* 01/29/00 and that to the best of my knowledge the employee is eligible to work in the United States. (State employment agencies may omit the date the employee began employment).

Signature of Employer or Authorized Representative *Sidney Bones*	Print Name Sidney Bones	Title owner

Business or Organization Name Sid's Bones	Address (Street Name and Number, City, State, Zip Code) 6789 Graves Ave., Chicago, IL 60601	Date (month/day/year) 01/29/00

Section 3. Updating and Reverification. To be completed and signed by employer

A. New Name (if applicable)	B. Date of rehire (month/day/year) (if applicable)

C. If employee's previous grant of work authorization has expired, provide the information below for the document that establishes current employment eligibility.

Document Title: _____ Document #: _____ Expiration Date (if any): ___/___/___

I attest, under penalty of perjury, that to the best of my knowledge, this employee is eligible to work in the United States, and if the employee presented document(s), the document(s) I have examined appear to be genuine and to relate to the individual.

Signature of Employer or Authorized Representative	Date (month/day/year)

Form I-9 (Rev. 11-21-91) N

U.S. Department of Justice
Immigration and Naturalization Service

OMB No. 1115-0136
Employment Eligibility Verification

INSTRUCTIONS
PLEASE READ ALL INSTRUCTIONS CAREFULLY BEFORE COMPLETING THIS FORM.

Anti-Discrimination Notice. It is illegal to discriminate against any individual (other than an alien not authorized to work in the U.S.) in hiring, discharging, or recruiting or referring for a fee because of that individual's national origin or citizenship status. It is illegal to discriminate against work eligible individuals. Employers **CANNOT** specify which document(s) they will accept from an employee. The refusal to hire an individual because of a future expiration date may also constitute illegal discrimination.

Section 1 - Employee. All employees, citizens and noncitizens, hired after November 6, 1986, must complete Section 1 of this form at the time of hire, which is the actual beginning of employment. **The employer is responsible for ensuring that Section 1 is timely and properly completed.**

Preparer/Translator Certification. The Preparer/Translator Certification must be completed if Section 1 is prepared by a person other than the employee. A preparer/translator may be used only when the employee is unable to complete Section 1 on his/her own. However, the employee must still sign Section 1 personally.

Section 2 - Employer. For the purpose of completing this form, the term "employer" includes those recruiters and referrers for a fee who are agricultural associations, agricultural employers, or farm labor contractors.

Employers must complete Section 2 by examining evidence of identity and employment eligibility within three (3) business days of the date employment begins. If employees are authorized to work, but are unable to present the required document(s) within three business days, they must present a receipt for the application of the document(s) within three business days and the actual document(s) within ninety (90) days. However, if employers hire individuals for a duration of less than three business days, Section 2 must be completed at the time employment begins. **Employers must record: 1)** document title; **2)** issuing authority; **3)** document number, **4)** expiration date, if any; and **5)** the date employment begins. Employers must sign and date the certification. Employees must present original documents. Employers may, but are not required to, photocopy the document(s) presented. These photocopies may only be used for the verification process and must be retained with the I-9. **However, employers are still responsible for completing the I-9.**

Section 3 - Updating and Reverification. Employers must complete Section 3 when updating and/or reverifying the I-9. Employers must reverify employment eligibility of their employees on or before the expiration date recorded in Section 1. Employers **CANNOT** specify which document(s) they will accept from an employee.

- If an employee's name has changed at the time this form is being updated/ reverified, complete Block A.

- If an employee is rehired within three (3) years of the date this form was originally completed and the employee is still eligible to be employed on the same basis as previously indicated on this form (updating), complete Block B and the signature block.

- If an employee is rehired within three (3) years of the date this form was originally completed and the employee's work authorization has expired **or** if a current employee's work authorization is about to expire (reverification), complete Block B and:
  - examine any document that reflects that the employee is authorized to work in the U.S. (see List A **or** C),
  - record the document title, document number and expiration date (if any) in Block C, and
  - complete the signature block.

Photocopying and Retaining Form I-9. A blank I-9 may be reproduced provided both sides are copied. The Instructions must be available to all employees completing this form. Employers must retain completed I-9s for three (3) years after the date of hire **or** one (1) year after the date employment ends, whichever is later.

For more detailed information, you may refer to the INS Handbook for Employers, (Form M-274). You may obtain the handbook at your local INS office.

Privacy Act Notice. The authority for collecting this information is the Immigration Reform and Control Act of 1986, Pub. L. 99-603 (8 U.S.C. 1324a).

This information is for employers to verify the eligibility of individuals for employment to preclude the unlawful hiring, or recruiting or referring for a fee, of aliens who are not authorized to work in the United States.

This information will be used by employers as a record of their basis for determining eligibility of an employee to work in the United States. The form will be kept by the employer and made available for inspection by officials of the U.S. Immigration and Naturalization Service, the Department of Labor, and the Office of Special Counsel for Immigration Related Unfair Employment Practices.

Submission of the information required in this form is voluntary. However, an individual may not begin employment unless this form is completed since employers are subject to civil or criminal penalties if they do not comply with the Immigration Reform and Control Act of 1986.

Reporting Burden. We try to create forms and instructions that are accurate, can be easily understood, and which impose the least possible burden on you to provide us with information. Often this is difficult because some immigration laws are very complex. Accordingly, the reporting burden for this collection of information is computed as follows: **1)** learning about this form, 5 minutes; **2)** completing the form, 5 minutes; and **3)** assembling and filing (recordkeeping) the form, 5 minutes, for an average of 15 minutes per response. If you have comments regarding the accuracy of this burden estimate, or suggestions for making this form simpler, you can write to both the Immigration and Naturalization Service, 425 I Street, N.W., Room 5304, Washington, D. C. 20536; and the Office of Management and Budget, Paperwork Reduction Project, OMB No. 1115-0136, Washington, D.C. 20503.

Form I-9 (Rev. 11-21-91) N

EMPLOYERS MUST RETAIN COMPLETED I-9
PLEASE DO NOT MAIL COMPLETED I-9 TO INS

LISTS OF ACCEPTABLE DOCUMENTS

LIST A		LIST B		LIST C
Documents that Establish Both Identity and Employment Eligibility	**OR**	**Documents that Establish Identity**	**AND**	**Documents that Establish Employment Eligibility**

LIST A — Documents that Establish Both Identity and Employment Eligibility

1. U.S. Passport (unexpired or expired)

2. Certificate of U.S. Citizenship (INS Form N-560 or N-561)

3. Certificate of Naturalization (INS Form N-550 or N-570)

4. Unexpired foreign passport, with I-551 stamp or attached INS Form I-94 indicating unexpired employment authorization

5. Alien Registration Receipt Card with photograph (INS Form I-151 or I-551)

6. Unexpired Temporary Resident Card (INS Form I-688)

7. Unexpired Employment Authorization Card (INS Form I-688A)

8. Unexpired Reentry Permit (INS Form I-327)

9. Unexpired Refugee Travel Document (INS Form I-571)

10. Unexpired Employment Authorization Document issued by the INS which contains a photograph (INS Form I-688B)

LIST B — Documents that Establish Identity

1. Driver's license or ID card issued by a state or outlying possession of the United States provided it contains a photograph or information such as name, date of birth, sex, height, eye color, and address

2. ID card issued by federal, state, or local government agencies or entities provided it contains a photograph or information such as name, date of birth, sex, height, eye color, and address

3. School ID card with a photograph

4. Voter's registration card

5. U.S. Military card or draft record

6. Military dependent's ID card

7. U.S. Coast Guard Merchant Mariner Card

8. Native American tribal document

9. Driver's license issued by a Canadian government authority

For persons under age 18 who are unable to present a document listed above:

10. School record or report card

11. Clinic, doctor, or hospital record

12. Day-care or nursery school record

LIST C — Documents that Establish Employment Eligibility

1. U.S. social security card issued by the Social Security Administration (other than a card stating it is not valid for employment)

2. Certification of Birth Abroad issued by the Department of State (Form FS-545 or Form DS-1350)

3. Original or certified copy of a birth certificate issued by a state, county, municipal authority or outlying possession of the United States bearing an official seal

4. Native American tribal document

5. U.S. Citizen ID Card (INS Form I-197)

6. ID Card for use of Resident Citizen in the United States (INS Form I-179)

7. Unexpired employment authorization document issued by the INS (other than those listed under List A)

Illustrations of many of these documents appear in Part 8 of the Handbook for Employers (M-274)

ADVERTISING AND PROMOTION LAWS

12

ADVERTISING LAWS AND RULES

FEDERAL LAWS

The federal government regulates advertising through the Federal Trade Commission (FTC), with rules contained in the Code of Federal Regulations (CFR). You can find these rules in most law libraries and many public libraries. If you plan any advertising that you think may be questionable, you might want to check these rules.

Federal rules do not apply to every business. Small businesses that operate only within the state and do not use the postal service may be exempt. However, many of the federal rules have been adopted into law by the state of Illinois. Therefore, a violation could be prosecuted by the state rather than the federal government.

Some of the important rules are summarized below. If you wish to learn more details about the rules you should obtain copies from your library, or visit the FTC's website for further information:

http://www.ftc.gov/ftc/business.htm.

Deceptive pricing (CFR Title 16 Ch. I Part 233). When prices are being compared, it is required that actual and not inflated prices are used. For example, if an object would usually be sold for $7, you should not first offer it for $10 and then start offering it at 30% off. It is considered misleading to suggest that a discount from list price is a bargain if the item is rarely actually sold at list price. If most surrounding stores sell an item for $7, it is considered misleading to say it has a "retail value of $10," even if there are some stores elsewhere selling it at that price.

Bait advertising (CFR Title 16 Ch. I Part 238). Bait advertising is placing an ad when you don't really want the respondents to buy the product offered but to switch to another item. The factors used to determine if there was a violation are similar to those used by Illinois.

Use of "free," "half-off," or similar words (CFR Title 16 Ch. I Part 251). Use of words such as "free," "1¢ sale" and the like must not be misleading. This means that the regular price must not include a mark-up to cover the free item. The seller must also expect to sell the product without the free item at some time in the future.

Substantiation of claims (CFR Title 16, Section 3.40, Federal Register (FR) Volume 48, Page 10471, March 11, 1983). The FTC requires that advertisers be able to substantiate their claims.

Endorsements (CFR Title 16 Ch. I Part 255). This rule forbids endorsements that are misleading. It is not necessary to use the exact words of the person endorsing the product as long as the opinion is not distorted. If a product is changed, an endorsement that does not apply to the new version cannot be used. For some items, such as drugs, claims cannot be used without scientific proof. Endorsements by organizations cannot be used unless you are sure that the membership holds the same opinion.

Unfairness (USC Title 15, Section 45). Any advertising practices which can be deemed to be "unfair" are forbidden by the FTC.

Negative option plans (CFR Title 16 Ch. I Part 425). When a seller uses a sales system in which the buyer must notify the seller if he does not want the goods, the seller must provide the buyer with a form to decline the sale and at least ten days in which to decline. Bonus merchandise must be shipped promptly and the seller must promptly terminate any who so request after completion of the contract.

Laser eye surgery (USC Title 15, Sections 45, 52-57). Under the laws governing deceptive advertising, the FTC and the FDA are regulating the advertising of laser eye surgery. Anyone involved in this area should obtain a copy of these rules.

Food and dietary supplements (USC Title 21, Sections 343). Under the Nutritional Labeling Education Act of 1990, the FTC and the FDA regulate the packaging and advertising of food and dietary products. Anyone involved in this area should obtain a copy of these rules.

Jewelry and precious metals (FR Vol. 61 Page 27212). The FTC has numerous rules governing the sale and advertising of jewelry and precious metals. Anyone in this business should obtain a copy of these rules.

ILLINOIS LAWS   *Misleading advertising* (Ill. Comp. Stat. Title 720, Section 295/1a). It is illegal to use advertising that is untrue, misleading or deceptive. Violation of the act is a misdemeanor.

Free gifts (Ill. Comp. Stat. Title 815, Section 505/2P). It is an unlawful practice for any person to promote or advertise any business or product by means of offering free prizes or gifts, unless all material terms and conditions relating to the offer are clearly and conspicuously disclosed at the offset of the offer.

Going-out-of-business sales (Ill. Comp. Stat. Title 815, Section 350). No person may advertise or represent to the public that any sale of goods is a going-out-of-business, creditor's, or insolvent's sale of goods, unless a license is first obtained. The license must be prominently displayed. Violation is subject to a misdemeanor, injunction, or both.

Bait and switch (Ill. Comp. Stat. Title 720, Section 295/16). It is forbidden to advertise a product or service when there is no intention to fulfill the offer in the ad. Violators are subject to a misdemeanor, injunction, or both.

INTERNET SALES LAWS

There are not yet specific laws governing Internet transactions that are different from laws governing other transactions. The FTC feels that its current rules regarding deceptive advertising, substantiation, disclaimers, refunds, and related matters must be followed by Internet businesses and that consumers are adequately protected by them. See the first three pages of this chapter for that information.

For some specific guidelines on Internet advertising, see the FTC's site at:

http://www.ftc.gov/ftc/business.htm

HOME SOLICITATION LAWS

FEDERAL LAWS   The Federal Trade Commission has rules governing door-to-door sales. In any such sale, failure to furnish a receipt explaining the sale (in the language of the presentation) and giving notice that there is a three day right of recision is a deceptive trade practice. The notice must be supplied in duplicate, must be in at least 10-point type, and must be captioned either "Notice of Right to Cancel" or "Notice of Cancellation." The notice must be worded similar to the one on the following page.

The seller must complete the notice and orally inform the buyer of the right to cancel. He or she cannot misrepresent the right to cancel, assign the contract until the fifth business day, or include a confession of judgment in the contract. (For more specific details see the rules contained in CFR Title 16 Ch. I Part 429.)

```
NOTICE OF CANCELLATION

                              _____
                                      Date
        YOU MAY CANCEL THIS TRANSACTION, WITHOUT ANY PENALTY
OR OBLIGATION, WITHIN THREE BUSINESS DAYS FROM THE ABOVE
DATE.
        IF YOU CANCEL, ANY PROPERTY TRADED IN, ANY PAYMENTS
MADE BY YOU UNDER THE CONTRACT OR SALE, AND ANY NEGO-
TIABLE INSTRUMENT EXECUTED BY YOU WILL BE RETURNED TO YOU
WITHIN 10 BUSINESS DAYS FOLLOWING RECEIPT BY THE SELLER OF
YOUR CANCELLATION NOTICE, AND ANY SECURITY INTEREST ARIS-
ING OUT OF THE TRANSACTION WILL BE CANCELLED.
        IF YOU CANCEL, YOU MUST MAKE AVAILABLE TO THE SELLER AT
YOUR RESIDENCE, IN SUBSTANTIALLY AS GOOD CONDITION AS WHEN
RECEIVED, ANY GOODS DELIVERED TO YOU UNDER THIS CONTRACT
OR SALE; OR YOU MAY, IF YOU WISH, COMPLY WITH THE INSTRUC-
TIONS OF THE SELLER REGARDING THE RETURN SHIPMENT OF THE
GOODS AT THE SELLER'S EXPENSE AND RISK.
        IF YOU DO MAKE THE GOODS AVAILABLE TO THE SELLER AND
THE SELLER DOES NOT PICK THEM UP WITHIN 20 DAYS OF THE DATE
OF YOUR NOTICE OF CANCELLATION, YOU MAY RETAIN OR DISPOSE
OF THE GOODS WITHOUT ANY FURTHER OBLIGATION. IF YOU FAIL TO
MAKE THE GOODS AVAILABLE TO THE SELLER, OR IF YOU AGREE TO
RETURN THE GOODS AND FAIL TO DO SO, THEN YOU REMAIN LIABLE
FOR PERFORMANCE OF ALL OBLIGATIONS UNDER THE CONTRACT.
        TO CANCEL THIS TRANSACTION, MAIL OR DELIVER A SIGNED
AND DATED COPY OF THIS CANCELLATION NOTICE OR ANY OTHER
WRITTEN NOTICE, OR SEND A TELEGRAM, TO [name of seller], AT [address
of seller's place of business] NOT LATER THAN MIDNIGHT OF
_____ (date).
        I HEREBY CANCEL THIS TRANSACTION.
        (DATE) _____


                              _____
                              (Buyer's signature)
```

ILLINOIS LAWS   ***Right to cancel*** (Ill. Comp. Stat. Title 815, Section 505/2B). The buyer
may cancel in writing any sale over $25 solicited at the buyer's home.
The notice must be postmarked any time before midnight of the third
business day after the sales day.

Written agreement. Every sale solicited at the buyer's home must be in writing and must contain a similar notice as the following:

> **You, the consumer, may cancel this transaction at any time prior to midnight of the third business day after the date of this transaction. See the attached notice of cancellation form for an explanation of this right.**

The notice should appear in bold, 10-point type. You will need to consult the statute to obtain the additional language required for the cancellation form.

Refund. The refund must be made to the buyer within ten days of receiving the notice of cancellation. If it is not, the seller may be subject to criminal and civil penalties.

TELEPHONE SOLICITATION LAWS

FEDERAL LAWS

Phone calls. Telephone solicitations are governed by the Telephone Consumer Protection Act (USC Title 47, Section 227) and the Federal Communications Commission rules implementing the act (CFR Title 47, Section 64.1200). Violators of the act can be sued for $500 in damages by consumers and can be fined $10,000 by the FCC. Some of the requirements under the law are:

- calls can only be made between 8 A.M. and 9 P.M;
- solicitors must keep a "do not call" list and honor requests to not call;
- there must be a written policy stating that the parties called are told the name of the caller, the caller's business name, and the phone number or address. They must also be informed that the call is a sales call and the nature of the goods or services;
- personnel must be trained in the policies, and,
- recorded messages cannot be used to call residences.

Faxes. It is illegal under the act to send advertising faxes to anyone who has not consented to receiving such faxes or is an existing customer.

ILLINOIS LAWS   The Telephone Solicitation Act (Ill. Comp. Stat. Title 815, Section 420) applies to any telephone communication to solicit the sale of goods. Penalties for violations include:

- a judgment for three times the amount of damages;
- attorney's fees; and,
- court costs.

The law contains these main provisions:

Identification. Any person who makes a telephone solicitation call must identity himself or herself by true first and last name, and the name of the business represented, immediately upon making contact.

Time. No calls may be made between the hours of 9 P.M. and 8 A.M.

Consent. The person who makes a telephone solicitation call must obtain the consent of the person called at the beginning of the call.

Exceptions. This law does not apply to telephone calls made by registered investment advisors or brokers.

Faxes. It is illegal to send unsolicited advertising materials by fax within the state of Illinois (Ill. Comp. Stat. Title 720, Section 5/26-3).

Illinois recently passed a law providing for a "do not call" list to be published. Businesses calling persons on this list are subject to fines (Ill Comp. Stat. Title 815, Section 413/1).

WEIGHTS AND LABELING

FEDERAL LAWS   *Food products.* Beginning in 1994, all food products were required to have labels with information on the nutritional values, such as calories, fat, and protein. For most products, the label must be in the required format so that consumers can easily compare products. However, if such a format will not fit on the product label, the information may be presented in another form that is easily readable.

Metric measures. In 1994, federal rules requiring metric measurement of products took effect. The Federal Trade Commission (FTC) and the Food and Drug Administration enforce these rules against businesses.

Metric measures do not have to be the first measurement on the container, but they must be included. Food items that are packaged as they are sold, such as delicatessen items, do not have to contain metric labels.

ILLINOIS LAW Illinois has the Weights and Measures Act (Ill. Comp. Stat. Title 220, Section 470), which governs many specific aspects of weighing and packaging, especially food and agricultural products. If your product fits into one of these categories, you might want to consult this statute.

DECEPTIVE PRACTICES

ILLINOIS LAW If a business engages in deceptive or unfair practices in a consumer transaction, the Attorney General or a State's Attorney may bring court action against the business for *injunctions*, damages to consumers, and fines of up to $50,000. If the court finds that the practice in question was entered into with an intent to defraud, it may impose a penalty up to $50,000 per violation (Ill. Comp. Stat. Title 815, Section 505).

No damages can be recovered against a retailer who acted in *good faith* in repeating claims of a manufacturer or wholesaler, and did not know they were in violation of this law.

Payment and Collections Laws 13

Depending on the business you are in, you may be paid by cash, checks, credit cards, or some sort of financing arrangement, such as a promissory note or mortgage. Both state and federal laws affect the type of payments you collect, and failure to follow these laws can cost you considerably.

Cash

Cash is probably the easiest form of payment and it is subject to few restrictions. The most important of these are:

- that you keep an accurate accounting of your cash transactions; and,
- report all of your cash income on your tax return.

Recent efforts to stop the drug trade have resulted in some serious penalties for failure to report cash transactions and for money laundering. The laws are so sweeping that even if you deal with cash in an ordinary business, you may violate the law and be subject to substantial fines.

The most important law to be concerned with is the one requiring the filing of THE REPORT OF CASH PAYMENTS OVER $10,000 (IRS FORM 8300) for cash transactions of $10,000 or more. (see form 13, p.222.)

A transaction does not have to happen in one day. If a person brings you smaller amounts of cash which add up to $10,000 and the government can construe them as one transaction, the form must be filed. Under this law, "cash" also includes travelers' checks and money orders, but not cashier's checks or bank checks. For more information, obtain **IRS FORM 8300** and instructions from the IRS.

CHECKS

ACCEPTING
CHECKS

It is important to accept checks in your business. While there is a small percentage that will be bad, most checks will be good, and you will be able to accommodate more customers. To avoid having problems with checks, you should follow the following rules.

Illinois law forbids a business from requiring a customer to provide a credit card number or expiration date in order to pay by or cash a check. (Ill. Comp. Stat. Title 810 Section 5/3-505A.) The business can request to see a card to establish that the customer is credit-worthy, or for additional identification, and can record the type of credit card and issuing company. The business cannot record the number of the card. The penalty for the first violation a fine of $500.

BAD CHECKS

Illinois has a fairly effective bad check collection process. If you follow the rules, you will probably be able to collect on a bad check. Some counties even have special divisions of the sheriff's department which actively help you collect on bad checks.

The first rule is that you must be able to identify the person who gave you the check. To do this, you should require identification and write down the sources of identification on the face of the check, such as their phone, drivers license, and social security numbers. Another rule is that you cannot accept post-dated checks. Also, you must send a demand to the person by certified mail, return receipt requested, that they pay the amount of the check plus a penalty of $25 (Ill. Comp. Stat. Title 810 Section 5/3-806). If the customer fails to pay the amount of the written check within thirty days, he is liable for costs and expenses, including reasonable attorneys fees, incurred in collection proceedings. Another option is to contact the local State's Attorney's Office to initiate criminal prosecution.

REFUNDS AFTER CASHING A CHECK

A popular scam is for a person to purchase something by using a check, only to return the next day demanding a refund. After making the refund, the business discovers the initial payment check bounced. Do not make refunds until checks clear!

CREDIT CARDS

In our buy-now, pay-later society, charge cards can add greatly to your sales potential, especially with large, discretionary purchases. For MasterCard, Visa and Discover, the fees you pay are about two percent, and this amount is easily paid for by the extra purchases that the cards allow. (American Express, however, charges four to five percent.)

For businesses that have a *retail outlet* there is usually no problem getting merchant status. Most commercial banks can handle it. Discover can also set you up to accept their card as well as MasterCard and Visa, and they will wire the money into your bank account daily. However, for mail order businesses, especially those operating out of the home, it is much harder to get merchant status.

Today things are a little better. Some companies are even soliciting merchants. But beware of those that charge exorbitant fees (such as $5 or $10 per order for "processing"). American Express will accept mail order companies operating out of the home. However, not as many people have their cards.

Some companies open a small storefront (or share one) to get merchant status, and then process mostly mail orders. The processors usually do not want to accept you if you will do more than fifty percent mail order; but if you do not have many complaints, you may be allowed to process mostly mail orders.

You might be tempted to try to run your charges through another business. This may be okay if you actually sell your products through them; however, if you run your business charges through their account, the other business may lose its merchant status. People who bought a book by mail from you and then have a charge on their statement from a florist shop will probably call the credit card company saying that they never bought anything from the florist shop. Too many of these complaints and the account will be closed.

FINANCING LAWS

Some businesses can make sales more easily if they finance the purchases themselves. If the business has enough capital to do this, it can earn extra profits on the financing terms. However, because of abuses, many consumer protection laws have been passed by both the federal and state governments.

FEDERAL LAWS

Reg. Z. Two important federal laws regarding financing are called the Truth in Lending Act and the Fair Credit Billing Act. These are implemented by what is called Regulation Z (commonly known as Reg. Z), issued by the Board of Governors of the Federal Reserve System. It is contained in Volume 12 of the Code of Federal Regulations, page 226 (CFR Vol. 12, Page 226).

The regulation covers all transactions in which the following four conditions are met:

- credit is offered;
- the offering of credit is regularly done;
- there is a finance charge for the credit or there is a written agreement with more than four payments; and,
- the credit is for personal, family, or household purposes.

It also covers credit card transactions where only the first two conditions are met. It applies to leases if the consumer ends up paying the full value and keeping the item leased. It does not apply to the following transactions:

- transactions with businesses or agricultural purposes;

- transactions with organizations such as corporations or the government;

- transactions of over $25,000 which are not secured by the consumer's dwelling;

- credit involving public utilities;

- credit involving securities or commodities; and,

- home fuel budget plans.

The way for a small business to avoid Reg. Z violations is to avoid transactions which meet the conditions or to make sure all transactions fall under the exceptions. This is easy for many businesses. Instead of extending credit to customers, accept credit cards and let the credit card company extend the credit. However, if your customers usually do not have credit cards, or if you are in a business which often extends credit (such as used car sales), you should consult a lawyer knowledgeable about Reg. Z. Or, if you dare, get a copy for yourself.

ILLINOIS LAWS   Illinois also has laws regarding financing arrangements. The law specifies what size type must be used in printed contracts, what notices must be included in them, as well as many other details. Anyone engaged in installment sales in Illinois should carefully review the latest versions of the following statutes:

- Consumer Installment Loan Act
  (Ill. Comp. Stat. Title 205, Section 670)

- Motor Vehicle Retail Installment Sales Act
  (Ill. Comp. Stat. Title 815, Section 375)

- Rental-Purchase Agreement Act
  (Ill Comp Stat. Title 815, Section 655)

- Retail Installment Sales Act
  (Ill. Comp. Stat. Title 815, Section 405)

In addition to these acts, Ill. Comp. Stat. Title 775, Section 5/4-102 forbids discrimination based upon sex, marital status, or race in the areas of loaning money and granting credit. And Ill. Comp. Stat. Title 775,

Section 5/3-102 forbids discrimination in the financing of residential real estate based upon race, color, national origin, sex, handicap, familial status, or religion.

USURY

Usury is the charging of an illegally high rate of interest. In Illinois, the maximum rate of interest you may charge is twenty percent. In some cases, the maximum rate is nine percent (see 815 ILCS 205/4, 4a). If there is no written agreement as to the rate of interest, the rate is set by law.

The penalty for charging above the legal rate is that the borrower may recover twice the total of all interest and charges, plus attorney's fees and court costs.

Anyone charging or receiving interest at a rate of over twenty percent is guilty of a felony.

COLLECTIONS

FEDERAL LAW   The Fair Debt Collection Practices Act of 1977 bans the use of deception, harassment, and other unreasonable acts in the collection of debts. It has strict requirements whenever someone is collecting a debt for someone else. If you are in the collection business, you must obtain a copy of this law.

The Federal Trade Commission has issued some rules that prohibit deceptive representations, such as:

- pretending to be in the motion picture industry, the government, or a credit bureau;
- using questionnaires that do not say their purpose is collecting a debt; or,
- any combination of these (CFR Title 16, Ch. I Part 237).

ILLINOIS LAWS

The Collection Agency Act (Ill. Comp. Stat. Title 225, Section 425) applies to debts owed by persons (not corporations) for transactions that were for personal, family, or household purposes. The law forbids:

- simulating a law enforcement officer or government agency;

- using or threatening force or violence;

- threatening to disclose the debt to others without explaining that the dispute over the debt will also be disclosed;

- contacting or threatening to contact a debtor's employer prior to obtaining a final judgment after the debt went to collection (unless the debtor gave permission in writing or agreed in writing as to the debt);

- disclosing information affecting the debtor's reputation to persons outside the debtor's family who do not have a legitimate business need for the information;

- disclosing false information affecting the debtor's reputation;

- disclosing information about a disputed debt without disclosing the dispute;

- willfully harassing the debtor or his or her family;

- using profane, obscene, vulgar, or willfully abusive language with the debtor or his or her family;

- attempting to collect a debt that is not legitimate;

- claiming a legal right, knowing that this right does not exist;

- using communication that looks like it is from a court, government, or attorney if it is not;

- pretending to be an attorney by using attorney's stationery or forms;

- orally pretending to be an attorney or associated with an attorney;

- advertising or threatening to advertise the sale of a claim, unless under court order or as assignee;

- publishing or posting a deadbeat list;

- refusing to identify one's self or employer when requested by a debtor;

- mailing any communication to a debtor that contains embarrassing words on the outside of the envelope; and,

- communicating with a debtor between 9 P.M. and 8 A.M. without prior consent of the debtor.

Violation of any of the above is subject to a fine of not more than $1000. The Division of Consumer Services also investigates the debtors' complaints of violations of this law. The agency may issue warnings, reprimands, revocation of licensing, and fines. The State's Attorney may seek criminal penalties and injunctions for certain violations.

Business Relations Laws 14

The Uniform Commercial Code

The Uniform Commercial Code is a set of laws regulating numerous aspects of business. A national group drafted this set of uniform laws to avoid having a patchwork of different laws around the fifty states. Although some states modified some sections of the laws, the code is basically the same in most of the states. In Illinois the "UCC," as it is called, is contained in Illinois Compiled Statutes Title 810, Section 512. Each chapter is concerned with a different aspect of commercial relations, such as sales, warranties, bank deposits, commercial paper, and bulk transfers.

Businesses that wish to know their rights in all types of transactions should obtain a copy of the UCC. It is especially useful in transactions between merchants. However, the meaning is not always clear from a reading of the statutes.

Commercial Discrimination

FEDERAL LAWS The Robinson-Patman Act of 1936 prohibits businesses from injuring competition by offering the same goods at different prices to different buyers. This means that the large chain stores should not be getting a better price than your small shop. It also requires that promotional allowances must be made on proportionally the same terms to all buyers.

As a small business, you may be the victim of Robinson-Patman Act violations. A good place to look for information on the act is the following web site:

http://www.lawmall.com/rpa/.

ILLINOIS LAW   Unlike some states, Illinois has not enacted a counterpart to the Robinson-Patman Act.

RESTRAINING TRADE

FEDERAL LAWS   One of the earliest federal laws affecting business is the Sherman Antitrust Act of 1890. The purpose of the law was to protect competition in the marketplace by prohibiting monopolies. For example, one large company might buy out all of its competitors and then raise prices to astronomical levels. In recent years, this law was used to break up AT&T.

Examples of some prohibited actions are:

- agreements between competitors to sell at the same prices;
- agreements between competitors on how much will be sold or produced;
- agreements between competitors to divide up a market;
- refusing to sell one product without a second product; and,
- exchanging information among competitors that results in similarity of prices.

As a new business, you probably will not be in a position to violate the act, but you should be aware of it in case a larger competitor tries to put you out of business. A good place to find information on the act is the following Internet site:

http://www.lawmall.com/sherman.act/index.html.

ILLINOIS LAWS   Under the Illinois Antitrust Act (Ill. Comp. Stat. Title 740, Section10), it is unlawful to have any contract, combination, or conspiracy to restrain trade. It is also unlawful to monopolize, attempt to monopolize, or combine or conspire with any other person to monopolize, any part of trade or commerce.

- The penalty for any violation is up to $100,000 for a person, and up to $1,000,000 for a company.

- A person whose business is hurt by a violation can seek an injunction to prohibit violations. In a suit against a violator, he or she may collect triple damages, plus costs and attorney fees.

COMMERCIAL BRIBERY

ILLINOIS LAWS   A person commits commercial bribery when he or she confers any benefit upon any employee without the consent of the employer with intent to influence his conduct in relation to his employer's affairs. Violations result in a fine of up to $5,000 (Ill. Comp. Stat. Title 720, Section 5/29A-1).

INTELLECTUAL PROPERTY PROTECTION

As a business owner, you should know enough about intellectual property laws to protect your own creations and to keep from violating the rights of others. Intellectual property is the product of human creativity, such as writings, designs, inventions, melodies, and processes. Intellectual property are things which can be stolen without being physically taken. For example, if you write a book, someone can steal the words from your book without stealing a physical copy of it.

As the Internet grows, intellectual property is becoming more valuable. Smart business owners will take the actions necessary to protect their company's intellectual property. Additionally, business owners should know intellectual property laws to make certain they do not violate the rights of others. Even an unknowing violation of the law can result in stiff fines and penalties.

The following paragraphs explain the types of intellectual property and the ways to protect them.

PATENT A *patent* is protection given to new and useful inventions, discoveries and designs. To be entitled to a patent, a work must be completely new and "unobvious." The first inventor who files for a patent gets it. Once an invention is patented, no one else can make use of that invention, even if they discover it independently. A patent protects an invention for 17 years; designs it protects for 3 1/2, 7 or 14 years. Patents cannot be renewed. The patent application must clearly explain how to make the invention, so when the patent expires, others will be able to freely make and use the invention. Patents are registered with the United States Patent and Trademark Office (PTO). Patentable items include mechanical devices or new drug formulas.

COPYRIGHT A *copyright* is protection given to "original works of authorship," such as written works, musical works, visual works, performance works, or computer software programs. A copyright exists from the moment of creation, but one cannot register a copyright until it has been fixed in tangible form. Also, titles, names, or slogans cannot be copyrighted. A copyright currently gives the author and his or her heirs exclusive right to the work for the life of the author plus seventy years. Copyrights first registered before 1978 last for 95 years. This was previously 75 years, but was extended 20 years to match the European system. Copyrights are registered with the Register of Copyrights at the Library of Congress. The fee to register a copyright is $20.00. Examples of works that are copyrightable include books, paintings, songs, poems, plays, drawings, and films.

TRADEMARK A *trademark* is protection given to a name or symbol that is used to distinguish one person's goods or services from those of others. It can consist of letters, numbers, packaging, labeling, musical notes, colors, or a combination of these. If a trademark is used on services, as opposed to goods, it is called *service mark*. A trademark lasts indefinitely if it is used continuously and renewed properly. Trademarks are registered with the United States Patent and Trademark Office and with individual states. This is explained further in Chapter 3. Examples of trademarks include the "Chrysler" name on automobiles, the red border on TIME magazine, and the shape of the Coca-Cola bottle.

TRADE SECRETS
A *trade secret* is information or process that provides a commercial advantage that is protected by keeping it a secret. Examples of trade secrets may be a list of successful distributors, the formula for Coca-Cola, or some unique source code in a computer program. Trade secrets are not registered anywhere, but they are protected by the fact that they are not disclosed. They are protected only for as long as they are kept secret. If you independently discover the formula for Coca-Cola tomorrow, you can freely market it. (But you can't use the trademark "Coca-Cola" on your product to market it.)

Illinois law. Illinois has passed the UNIFORM TRADE SECRETS ACT, which protects trade secrets from appropriation by other businesses. The law is contained at 765ILCS1065/1 of the Illinois Statutes. It provides for injunctions, damages, and attorneys fees for violation of the act.

There are numerous other Illinois laws dealing with trade secrets. If you have some concerns about trade secrets in your business, you should check the index to Illinois statutes under "trade secrets."

NON-PROTECTABLE
CREATIONS
Some things are just not protectable, such as ideas, systems, and discoveries which are not allowed any protection under law. If you have a great idea, such as selling packets of hangover medicine in bars, you cannot stop others from doing the same thing. If you invent a new medicine you can patent it, and if you pick a distinctive name for it you can register the name as a trademark. Also, you can copyright any unique pictures or instructions you create for the package. However, you cannot stop others from using your basic business idea of marketing hangover medicine in bars.

Notice the subtle differences between the protective systems available. If you invent something two days after someone else does and that person has patented it, you cannot even use it for yourself, but if you write the same poem as someone else and neither of you copied the other, both of you can copyright the poem. If you patent something, you can have the exclusive rights to it for the term of the patent, but you must disclose how others can recreate it after the patent expires. However, if you keep it a trade secret, you have exclusive rights as long as no one learns the secret.

We are in a time of transition of the law of intellectual property. Every year new changes are made in the laws and new forms of creativity win protection. For more information you should consult a new edition of a book on these types of property. Some are listed in the section of this book entitled "for further reading."

ENDLESS LAWS 15

The state of Illinois and the federal government have numerous laws and rules that apply to every aspect of every type of business. There are laws governing such things as fence posts, hosiery, rabbit raising, refund policies, frozen desserts and advertising. Every business is affected by one or another of these laws.

Some activities are covered by both state and federal laws. In such cases, you must obey the stricter of the rules. In addition, more than one agency of the state or federal government may have rules governing your business. Each of these may have the power to investigate violations and impose fines or other penalties.

Penalties for violations of these laws can range from a warning to a criminal fine, or even jail time. In some cases, employees can sue for damages. Recently, employees have been given awards of millions of dollars from employers who violated the law. Since "ignorance of the law is no excuse," it is your duty to learn what laws apply to your business.

Very few people in business know the laws that apply to their businesses. If you take the time to learn them, you can become an expert in your field and avoid problems with regulators. You can also fight back if one of your competitors uses an illegal method to compete with you.

The laws and rules that affect most businesses are explained in this section. Following the explanation is a list of more specialized laws. You should read through this list and see which ones may apply to your business. Then go to your public library or law library and read them. Some may not apply to your phase of the business. If any of them do apply, you should make copies to keep on hand.

No one could possibly know all the rules that affect business, much less comply with all of them. The Interstate Commerce Commission alone has 40 trillion rates on its books telling the transportation industry what it should charge! You will stay out of trouble and have more chance of success if you keep up with the important rules.

FEDERAL LAWS

The federal laws that are most likely to affect small businesses are rules of the Federal Trade Commission (FTC). The FTC has some rules that affect many businesses, the rules about labeling, warranties, and mail order sales are just some examples. Other rules affect only certain industries.

If you sell goods by mail you should send for their booklet, *A Business Guide to the Federal Trade Commission's Mail Order Rule*. You should ask for their latest information on the subject if you are going to be involved in an industry such as those listed below, or using warranties or your own labeling. The address is:

Federal Trade Commission
Washington, DC 20580

The rules of the FTC are contained in the Code of Federal Regulations (CFR) in Chapter 16. Some of the industries covered are:

Industry	Part
Adhesive Compositions	235
Aerosol Products Used for Frosting Cocktail Glasses	417
Automobiles (New car fuel economy advertising)	259
Barber Equipment and Supplies	248
Binoculars	402
Business Opportunities and Franchises	436
Cigarettes	408
Decorative Wall Paneling	243
Dog and Cat Food	241
Dry Cell Batteries	403
Extension Ladders	418

Some other federal laws which affect businesses are as follows:

- Alcohol Administration Act (U.S.C. Title 29, Section 201 et seq.).
- Child Protection and Toy Safety Act (1969).
- Clean Water Act (U.S.C. Title 33).
- Comprehensive Smokeless Tobacco Health Education Act (1986). See also CFR Title 16, Ch. I, Part 307 for rules.
- Consumer Credit Protection Act (1968).
- Consumer Product Safety Act (1972).
- Energy Policy and Conservation Act. See also CFR Title 16, Ch. I, Part 305 for rules about energy cost labeling.
- Environmental Pesticide Control Act of 1972.
- Fair Credit Reporting Act (1970).
- Fair Packaging and Labeling Act (1966). See also CFR Title 16, Ch. I, Parts 500-503 for rules.
- Flammable Fabrics Act (1953). See also CFR Title 16, Ch. II, Parts 1602-1632 for rules.
- Food, Drug, and Cosmetic Act (U.S.C. Title 21, Section 301 et seq.).
- Fur Products Labeling Act (1951). See also CFR Title 16, Ch. I, Part 301 for rules.
- Hazardous Substances Act (1960).
- Hobby Protection Act. See also CFR Title 16 Ch. I, Part 304 for rules.
- Insecticide, Fungicide, and Rodenticide Act (U.S.C. Title 7, Section136 et seq.).
- Magnuson-Moss Warranty Act. See also CFR Title 16, Ch. I, Part 239 for rules.
- Poison Prevention Packaging Act of 1970. See also CFR Title 16, Ch. II, Parts 1700-1702 for rules.
- Solid Waste Disposal Act (U.S.C. Title 42, Section 6901 et seq.).
- Textile Fiber Products Identification Act. See also CFR Title 16, Ch. I, Part 303 for rules.
- Toxic Substance Control Act (U.S.C. Title 15).

- Wool Products Labeling Act (1939). See also CFR Title 16 Ch. I, Part 300 for rules.
- Nutrition Labeling and Education Act of 1990 (CFR Title 21, Ch. I, Subch. B.
- Food Safety Enforcement Enhancement Act of 1997.

ILLINOIS LAWS

Illinois has numerous laws regulating specific types of businesses or certain activities of businesses. The following is a list of the laws that are most likely to affect small businesses.

Citations refer to a version of Illinois laws called the Illinois Compiled Statutes.

Adoption agencies	Ill. Comp. Stat. Title 750, Section 50/4.1
Adult congregate living facilities	Ill. Comp. Stat. Title 210, Section 35
Adult foster care	Ill. Comp. Stat. Title 210, Section 135/3
Air conditioning	Ill. Comp. Stat. Title 65, Section 5/11-32-1, Ill. Comp. Stat. Title 720, Section 220, Ill. Comp. Stat. Title 235, Section 5
Alarm contractors	Ill. Comp. Stat. Title 225, Section 446
Ambulance services	Ill. Comp. Stat. Title 210, Section 50/9
Animals	Ill. Comp. Stat. Title 510, Section 5
Bail bondsmen	Ill. Comp. Stat. Title 725, Section 5/103-9
Banking	Ill. Comp. Stat. Title 810, Section 5/4
Bed and breakfast establishments	Ill. Comp. Stat. Title 50, Section 820
Boiler safety	Ill. Comp. Stat. Title 430, Section 75
Boxing and fighting	Ill. Comp. Stat. Title 225, Section 105
Brake fluid	Ill. Comp. Stat. Title 625, Section 5/12-302
Business records	Ill. Comp. Stat. Title 805, Section 410
Cemeteries	Ill. Comp. Stat. Title 410, Section 535
Charitable solicitation	Ill. Comp. Stat. Title 225, Section 460
Child day care	Ill. Comp. Stat. Title 225, Section 10/3
Collections	Ill. Comp. Stat. Title 225, Section 425
Commissions merchants	Ill. Comp. Stat. Title 225, Section 615
Condominiums	Ill. Comp. Stat. Title 765, Section 605
Construction	Ill. Comp. Stat. Title 225, Section 335
Consumer finance	Ill. Comp. Stat. Title 205, Section 660
Cosmetics	Ill. Comp. Stat. Title 610, Section 420
Credit cards	Ill. Comp. Stat. Title 720, Section 250
Credit services organizations	Ill. Comp. Stat. Title 815, Section 605

Dairies	Ill. Comp. Stat. Title 410, Section 635
Dance studio	Ill. Comp. Stat. Title 815, Section 610
Dating referral services	Ill. Comp. Stat. Title 815, Section 615
Drugs	Ill. Comp. Stat. Title 30, Section 580, Ill. Comp. Stat. Title 410, Section 620, Ill. Comp. Stat. Title 720, Section 570
Elevators	Ill. Comp. Stat. Title 430, Section 80, Ill. Comp. Stat. Title 410, Section 30
Energy conservation standards	Ill. Comp. Stat. Title 20, Section 1115
Explosives	Ill. Comp. Stat. Title 225, Section 210
Farm produce	Ill. Comp. Stat. Title 225, Section 615
Fences	Ill. Comp. Stat. Title 765, Section 130
Fertilizers	Ill. Comp. Stat. Title 505, Section 80
Fiduciaries	Ill. Comp. Stat. Title 205, Section 620
Fireworks	Ill. Comp. Stat. Title 425, Section 30
Food	Ill. Comp. Stat. Title 410, Section 620
Franchises	Ill. Comp. Stat. Title 815, Section 705
Fruits and vegetables	Ill. Comp. Stat. Title 505, Section 65
Fuels	Ill. Comp. Stat. Title 430, Section 30
Gambling and lotteries	Ill. Comp. Stat. Title 720 , Section 5/28
Gas, liquefied petroleum	Ill. Comp. Stat. Title 430, Section 75/5
Gasoline and oil	Ill. Comp. Stat. Title 220, Section 5/9
Glass	Ill. Comp. Stat. Title 430, Section 60
Hazardous substances	Ill. Comp. Stat. Title 430, Section 35, Ill. Comp. Stat. Title 415, Section 5
Health care	Ill. Comp. Stat. Title 20, Section 3960 Ill. Comp. Stat. Title 305, Section 5/5
Health clubs	Ill. Comp. Stat. Title 815, Section 645
Home health agencies	Ill. Comp. Stat. Title 210, Section 55
Honey	Ill. Comp. Stat. Title 410, Section 620/11
Horse sales, shows, exhibitions	Ill. Comp. Stat. Title 510, Section 65
Hospices	Ill. Comp. Stat. Title 210, Section 60
Hotels	Ill. Comp. Stat. Title 740, Section 90
Household products	Ill. Comp. Stat. Title 720, Section 5/16C-1
Identification cards	Ill. Comp. Stat. Title 15, Section 335
Insurance and service plans	Ill. Comp. Stat. Title 215, Section 5
Invention development	Ill. Comp. Stat. Title 815, Section 620/101
Job referral services	Ill. Comp. Stat. Title 815, Section 630
Land sales	Ill. Comp. Stat. Title 765, Section 85
Lasers and non-ionizing radiation	Ill. Comp. Stat. Title 420, Section 55
Lead acid batteries	Ill. Comp. Stat. Title 415, Section 5/22, 23
Legal services	Ill. Comp. Stat. Title 705, Section 210
Linen suppliers	Ill. Comp. Stat. Title 765, Section 1045
Liquor	Ill. Comp. Stat. Title 235, Section 5

POSTER LAWS

Illinois requires that employers post certain notices in the workplace. Some of these notices have been previously discussed, for example, posters relating to discrimination, wage and hour laws, worker's compensation, etc. These may be obtained from the Commission of Human Rights:

Department of Human Rights
222 S. College, Rm. 101A
Springfield, IL 62704

Bookkeeping and Accounting 16

Without accurate records of where your income is coming from and where it is going, you will be unable to increase your profits, lower your expenses, obtain needed financing, or make the right decisions in all areas of your business. The time to decide how you will handle your bookkeeping is when you open your business, not a year later during tax time.

Initial Bookkeeping

If you do not understand business taxation, you should pick up a good book on the subject, as well as the IRS tax guide for your type of business (proprietorship, partnership, or corporation).

The IRS tax book for small businesses is Publication 334, *Tax Guide for Small Businesses*. There are also instruction booklets for each type of business's form: Schedule C for proprietorships, Form 1120 or 1120S for C corporations and S corporations, and 1165 for partnerships and businesses, which are taxed like partnerships (LLCs, LLPs).

Keep in mind that the IRS does not give you the best advice for saving on taxes, and does not give you the other side of contested issues. You need a private tax guide or advisor to assist you in these areas.

The most important thing to do is to set up your bookkeeping so that you can easily fill out your monthly, quarterly, and annual tax returns. The best way to do this is to get copies of the returns, note the categories that you will need to supply, and set up your bookkeeping system to arrive at those totals.

For example, a sole proprietorship will use "Schedule C" to report business income and expenses to the IRS at the end of the year. Use the categories on that form to sort your expenses. To make your job especially easy every time you pay a bill, put the category number on the check.

ACCOUNTANTS

In the beginning it is likely that your new business will not be able to afford an accountant to handle your books. Doing them yourself will force you to learn about business accounting and taxation. The worst way to run a business knowing nothing about the tax laws and turning everything over to an accountant at the end of the year.

You should know the basics of tax law before making basic decisions like buying or renting equipment or premises. You should understand accounting so you can time your financial affairs appropriately. You need to have at least a basic understanding of the system within which you are working if your business buys supplies, inventory, or equipment and provides goods or services throughout the year.

Once you can afford an accountant, you should weigh the cost against your time and the risk that you may make an error. Even if you think you know enough to do your own corporate tax return, you should still take it to an accountant one year to see if you have been missing any deductions. You might decide that the money saved is worth the cost of the accountant's services.

Computer Programs

Today every business should keep its books by computer. There are inexpensive programs such as Quicken that can instantly provide you with reports of your income and expenses and the right figures to plug into your tax returns.

Most programs even offer a tax program each year that will take all of your information and print it out on the current year's tax forms. It sure beats sorting through shoe boxes of receipts with an adding machine!

Tax Tips

Here are a few tax tips for small businesses that will help you save money:

- Usually when you buy equipment for a business you must amortize the cost over several years. That is, you do not deduct it all when you buy it, you take, say, twenty-five percent of the cost off your taxes each year for four years. (The time is determined by the theoretical usefulness of the item.) However, small businesses are allowed to write off the entire cost of a limited amount of items under Internal Revenue Code 179. If you have income to shelter, use it.

- Owners of S corporations do not have to pay social security or medicare taxes on the part of their profits that is not considered salary. As long as you pay yourself a reasonable salary, other money you take out is not subject to these taxes.

- You should not neglect to deposit withholding taxes for your own salary or profits. You will not only be forced to produce a large amount of money in April, but there are penalties that must also be paid for the failure to do so.

- Do not fail to keep track of and remit your employees' withholding. You will be personally liable for them even if you are a - corporation.

- If you keep track of the use of your car for business, you can deduct 31.5¢ per mile (this may go up or down each year). If you use your car for business within a considerable amount of time, you may be able to depreciate it.

- If your business is a corporation and you designate the stock as "section 1244 stock," and the business fails, you are able to get a much better deduction for the loss.

- By setting up a retirement plan, you can exempt up to twenty percent of your salary from income tax. See Chapter 10. But don't use money you might need later. There are penalties for taking it out of the retirement plan.

- When you buy things which will be resold or made into products which will be resold, you do not have to pay sales taxes on those purchases. See Chapter 17.

Paying Federal Taxes 17

Federal Income Tax

The following section describes the manner in which each type of business pays taxes.

PROPRIETORSHIP

A proprietor reports profits and expenses on Schedule C attached to the usual Form 1040 and pays tax on all of the net income of the business. Each quarter Form 1040-ES must be filed along with payment of one-quarter of the amount of income tax and social security taxes estimated to be due for the year.

PARTNERSHIP

The partnership files a return showing the income and expenses but pays no tax. Each partner is given a form showing his share of the profits or losses and reports these on Schedule E of Form 1040. Each quarter, Form 1040-ES must be filed by each partner along with payment of one-quarter of the amount of income tax and social security taxes estimated to be due for the year.

C CORPORATION

A regular corporation is a separate taxpayer, and pays tax on its profits after deducting all expenses, including officers' salaries. If dividends are distributed, they are paid out of after-tax dollars, and the shareholders pay tax a second time when they receive the dividends. If a corporation needs to accumulate money for investment, it may be able to do so at lower tax rates than the shareholders. But if all profits will be distributed to shareholders, the double-taxation may be excessive unless all income is paid as salaries. A C corporation files Form 1120.

S CORPORATION

A small corporation has the option of being taxed like a partnership. If Form 2553 is filed by the corporation and accepted by the Internal Revenue Service, the S corporation will only file an informational return listing profits and expenses. Each shareholder will be taxed on a proportional share of the profits (or be able to deduct a proportional share of the losses). Unless a corporation will make a large profit that will not be distributed, S-status is usually best in the beginning. An S corporation files Form 1120S and distributes Form K-1 to each shareholder. If any money is taken out by a shareholder that is not listed as wages subject to withholding, the shareholder will usually have to file form ES-1040 each quarter along with payment of the estimated withholding on the withdrawals.

LIMITED LIABILITY COMPANIES AND PARTNERSHIPS

Limited liability companies and limited liability partnerships are allowed to elect to be taxed either as a partnership or a corporation by the IRS. To make this election, you file Form 8832, ENTITY CLASSIFICATION ELECTION with the IRS.

TAX WORKSHOPS AND BOOKLETS

The IRS conducts workshops to inform businesses about the tax laws. (Do not expect in-depth study of the loopholes.) For more information, call the IRS toll free at 1-800-829-1040 or write to the IRS at the following addresses:

Internal Revenue Service
230 S. Dearborn St., Rm. 1710
Chicago, IL 60604-1132
312-886-1572

Internal Revenue Service
320 W. Washington St.,
Springfield, IL 62701
217-527-6366

FEDERAL WITHHOLDING, SOCIAL SECURITY, AND MEDICARE TAXES

If you need basic information on business tax returns, the IRS publishes a rather large booklet that answers most questions and is available free of charge. Call or write the IRS and ask for Publication No. 334. If you have any questions, look up their toll-free number in the phone book under United States Government/Internal Revenue Service. If you want more creative answers and tax saving information, you should find a good accountant. However, to get started, you will need the following:

EMPLOYER IDENTIFICATION NUMBER

If you are a sole proprietor with no employees, you can use your social security number for your business. If you are a corporation, a partnership, or a proprietorship with employees, you must obtain an "Employer Identification Number." This is done by filing the **APPLICATION FOR EMPLOYER IDENTIFICATION NUMBER (IRS FORM SS-4)**. (see form 5, p.203.) It usually takes a week or two to receive. You will need this number to open bank accounts for the business, so you should file this form a soon as you decide to go into business. A sample filled-in form and instructions are in Appendix C.

EMPLOYEE'S WITHHOLDING ALLOWANCE CERTIFICATE

You must have each employee fill out a W-4 form to calculate the amount of federal taxes to be deducted and to obtain their social security numbers. (The number of allowances on this form is used with IRS Circular E, Publication 15, to figure out the exact deductions.) A sample filled-in is included in Appendix C.

FEDERAL TAX DEPOSIT COUPONS

After taking withholdings from employees' wages, you must deposit them at a bank that is authorized to accept such funds. If at the end of any month you have over $1000 in withheld taxes (including your contribution to FICA), you must make a deposit prior to the 15th of the following month. If on the 3rd, 7th, 11th, 15th, 19th, 22nd, or 25th of any month you have over $3,000 in withheld taxes, you must make a deposit within three banking days. The deposit is made using the coupons in the Form 8109 booklet. A sample 8109-B coupon, which you will use to order your booklet, is shown in Appendix C.

ESTIMATED TAX PAYMENT VOUCHER
Sole proprietors and partners usually take draws from their businesses without the formality of withholding. However, they are still required to make deposits of income and FICA taxes each quarter. If more than $500 is due in April on a person's 1040 form, not enough money was withheld each quarter. In this situation, a penalty is assessed, unless the person falls under an exception. The quarterly withholding is submitted on Form 1040-ES on April 15th, June 15th, September 15th, and January 15th each year. If these days fall on a weekend, the due date is the following Monday. The worksheet with Form 1040-ES can be used to determine the amount to pay.

NOTE: *One exception to the rule is that if you withhold the same amount as last year's tax bill, you do not have to pay a penalty. This is usually much easier than filling out the 1040-ES worksheet.*

EMPLOYER'S QUARTERLY TAX RETURN
Each quarter you must file Form 941 to report your federal withholding and FICA taxes. If you owe more than $1000 at the end of a quarter, you are required to make a deposit at the end of any month that you have $1000 in withholding. These deposits are made to the Federal Reserve Bank or an authorized financial institution on Form 501. Most banks are authorized to accept deposits. If you owe more than $3,000 for any month, you must make a deposit at any point in the month in which you owe $3,000. After you file IRS form SS-4, the 941 forms will be sent to you automatically, as long as you checked the box saying that you expect to have employees.

WAGE AND TAX STATEMENT
At the end of each year, you are required to issue a W-2 Form to each employee. This form shows the amount of wages paid to the employee during the year, as well as the amounts withheld for taxes, social security, medicare, and other purposes. A sample W-2 is in Appendix C.

MISCELLANEOUS
If you pay at least $600 to a person (not a corporation) who is not an employee (such as independent contractors), you are required to file a Form 1099 for that person. Along with the 1099s, you must file a form 1096, which is a summary sheet.

Many people are not aware of this law and fail to file these forms, but the forms are required for such things as services, royalties, rents, awards and prizes that you pay to individuals (but not corporations). The rules for this are quite complicated, so you should either obtain "Package 1099" from the IRS or consult your accountant. Sample forms 1099 and 1096 are in Appendix C.

EARNED
INCOME CREDIT

People who are not liable to pay income tax may have the right to a check from the government because of the "Earned Income Credit." You are required to notify your employees of this in one of the following ways:

- a W-2 Form with the notice on the back;

- a substitute for the W-2 Form with the notice on it;

- a copy of Notice 797; or

- a written statement with the wording from Notice 797.

A Notice 797 can be obtained by calling 1-800-829-3676.

FEDERAL EXCISE TAXES

Excise taxes are taxes on certain activities or items. A few remain, but most federal excise taxes have been eliminated since World War II.

Some of the things that are subject to federal excise taxes are tobacco and alcohol, gasoline, tires and inner tubes, some trucks and trailers, firearms, ammunition, bows, arrows, fishing equipment, the use of highway vehicles of over 55,000 pounds, aircraft, wagering, telephone and teletype services, coal, hazardous wastes, and vaccines. If you are involved with any of these, you should obtain from the IRS publication No. 510, *Information on Excise Taxes.*

UNEMPLOYMENT COMPENSATION TAXES

You must pay federal unemployment taxes if you paid wages of $1,500 in any quarter, or if you had at least one employee for twenty calendar weeks. The federal tax amount is 0.8% of the first $7,000 of wages paid each employee. If more than $100 is due by the end of any quarter (if you paid $12,500 in wages for the quarter), then Form 508 must be filed with an authorized financial institution or the Federal Reserve Bank in your area. You will receive Form 508 when you obtain your employer identification number.

At the end of each year, you must file Form 940 or Form 940EZ. This is your annual report of federal unemployment taxes. You will receive an original form from the IRS.

PAYING ILLINOIS TAXES 18

SALES AND USE TAX

If you will be selling or renting goods or services at retail, you must collect Illinois Sales and Use Tax. Some services, such as doctors and lawyers fees and newspaper advertising, are not taxed. If you have any doubt, check with the Illinois Department of Revenue.

First, you must obtain a tax number by filling out form NUC-1. A sample filled-in copy of the form is in Appendix C. For more details about the tax you should obtain the ST-19 Retailer's Tax Booklet from the Department of Revenue. Call their main number, 1-800-732-8866, or get their forms online at:

http://www.commerce.state.il.us/bus/state_bus_form.html

Their address is:

Illinois Department of Revenue
Central Registration Division,
P.O. Box 19030,
Springfield, IL 62794-9030.

The sales and use tax returns are due for each month on the 20th of the following month. You are allowed to deduct 2.5% of the tax as your reimbursement for collecting the tax. In some cases, if your sales are very limited (under $100 a quarter) you may be allowed to file returns quarterly.

Once you file your APPLICATION FOR SALES AND USE TAX REGISTRATION, you will have to start filing monthly returns (use Illinois Use Tax Return (ST-44)) whether you have any sales or not. (see form 11, p.219.) Regardless of your amount of sales, if you do not file the return, you must pay a $5 penalty. If you do not expect to have any sales for the first few months while you are setting up your business, you probably should wait before sending in the registration. Otherwise you may forget to file the returns marked with zeros and end up paying the penalties.

One reason to get a tax number early is to exempt your purchases from tax. When you buy a product that you will resell, or use as part of a product that you will sell, you are exempt from paying tax on it. To get the exemption, you need to submit an ILLINOIS CERTIFICATE OF RESALE (CRT-61) to the seller. (see form 12, p.221.) This form must contain your sales and use tax registration number.

If you will only be selling items wholesale or out of state, you might think that you would not need a tax number or to submit returns. However, you will need to be registered to obtain the tax number to exempt your purchases.

If you have any sales before you get your monthly tax return forms, you should calculate the tax and submit it anyway. Otherwise, you will be charged a penalty, even if it was not your fault that you did not have the forms. FORM ST-44 is included in Appendix D. (see form 11, p.219.)

After you obtain your tax number, you will be required to collect sales tax on all sales that are not exempt.

If you sell to someone who claims to be exempt from sales and use taxes (for example, if they plan to resell merchandise they have purchased from you), you must have them complete the CERTIFICATE OF RESALE mentioned above.

INCOME TAX

If you have employees, you will have to withhold Illinois Income Tax from their salaries and remit it to the state Department of Revenue. Tax on the business' profits will also need to be paid either by the business (if taxed as a corporation), or by the owners (if set up as a pass-through entity). When you file form **NUC-1** (as discussed on page 143), you will receive forms and instructions for the Illinois Income Tax.

You should also be aware that some municipalities and counties impose their own taxes in addition to the state and federal taxes previously discussed. You should contact your local revenue department to determine if additional taxes apply to your business activities.

EXCISE TAXES

Illinois imposes taxes on the following businesses:

- wholesale tobacco dealers and tobacco vending machine operators;
- alcohol manufacturers and distributors;
- motor fuel dealers;
- telecommunications; and,
- charitable games

For more information and registration forms, contact the Department of Revenue at 800-732-8866.

SELLING TO TAX
EXEMPT PURCHASERS

You are required to collect sales and use taxes for all sales you make, unless you have documentation on file proving that a purchase was exempt from the tax. A person can fill out a form for a particular sale, or they can fill out one form to be used for all their interactions with you. The latter is called a **BLANKET CERTIFICATE OF RESALE**. A suggested form for this purpose is included in Appendix D. (see form 12, p.221.)

UNEMPLOYMENT COMPENSATION TAXES

You are not liable to pay unemployment compensation taxes until you have had an employee work a part of a day in any twenty calendar weeks, or paid $1500 in wages in a quarter. But once you reach that point you are liable for all back taxes. The rate starts at 2.7%, but if your record is clear it may drop to 0.1%. The tax is paid on the first $7000 of wages of each employee.

When you have had an employee work for twenty weeks, you should send in a form UI-1 Report to Determine Liability. A sample filled-in form is in Appendix C. You can use the blank form in Appendix D. (see form 9, p.214.) You will be sent quarterly returns to fill out.

Some businesses try to keep taxes low by having all their work done by independent contractors instead of employees. One thing to be aware of is if a business has no employees for several quarters, the Illinois unemployment tax rate increases. A payment of a small wage to someone each quarter will avoid this problem.

For more information on unemployment compensation, contact:

> Department of Employment Security
> 400 W. Monroe, Suite 303
> Springfield, IL 62704

For more information on Illinois taxes, contact:

> Department of Revenue
> 101 W. Jefferson
> Springfield, IL 62794

Out-of-State Taxes 19

State Sales Taxes

In 1992, the United States Supreme Court struck a blow for the rights of small businesses by ruling that state tax authorities cannot force them to collect sales taxes on interstate mail orders (*Quill Corporation v. North Dakota*).

Unfortunately, the court left open the possibility that Congress could allow interstate taxation of mail order sales, and since then several bills have been introduced that would do so. One bill, introduced by Arkansas senator Dale Bumpers, was given an Orwellian "newspeak" title, *The Consumer and Main Street Protection Act*.

At present, companies are only required to collect sales taxes for states in which they do business. Exactly what business is enough to trigger taxation is a legal question, and some states try to define it as broadly as possible.

If you have an office in a state, clearly you are doing business there. Any goods shipped to consumers in that state are subject to sales taxes. If you have a full time employee working in the state for a great part of the year, many states will consider you doing business there. In some states, attending a two-day trade show is enough business to trigger taxation for the entire year for every order shipped to the state. One loophole that often works is to be represented at shows by persons who are not your employees.

Because the laws are different in each state, you will have to do some research on a state-by-state basis to find out how much business you can do in a state without being subject to their taxation. You can request a state's rules from its department of revenue. Keep in mind that what the Department of Revenue wants the law to be is not always agreed by the courts.

BUSINESS TAXES

Being subject to a state's income or other business taxes is even worse than being subject to their sales taxes. For example, California charges every company doing business in the state a minimum $800 a year fee, and charges income tax on a portion of the company's worldwide income. Doing a small amount of business in that state is clearly not worth getting mixed up in California taxation.

For this reason some trade shows have been moved from the state. This has resulted in a review of the tax policies and the creation of some "safe-harbor" guidelines to advise companies on what they can do without becoming subject to taxation.

Write to the Department of Revenue of any state with which you have business contacts to see what might trigger your taxation.

CANADIAN TAXES

The Canadian government expects American companies, which sell goods by mail order to Canadians, to collect taxes for them and file returns with Revenue Canada, their tax department.

Those that receive an occasional unsolicited order are not expected to register, and Canadian customers, who order things from the U.S., pay the tax plus a $5 fee upon receipt of the goods. But companies that solicit Canadian orders are expected to be registered if their worldwide income is $30,000 or more per year. In some cases, a company may be required to post a bond and to pay for the cost of Canadian auditors visiting its premises and auditing its books. For these reasons, you may notice that some companies decline to accept orders from Canada.

THE END...AND THE BEGINNING 20

If you have read through this whole book, you know more about the rules and laws for operating an Illinois business than most people in business today. However, after learning about all the governmental regulations, you may become discouraged. You are probably wondering how you can keep track of all the laws and how you will have any time left to make money after complying with the laws. It is not that bad. People are starting businesses every day and they are making money, lots of money. American business owners are lucky. Some countries have marginal tax rates as high as 105%!

The regulations that exist right now are enough to strangle some businesses. Consider the Armour meat-packing plant. The Federal Meat Inspection Service required that an opening be made in a conveyor to allow inspection or they would shut down the plant. OSHA told them that if they made that opening they would be shut down for safety reasons. Government regulations made it impossible for that plant to be in business!

But what you must realize is that the same bureaucrats who are creating laws to slow down businesses are the ones who responsible for enforcing the laws. And just as most government programs cost more than expected and fail to achieve their goals, most government regulations cannot be enforced against millions of people.

In a pure democracy, fifty-one percent of the voters can decide that all left-handed people must wear green shirts and that everyone must go to church three days a week. It is the Bill of Rights in our constitution that protects us from the whims of the majority.

In America today, there are no laws regarding left-handed people or going to church but there are laws controlling minute aspects of our personal and business lives. Does a majority have the right to decide what hours you can work, what you can sell, or where you can sell it? You must decide for yourself and act accordingly.

One way to avoid problems with the government is to keep a low profile and avoid open confrontation. For a lawyer, it can be fun going to appeals court over an unfair parking ticket or making a federal case out of a $25 fine. But for most people the expenses of a fight with the government are unbearable. If you start a mass protest against the IRS or OSHA they will have to make an example of you.

The important thing is that you know the laws and the penalties for violations before making your decision. Knowing the laws will also allow you to use the loopholes in the laws to avoid violations.

Congratulations on deciding to start a business in Illinois! If you have any unusual experiences along the way, drop us a line at the following address. The information may be useful for a future book.

Sphinx Publishing/Sourcebooks, Inc.
P. O. Box 4410
Naperville, IL 60567-4410

GLOSSARY

A

acceptance.   Agreeing to the terms of an offer and creating a contract.

affirmative action.   Hiring an employee to achieve a balance in the workplace, and avoid existing or continuing discrimination based on minority status.

alien.   A person who is not a citizen of the country.

articles of incorporation.   The document that sets forth the organization of a corporation.

B

bait advertising.   Offering a product for sale with the intention of selling another product.

bulk sales.   Selling substantially all of a company's inventory.

C

C corporation.   A corporation that pays taxes on its profits.

collections.   The gathering of money owed to a business.

common law. Laws that are determined in court cases rather than statutes.

consideration. The exchange of value or promises in a contract.

contract. An agreement between two or more parties.

copyright. Legal protection given to "original works of authorship."

corporation. An "artificial person" that is set up to conduct a business owned by shareholders and run by officers and directors.

D

deceptive pricing. Pricing goods or services in a manner intended to deceive the customers.

discrimination. The choosing among various options based on their characteristics.

domain name. The address of a website.

E

employee. Person who works for another, under that person's control and direction.

endorsements. Positive statements about goods or services.

excise tax. A tax paid on the sale or consumption of goods or services.

express warranty. A specific guarantee of a product or service.

F

fictitious name. A name used by a business that is not its personal or legal name.

G

general partnership. A business that is owned by two or more persons.

goods. Items of personal property.

guarantee/guaranty. A promise of quality of a good or service.

I

implied warranty. A guarantee of a product or service that is not specifically made, but can be implied from the circumstances of the sale.

independent contractor. Person who works for another as a separate business, not as an employee.

intangible property. Personal property that does not have physical presence, such as the ownership interest in a corporation.

intellectual property. Legal rights to the products of the mind, such as writings, musical compositions, formulas and designs.

L

liability. The legal responsibility to pay for an injury.

limited liability company. An entity recognized as a legal "person" that is set up to conduct a business owned and run by members.

limited liability partnership. An entity recognized as a legal "person" that is set up to conduct a business owned and run by members that is set up for professionals such as attorneys or doctors.

limited partnership. A business that is owned by two or more persons of which one or more is liable for the debts of the business and one or more has no liability for the debts.

limited warranty. A guarantee covering certain aspects of a good or service.

M

merchant. A person who is in business.

merchant's firm offer. An offer by a business made under specific terms.

N

nonprofit corporation. An entity recognized as a legal "person" that is set up to run an operation in which none of the profits are distributed to controlling members.

O

occupational license. A government-issued permit to transact business.

offer. A proposal to enter into a contract.

overtime. Hours worked in excess of forty hours in one week, or eight hours in one day.

P

partnership. A business formed by two or more persons.

patent. Protection given to inventions, discoveries and designs.

personal property. Any type of property other than land and the structures attached to it.

pierce the corporate veil. When a court ignores the structure of a corporation and holds its owners responsible for its debts or liabilities.

professional association. An entity recognized as a legal "person" that is set up to conduct a business of professionals such as attorneys or doctors.

proprietorship. A business that is owned by one person.

R

real property. Land and the structures attached to it.

resident alien. A person who is not a citizen of the country but who may legally reside and work there.

S

S corporation.   A corporation in which the profits are taxed to the shareholders.

sale on approval.   Selling an item with the agreement that it may be brought back and the sale cancelled.

sale or return.   An agreement whereby goods are to be purchased or returned to the vendor.

securities.   Interests in a business such as stocks or bonds.

sexual harassment.   Activity that causes an employee to feel or be sexually threatened.

shares.   Units of stock in a corporation.

statute of frauds.   Law that requires certain contracts to be in writing.

stock.   Ownership interests in a corporation.

sublease.   An agreement to rent premises from an existing tenant.

T

tangible property.   Physical personal property such as desks and tables.

trade secret.   Commercially valuable information or process that is protected by being kept a secret.

trademark.   A name or symbol used to identify the source of goods or services.

U

unemployment compensation.   Payments to a former employee who was terminated from a job for a reason not based on his or her fault.

usury.   Charging an interest rate higher than that allowed by law.

W

withholding.   Money taken out of an employee's salary and remitted to the government.

workers compensation.   Insurance program to cover injuries or deaths of employees.

FOR FURTHER READING

The following books will provide valuable information to those who are starting new businesses. Some are out of print, but they are classics that are worth tracking down.

For inspiration to give you the drive to succeed:

Hill, Napoleon, *Think and Grow Rich*. New York: Fawcett Books, 1990, 233 pages.

Karbo, Joe, *The Lazy Man's Way to Riches*. Sunset Beach: F P Publishing, 1974, 156 pages.

Schwartz, David J., *The Magic of Thinking Big*. Fireside, 1987, 234 pages.

For hints on what it takes to be successful:

Carnegie, Dale, *How to Win Friends and Influence People*. New York: Pocket Books, 1994, 276 pages.

Ringer, Robert J., *Looking Out for #1*. New York: Fawcett Books, 1993.

Ringer, Robert J., *Million Dollar Habits*. New York: Fawcett Books, 1991.

Ringer, Robert J., *Winning Through Intimidation*. New York: Fawcett Books, 1993.

For advice on bookkeeping and organization:

Kamoroff, Bernard, *Small Time Operator (25th Edition)*. Bell Springs Publishing, 2000, 200 pages.

For a very practical guide to investing:

Tobias, Andrew, *The Only Investment Guide You'll Ever Need*. Harvest Books, 1999, 239 pages.

For advice on how to avoid problems with government agencies:

Browne, Harry, *How I Found Freedom in an Unfree World*. Great Falls: Liam Works, 1998, 387 pages.

The following are other books published by **Sphinx Publishing** that may be helpful to your business:

Eckert, W. Kelsea, Sartorius, Arthur, III, & Warda, Mark, *How to Form Your Own Corporation*. 2001.

Haman, Edward A., *How to Form Your Own Partnership*. 2002.

Ray, James C., *The Most Valuable Business Legal Forms You'll Ever Need*. 2001.

Ray, James C., *The Most Valuable Corporate Forms You'll Ever Need*. 2001.

Warda, Mark, *Incorporate in Delaware from Any State*. 2002.

Warda, Mark, *Incorporate in Nevada from Any State*. 2001.

Warda, Mark, *How to Form a Limited Liability Company*. 1999.

Warda, Mark, *How to Register Your Own Copyright*. 2002.

Warda, Mark, *How to Register Your Own Trademark*. 1999.

The following are books published by **Sourcebooks, Inc.** that may be helpful to your business:

Fleury, Robert E., *The Small Business Survival Guide.*. 1995.

Gutman, Jean E., *Accounting Made Easy*. 1998.

Milling, Bryan E., *How to Get a Small Business Loan (2nd Edition)*. 1998.

The following websites provide information that may be useful to you in starting your business:

Internal Revenue Service: http://www.irs.gov

Small Business Administration: http://www.sba.gov

Social Security Administration: http://www.ssa.gov

U. S. Business Advisor: http://www.business.gov

APPENDIX A
GOVERNMENT RESOURCES

FIRST-STOP BUSINESS INFORMATION CENTER OF ILLINOIS

Provides general information on business assistance programs and services, and information on related state agencies.

> 1-800-252-2923
>
> Internet: http://www.commerce.state.il.us/

INCORPORATION

> Secretary of State
> Department of Business Services
> 501 S. Second St. Suite 328
> Springfield, IL 62756
> 217-782-6961

> Secretary of State
> Department of Business Services
> 69 W. Washington Suite 1240
> Chicago, IL 60602
> 312-793-3380

BUSINESS TAX NUMBER

> Illinois Department of Revenue
> Income Tax Division
> 101 West Jefferson
> Springfield, IL 62702
> 1-800-732-8866
> 217-782-3336

> Illinois Department of Revenue
> 100 West Randolph
> Concourse Level
> Chicago, IL 60601
> 312-814-5258

ASSUMED NAMES (Cook County)

Cook County Building
118 North Clark - Lower Level
Chicago, IL 60602
312-603-5656

GENERAL BUSINESS LICENSE (Chicago)

City Hall
121 N. LaSalle St., Room 107
Chicago, IL 60602
312-744-3947

TRADEMARK INQUIRIES
Secretary of State's Office
Dept. of Business Services Trademarks
Howlett Building, Room 328
Springfield, IL 62756
217- 524-0400

ILLINOIS ATTORNEY GENERAL

1-800-243-0618

GENERAL GOVERNMENT INFORMATION

Federal: 1-800-366-2998
Illinois: 312-793-3500
1-800-642-3112
Cook County: 312-443-5500
Chicago: 312-744-5000

STATE OF ILLINOIS WEBSITES

http://www.commerce.state.il.us (business information center)

http://www.dpr.state.il.us (Department of Professional Regulation)

http://www.ides.state.il.us (unemployment insurance)

http://www.sos.state.il.us (business registration)

http://www.state.il.us/agency/iic (workers' compensation)

FEDERAL WEBSITES

http://www.ins.gov (INS - employee form I-9)

http://www.irs.gov (IRS forms)

http://www.sba.gov (Small Business Administration)

http://www.ftc.gov/ftc/business.htm (advertising guidelines)

MISCELLANEOUS WEBSITES

http://www.govspot.com (links to state, federal and foreign government sites)

Appendix B
Business Start-up Checklist

The following start-up checklist may be photocopied or removed from this book and used immediately.

❏ Make your plan
   ❏ Obtain and read all relevant publications on your type of business
   ❏ Obtain and read all laws and regulations affecting your business
   ❏ Calculate whether your plan will produce a profit
   ❏ Plan your sources of capital
   ❏ Plan your sources of goods or services
   ❏ Plan your marketing efforts
❏ Choose your business name
   ❏ Check other business names and trademarks
   ❏ Register your name, trademark, etc.
❏ Choose the business form
   ❏ Prepare and file organizational papers
   ❏ Prepare and file fictitious name if necessary
❏ Choose the location
   ❏ Check competitors
   ❏ Check zoning
❏ Obtain necessary licenses
   ❏ City?   ❏ State?
   ❏ County?   ❏ Federal?
❏ Choose a bank
   ❏ Checking
   ❏ Credit card processing
   ❏ Loans
❏ Obtain necessary insurance
   ❏ Worker's Comp   ❏ Automobile
   ❏ Liability   ❏ Health
   ❏ Hazard   ❏ Life/disability
❏ File necessary federal tax registrations
❏ File necessary state tax registrations
❏ Set up a bookkeeping system
❏ Plan your hiring
   ❏ Obtain required posters
   ❏ Obtain or prepare employment application
   ❏ Obtain new hire tax forms
   ❏ Prepare employment policies
   ❏ Determine compliance with health and safety laws
❏ Plan your opening
   ❏ Obtain all necessary equipment and supplies
   ❏ Obtain all necessary inventory
   ❏ Do all necessary marketing and publicity
   ❏ Obtain all necessary forms and agreements
   ❏ Prepare you company policies on refunds, exchanges, returns

Appendix C: Sample Filled-In Forms

The following forms are selected filled-in forms for demonstration purposes. Most have a corresponding blank form in Appendix D. The form numbers in this appendix correspond to the form numbers in Appendix D. If there is no blank for a particular form, it is because you must obtain it from a government agency. If you need instructions for these forms as you follow how they are filled out, they can be found in Appendix D, or in those pages in the chapters that discuss those forms.

STATE OF ILLINOIS)   File No._____

COUNTY OF __Cook__)SS.   Filing Fee $5.00

CERTIFICATE

It is hereby certified that the undersigned is/are conducting or transacting business under the Assumed Name of:

Doe Company   ;

(List the Business Name)

The Business is being conducted at the following locations: 1234 W. Main Street

Chicago, IL 60601   ;

(List all Business Addresses located in the County)

The nature of the Business being conducted or transacted is Construction

_____ ;

(Declare the Type of Business)

The true and real full name or names of the person or persons owning, conducting, or transacting the business are as follows:

PRINT NAME	PRINT RESIDENCE ADDRESS
John Doe	1234 W. Main Street
	Chicago, IL 60601
James Doe	2550 W. Maple Street
	Chicago, IL 60601

Dated this 15th day of __June__, 2002.

SIGNATURE ___*John Doe*___

SIGNATURE ___*James Doe*___

SIGNATURE _____

SIGNATURE _____

(All persons must sign)

STATE OF ILLINOIS)
COUNTY OF __Cook__)SS.

I, ___Jane Notary___, a Notary Public in and for said County and State, do hereby certify that ___John Doe and James Doe___

is/are the same person(s) whose name(s) is/are subscribed to the foregoing instrument, and that John Doe and James Doe

appeared before me this day in person and acknowledged that he/she/they has/have read and signed said instrument, and that each of the statement contained therein are true.

Jane Notary

Notary Public

Form AB2   My commission expires on the __30th__
FILE ONE COPY ONLY   day of __November__, 2004

STATE OF ILLINOIS
TRADEMARK OR SERVICEMARK APPLICATION
Complete and Return with $10 Fee and Three Specimens
<u>**Must be typewritten**</u>

1. Name of Registrant Sidney Bones

2. Business Address 6789 Graves Ave.
   Street

   Chicago   IL   60601
        City   State   ZIP Code

3. Is registrant a (**check one**)

   ❏ Corporation   ❏ Union   ❏ General Partnership   ❏ Limited Liability Partnership (LLP)

   ☒ Individual   ❏ Association   ❏ Limited Partnership (LP)   ❏ Limited Liability Company (LLC)

   ❏ Other (specify) _____

4. A. If a **Corporation, LP, LLP,** or **LLC,** in what state is it organized? _____

   B. If an **LP** or **LLP,** what is the name of one of the general partners? _____

   _____

5. Name of mark Sid's Bones

6. Describe the specific goods or services in connection with which mark is used novelty store

   _____

   _____

7. *Class No. _____ 40 _____ (**One classification number only; classes are listed on the back.**)

8. A. If a **Trademark**, check how the mark is used. (**check as many as apply**) By applying it: directly to the goods _____ , directly to the containers for the goods _____ , to tags or labels affixed to the goods __X__ , to tags or labels affixed to the containers for the goods __X__ , or by displaying it in physical association with the goods in the sale or distribution thereof __X__ .

   OR

   B. If a **Servicemark**, check how the mark is used. (**check as many as apply**) By displaying it: in advertisements of the service _____ , on documents, wrappers, or articles delivered in connection with the service rendered _____ , in other fashion _____ , if so, (**specify**): _____

9. Date of the first use of mark by applicant or predecessor. Mark must be used in Illinois prior to registration. (**If first use of mark was in Illinois, use same date in both A and B.**)

   A. Anywhere January 29, 2002 _____ (**month, day, and year**)

   B. In Illinois January 29, 2002 _____ (**month, day, and year**)

10. If either of the above first uses was by a predecessor of applicant, state which use or uses were by a predecessor and identify predecessor _____

The applicant hereby appoints the Secretary of State of Illinois as agent for service of process in an action relating only to the registration which may be issued pursuant to this application if the registrant be, or shall become, a non-resident individual, or foreign partnership, limited liability company, association, or corporation not licensed to do business in this State, or cannot be found in this State.

The undersigned hereby declares, under penalty of perjury, that the statements made in the foregoing application are true and that to his/her knowledge no other person has registered the mark, either federally or in this State, or has the right to use the mark either in the identical form thereof or in such near resemblance thereto as to be likely, when applied to the goods or services of such other person, to cause confusion or to cause mistake, or to deceive.

x   *Sidney Bones*
_____
                          Signature of Applicant

       Sidney Bones
_____
                     Type or Print Name of Applicant

       Owner
_____
                          Official Capacity

NOTE

The application must be accompanied by three specimens or facsimiles of the mark and by a filing fee of $10.00 payable to the Secretary of State. Clip specimens or facsimiles to application. DO NOT GLUE OR STAPLE.

Specimens larger than 3" x 3" will not be accepted. If the specimens are larger than that, send facsimiles such as photostats reduced in size of the actual specimens.

Send a separate check for each application. This will prevent return of multiple applications for correction.

The following general classes of goods and services are established for convenience of administration of this Act but not to limit or extend the applicant's or registrant's rights. A single application for registration of a mark may include any or all goods or services upon which the mark is actually being used and which are comprised in a single class. In no event shall a single application include goods or services upon which the mark is being used and which fall within different classes.

CLASSIFICATION OF GOODS FOR TRADEMARKS

(1) Chemicals
(2) Paints
(3) Cosmetics and cleaning preparations
(4) Lubricants and fuels
(5) Pharmaceuticals
(6) Metal goods
(7) Machinery
(8) Hand tools
(9) Electrical and scientific apparatus
(10) Medical apparatus
(11) Environmental control apparatus

(12) Vehicles
(13) Firearms
(14) Jewelry
(15) Musical instruments
(16) Paper goods and printed matter
(17} Rubber goods
(18) Leather goods
(19) Non-metallic building materials
(20) Furniture and articles not otherwise classified
(21) Housewares and glass
(22) Cordage and fibers

(23) Yarns and threads
(24) Fabrics
(25) Clothing
(26) Fancy goods
(27) Floor coverings
(28) Toys and sporting goods
(29) Meals and processed foods
(30) Staple foods
(31) Natural agricultural products
(32) Light beverages
(33) Wine and spirits
(34) Smoker's articles

CLASSIFICATION OF SERVICES FOR SERVICEMARKS

(35) Advertising and business
(36) Insurance and financial
(37) Building construction and repair

(38) Telecommunications
(39) Transportation and storage
(40) Treatment of materials

(41) Education and entertainment
(42) Miscellaneous

*The Secretary of State will fill in the answer to question #7 if no answer is given and has the right to change the classification if that furnished by applicant is not correct. *Each classification requires a separate application, set of three specimens, and fee.*

> **RETURN TO:**
> Secretary of State's Office
> Department of Business Services
> Trademark Division
> 3rd Floor, Howlett Building
> Springfield, IL 62756
>
> (217) 524-0400
> http://www.sos.state.il.us

C-246.3

Form **SS-4**

(Rev. December 2001)

Department of the Treasury
Internal Revenue Service

Application for Employer Identification Number

(For use by employers, corporations, partnerships, trusts, estates, churches, government agencies, Indian tribal entities, certain individuals, and others.)

· See separate instructions for each line.   · Keep a copy for your records.

EIN

OMB No. 1545-0003

Type or print clearly.

1 Legal name of entity (or individual) for whom the EIN is being requested
Sidney Bones

2 Trade name of business (if different from name on line 1)
Bones Enterprises

3 Executor, trustee, "care of" name

4a Mailing address (room, apt., suite no. and street, or P.O. box)
6789 Graves Avenue

4b City, state, and ZIP code
Chicago, Il 60601

5a Street address (if different) (Do not enter a P.O. box.)

5b City, state, and ZIP code

6 County and state where principal business is located
Cook, IL

7a Name of principal officer, general partner, grantor, owner, or trustor
Sidney Bones

7b SSN, ITIN, or EIN   123-45-6789

8a **Type of entity** (check only one box)
- [X] Sole proprietor (SSN) ___ 123 45 6789 ___
- [ ] Partnership
- [ ] Corporation (enter form number to be filed) · ___
- [ ] Personal service corp.
- [ ] Church or church-controlled organization
- [ ] Other nonprofit organization (specify) · ___
- [ ] Other (specify) · ___

- [ ] Estate (SSN of decedent) ___
- [ ] Plan administrator (SSN) ___
- [ ] Trust (SSN of grantor) ___
- [ ] National Guard   [ ] State/local government
- [ ] Farmers' cooperative   [ ] Federal government/military
- [ ] REMIC   [ ] Indian tribal governments/enterprises
- Group Exemption Number (GEN) · ___

8b If a corporation, name the state or foreign country (if applicable) where incorporated

State

Foreign country

9 **Reason for applying** (check only one box)
- [X] Started new business (specify type) · ___
  novelty store
- [ ] Hired employees (Check the box and see line 12.)
- [ ] Compliance with IRS withholding regulations
- [ ] Other (specify) · ___

- [ ] Banking purpose (specify purpose) · ___
- [ ] Changed type of organization (specify new type) · ___
- [ ] Purchased going business
- [ ] Created a trust (specify type) · ___
- [ ] Created a pension plan (specify type) · ___

10 Date business started or acquired (month, day, year)
01-29-01

11 Closing month of accounting year
December

12 First date wages or annuities were paid or will be paid (month, day, year). **Note:** *If applicant is a withholding agent, enter date income will first be paid to nonresident alien. (month, day, year)* . . . . ·   02-13-01

13 Highest number of employees expected in the next 12 months. **Note:** *If the applicant does not expect to have any employees during the period, enter "-0-."* . . . .

Agricultural	Household	Other

14 Check **one** box that best describes the principal activity of your business.
- [ ] Construction
- [ ] Real estate
- [ ] Rental & leasing
- [ ] Manufacturing
- [ ] Transportation & warehousing
- [ ] Finance & insurance
- [ ] Health care & social assistance
- [ ] Accommodation & food service
- [ ] Other (specify)
- [ ] Wholesale–agent/broker
- [ ] Wholesale–other
- [X] Retail

15 Indicate principal line of merchandise sold; specific construction work done; products produced; or services provided.
novelty sales

16a Has the applicant ever applied for an employer identification number for this or any other business? . . . . . [ ] Yes   [X] No
Note: *If "Yes," please complete lines 16b and 16c.*

16b If you checked "Yes" on line 16a, give applicant's legal name and trade name shown on prior application if different from line 1 or 2 above.
Legal name ·   Trade name ·

16c Approximate date when, and city and state where, the application was filed. Enter previous employer identification number if known.
Approximate date when filed (mo., day, year)   City and state where filed   Previous EIN

Third Party Designee

Complete this section **only** if you want to authorize the named individual to receive the entity's EIN and answer questions about the completion of this form.

Designee's name

Designee's telephone number (include area code)
(   )

Address and ZIP code

Designee's fax number (include area code)
(   )

Under penalties of perjury, I declare that I have examined this application, and to the best of my knowledge and belief, it is true, correct, and complete.

Name and title (type or print clearly) ·   Sidney Bones, owner

Applicant's telephone number (include area code)
(630) 962-0000

Signature ·   *Sidney Bones*   Date · 01/29/02

Applicant's fax number (include area code)
(   )

For Privacy Act and Paperwork Reduction Act Notice, see separate instructions.   Cat. No. 16055N   Form **SS-4** (Rev. 12-2001)

Form W-4 (2002)

Purpose. Complete Form W-4 so your employer can withhold the correct Federal income tax from your pay. Because your tax situation may change, you may want to refigure your withholding each year.

Exemption from withholding. If you are exempt, complete only lines 1, 2, 3, 4, and 7 and sign the form to validate it. Your exemption for 2002 expires February 16, 2003. See **Pub. 505,** Tax Withholding and Estimated Tax.

Note: *You cannot claim exemption from withholding if (a) your income exceeds $750 and includes more than $250 of unearned income (e.g., interest and dividends) and (b) another person can claim you as a dependent on their tax return.*

Basic instructions. If you are not exempt, complete the **Personal Allowances Worksheet** below. The worksheets on page 2 adjust your withholding allowances based on itemized deductions, certain credits, adjustments to income, or two-earner/two-job situations. Complete all worksheets that apply. **However, you may claim fewer (or zero) allowances.**

Head of household. Generally, you may claim head of household filing status on your tax return only if you are unmarried and pay more than 50% of the costs of keeping up a home for yourself and your dependent(s) or other qualifying individuals. See line **E** below.

Tax credits. You can take projected tax credits into account in figuring your allowable number of withholding allowances. Credits for child or dependent care expenses and the child tax credit may be claimed using the **Personal Allowances Worksheet** below. See **Pub. 919,** How Do I Adjust My Tax Withholding? for information on converting your other credits into withholding allowances.

Nonwage income. If you have a large amount of nonwage income, such as interest or dividends, consider making estimated tax payments using **Form 1040-ES,** Estimated Tax for Individuals. Otherwise, you may owe additional tax.

Two earners/two jobs. If you have a working spouse or more than one job, figure the total number of allowances you are entitled to claim on all jobs using worksheets from only one Form W-4. Your withholding usually will be most accurate when all allowances are claimed on the Form W-4 for the highest paying job and zero allowances are claimed on the others.

Nonresident alien. If you are a nonresident alien, see the **Instructions for Form 8233** before completing this Form W-4.

Check your withholding. After your Form W-4 takes effect, use Pub. 919 to see how the dollar amount you are having withheld compares to your projected total tax for 2002. See Pub. 919, especially if you used the **Two-Earner/Two-Job Worksheet** on page 2 and your earnings exceed $125,000 (Single) or $175,000 (Married).

Recent name change? If your name on line 1 differs from that shown on your social security card, call 1-800-772-1213 for a new social security card.

Personal Allowances Worksheet (Keep for your records.)

A Enter "1" for **yourself** if no one else can claim you as a dependent . . . . **A** _____

B Enter "1" if:
{
- You are single and have only one job; or
- You are married, have only one job, and your spouse does not work; or
- Your wages from a second job or your spouse's wages (or the total of both) are $1,000 or less.
}
. . **B** ___1___

C Enter "1" for your **spouse.** But, you may choose to enter "-0-" if you are married and have either a working spouse or more than one job. (Entering "-0-" may help you avoid having too little tax withheld.). . . . . **C** _____

D Enter number of **dependents** (other than your spouse or yourself) you will claim on your tax return . . . . **D** _____

E Enter "1" if you will file as **head of household** on your tax return (see conditions under **Head of household** above) . **E** _____

F Enter "1" if you have at least $1,500 of **child or dependent care expenses** for which you plan to claim a credit . . **F** _____

(**Note:** *Do **not** include child support payments. See **Pub. 503,** Child and Dependent Care Expenses, for details.*)

G **Child Tax Credit** (including additional child tax credit):
- If your total income will be between $15,000 and $42,000 ($20,000 and $65,000 if married), enter "1" for each eligible child plus **1 additional** if you have three to five eligible children or **2 additional** if you have six or more eligible children.
- If your total income will be between $42,000 and $80,000 ($65,000 and $115,000 if married), enter "1" if you have one or two eligible children, "2" if you have three eligible children, "3" if you have four eligible children, or "4" if you have five or more eligible children. **G** ___1___

H Add lines A through G and enter total here. **Note:** *This may be different from the number of exemptions you claim on your tax return.* ▶ **H** _____

For accuracy, complete all worksheets that apply.
{
- If you plan to **itemize or claim adjustments to income** and want to reduce your withholding, see the **Deductions and Adjustments Worksheet** on page 2.
- If you have **more than one job** or are **married and you and your spouse both work** and the combined earnings from all jobs exceed $35,000, see the **Two-Earner/Two-Job Worksheet** on page 2 to avoid having too little tax withheld.
- If **neither** of the above situations applies, **stop here** and enter the number from line H on line 5 of Form W-4 below.
}

- - - - - - - - - - - - - - - - - - - **Cut here and give Form W-4 to your employer. Keep the top part for your records.** - - - - - - - - - - - - - - - -

Form **W-4**	**Employee's Withholding Allowance Certificate**	OMB No. 1545-0010
Department of the Treasury Internal Revenue Service	▶ **For Privacy Act and Paperwork Reduction Act Notice, see page 2.**	2002

1 Type or print your first name and middle initial | Last name | **2** Your social security number

John A. | Smith | 321 54 6879

Home address (number and street or rural route)
567 Wharf Blvd.

3 [X] Single [ ] Married [ ] Married, but withhold at higher Single rate.
Note: *If married, but legally separated, or spouse is a nonresident alien, check the "Single" box.*

City or town, state, and ZIP code
Chicago, IL 60601

4 If your last name differs from that on your social security card, check here. You must call 1-800-772-1213 for a new card. ▶ [ ]

5 Total number of allowances you are claiming (from line **H** above **or** from the applicable worksheet on page 2) | **5** | 1

6 Additional amount, if any, you want withheld from each paycheck . . . . | **6** $ | 0

7 I claim exemption from withholding for 2002, and I certify that I meet **both** of the following conditions for exemption:
- Last year I had a right to a refund of **all** Federal income tax withheld because I had **no** tax liability **and**
- This year I expect a refund of **all** Federal income tax withheld because I expect to have **no** tax liability.

If you meet both conditions, write "Exempt" here . . . . ▶ | **7** |

Under penalties of perjury, I certify that I am entitled to the number of withholding allowances claimed on this certificate, or I am entitled to claim exempt status.

Employee's signature
(Form is not valid unless you sign it.) ▶ *John A. Smith*

Date ▶ *June 6, 2002*

8 Employer's name and address (Employer: Complete lines 8 and 10 only if sending to the IRS.) | **9** Office code (optional) | **10** Employer identification number

Cat. No. 10220Q

Deductions and Adjustments Worksheet

Note: *Use this worksheet only if you plan to itemize deductions, claim certain credits, or claim adjustments to income on your 2002 tax return.*

1	Enter an estimate of your 2002 itemized deductions. These include qualifying home mortgage interest, charitable contributions, state and local taxes, medical expenses in excess of 7.5% of your income, and miscellaneous deductions. (For 2002, you may have to reduce your itemized deductions if your income is over $137,300 ($68,650 if married filing separately). See **Worksheet 3** in Pub. 919 for details.)	**1** $ _____
2	Enter: $\left\{\begin{array}{l}\$7,850 \text{ if married filing jointly or qualifying widow(er)}\\ \$6,900 \text{ if head of household}\\ \$4,700 \text{ if single}\\ \$3,925 \text{ if married filing separately}\end{array}\right\}$	**2** $ _____
3	**Subtract** line 2 from line 1. If line 2 is greater than line 1, enter "-0-"	**3** $ _____
4	Enter an estimate of your 2002 adjustments to income, including alimony, deductible IRA contributions, and student loan interest	**4** $ _____
5	**Add** lines 3 and 4 and enter the total. Include any amount for credits from **Worksheet 7** in Pub. 919. .	**5** $ _____
6	Enter an estimate of your 2002 nonwage income (such as dividends or interest)	**6** $ _____
7	**Subtract** line 6 from line 5. Enter the result, but not less than "-0-"	**7** $ _____
8	**Divide** the amount on line 7 by $3,000 and enter the result here. Drop any fraction	**8** _____
9	Enter the number from the **Personal Allowances Worksheet,** line H, page 1	**9** _____
10	**Add** lines 8 and 9 and enter the total here. If you plan to use the **Two-Earner/Two-Job Worksheet,** also enter this total on line 1 below. Otherwise, **stop here** and enter this total on Form W-4, line 5, page 1 .	**10** _____

Two-Earner/Two-Job Worksheet

Note: *Use this worksheet only if the instructions under line H on page 1 direct you here.*

1	Enter the number from line H, page 1 (or from line 10 above if you used the **Deductions and Adjustments Worksheet**)	**1** _____
2	Find the number in **Table 1** below that applies to the **lowest** paying job and enter it here	**2** _____
3	If line 1 is **more than or equal to** line 2, subtract line 2 from line 1. Enter the result here (if zero, enter "-0-") and on Form W-4, line 5, page 1. **Do not** use the rest of this worksheet	**3** _____

Note: *If line 1 is **less than** line 2, enter "-0-" on Form W-4, line 5, page 1. Complete lines 4-9 below to calculate the additional withholding amount necessary to avoid a year end tax bill.*

4	Enter the number from line 2 of this worksheet . . . . **4** _____	
5	Enter the number from line 1 of this worksheet . . . . **5** _____	
6	**Subtract** line 5 from line 4	**6** _____
7	Find the amount in **Table 2** below that applies to the **highest** paying job and enter it here	**7** $ _____
8	**Multiply** line 7 by line 6 and enter the result here. This is the additional annual withholding needed . .	**8** $ _____
9	**Divide** line 8 by the number of pay periods remaining in 2002. For example, divide by 26 if you are paid every two weeks and you complete this form in December 2001. Enter the result here and on Form W-4, line 6, page 1. This is the additional amount to be withheld from each paycheck	**9** $ _____

Table 1: Two-Earner/Two-Job Worksheet

Married Filing Jointly				All Others			
If wages from **LOWEST** paying job are-	Enter on line 2 above	If wages from **LOWEST** paying job are-	Enter on line 2 above	If wages from **LOWEST** paying job are-	Enter on line 2 above	If wages from **LOWEST** paying job are-	Enter on line 2 above
$0 - $4,000	0	44,001 - 50,000	8	$0 - $6,000	0	75,001 - 95,000	8
4,001 - 9,000	1	50,001 - 55,000	9	6,001 - 11,000	1	95,001 - 110,000	9
9,001 - 15,000	2	55,001 - 65,000	10	11,001 - 17,000	2	110,001 and over	10
15,001 - 20,000	3	65,001 - 80,000	11	17,001 - 23,000	3		
20,001 - 25,000	4	80,001 - 95,000	12	23,001 - 28,000	4		
25,001 - 32,000	5	95,001 - 110,000	13	28,001 - 38,000	5		
32,001 - 38,000	6	110,001 - 125,000	14	38,001 - 55,000	6		
38,001 - 44,000	7	125,001 and over	15	55,001 - 75,000	7		

Table 2: Two-Earner/Two-Job Worksheet

Married Filing Jointly		All Others	
If wages from **HIGHEST** paying job are-	Enter on line 7 above	If wages from **HIGHEST** paying job are-	Enter on line 7 above
$0 - $50,000	$450	$0 - $30,000	$450
50,001 - 100,000	800	30,001 - 70,000	800
100,001 - 150,000	900	70,001 - 140,000	900
150,001 - 270,000	1,050	140,001 - 300,000	1,050
270,001 and over	1,150	300,001 and over	1,150

Illinois Department of Revenue
NUC-1 Illinois Business Registration

Read this information first

You must read the instructions before completing this form. Be sure to complete all of the information that relates to your business. If you omit any required information, we cannot properly register your business.

You may need the following information:
- a federal employer identification number (FEIN)
- an Employment Security account number
- a corporation number (corporate file no.)

If you photocopy this form, be sure to mail us the original.

Section 1: Identify your business

1 Business trade name: __Bones Enterprises__

Corporate or partnership name if other than above:

Principal business address: (Do not use a p.o. box number.)

6789 Graves Avenue
Number and street

Chicago   IL   60601
City   State   ZIP

2 Daytime phone no.: (312) 962-0000   Ext._____

3 FEIN: _5_ _9_ - _1_ _2_ _3_ _4_ _5_ _6_ _7_

4 Check one of the following categories which best describes your type of business:
- _____ Agricultural, forestry, or animal products services
- _____ Construction   __X__ Retail
- _____ Wholesale   _____ Service
- _____ Manufacturing

5 Describe your principal business activity:
__Novelty Sales__

6 Date business started in Illinois under your current ownership?
__01_/ _29_/ _02_
Month Day Year

7 The above business is located (check one and complete):

__X__ inside the city, village, or town limits of
__Chicago__

_____ outside the city, village or town limits in the county of
_____

8 Check your type of business ownership:

__X__	A1	Individual (sole proprietor)
_____	B0	Husband/wife (sole proprietors)
_____	C2	Partnership (no. of general partners: _____)
_____	D3	Corporation
_____	E4	Trust
_____	F5	Estate
_____	G6	Small business corporation (IRC 1361)
_____	H7	Exempt organization (IRC 501)
_____	I9	Government

9 You **must** complete the following information for all owners, general partners, executive officers, executors, and trustees. If your business ownership is a corporation, you must **at least** provide the information for the president, secretary, and treasurer. If a person holds more than one title, the name must appear separately with each title held. Attach additional sheets if necessary.

__Sidney Bones__   __123-45-6789__
Legal name (last, first, middle)   SSN/FEIN
__owner__   __3215 Ulna Lane__
Title   __Chicago, IL 60602__
   Home address

Legal name (last, first, middle)   SSN/FEIN

Title   Home address

Legal name (last, first, middle)   SSN/FEIN

Title   Home address

Legal name (last, first, middle)   SSN/FEIN

Title   Home address

10 Did you buy this business from someone? _____ yes __X__ no
If you answer "yes," complete the following information about the previous ownership:

Name: _____

Address: _____

City, state, ZIP: _____

Phone no.: ___(_____)_____

FEIN: _____ IBT:_____

Note: You must complete Form NUC-542-A, Notice of Sale/Purchase of Business Assets, if you bought the business from someone. If you do not complete Form NUC-542-A, you may have to pay any taxes, penalties, and interest owed to us by the former owner of the business.

Section 2: Sales Tax and Reseller Registration

If you do not make any sales (retail or wholesale) or inventory purchases, **do not** complete this section. Go to Section 3.

You **must** complete this section if you
- sell merchandise from a site in Illinois
- are a serviceperson who sells merchandise while performing your service (see instructions)
- use merchandise in Illinois that you buy from out-of-state businesses that do not collect Illinois tax,
- are an out-of-state business that sells or leases merchandise to Illinois customers or solicits orders.

Answer ALL of the following questions:

1 Do you sell any merchandise at retail from a site in Illinois? (A site can be permanent, such as an office or warehouse, or can be changeable, such as a fair, flea market, art show, or trade show.)
    _X_ yes   _____ no

2 Do you conduct business at more than one site in Illinois?
    _____ yes   _X_ no
If you answer "yes," you must attach Schedule M.

3 Are you a serviceperson who sells merchandise while performing your service? (see instructions)
    _____ yes   _X_ no

4 Do you ever purchase merchandise (that you will personally use in your business) from out-of-state businesses that do not collect Illinois tax from you?
    _____ yes   _X_ no

5 Is your business located outside Illinois?
    _____ yes   _X_ no

If you answer "yes,"
A do you have an office, agent, salesperson, or representative in Illinois? (see instructions)
    _____ yes   _____ no
B do you solicit orders for merchandise? (see instructions)
    _____ yes   _____ no
C will any of the merchandise that you sell to Illinois customers be delivered in your own vehicles?
    _____ yes   _____ no
D do you bring merchandise into Illinois that you will use or lease in Illinois? (see instuctions)
    _____ yes   _____ no

6 Do you sell all merchandise in such a way that no sales tax is due?
    _____ yes   _X_ no

If you answer "yes," will you make any withdrawals from your sales inventory for your own use in Illinois?
    _____ yes   _____ no

7 Are you a distributor, supplier, or reseller of motor fuels? (see instructions)
    _____ yes   _X_ no
If you answer "yes" and you are a distributor or supplier, what is your Illinois motor fuel license number?
_____

8 Do you own vending machines through which merchandise is sold?
    _____ yes   _X_ no
If you answer "yes," how many machines do you own?
_____

9 Do you sell new or used cars, trucks, motorcycles, watercraft, aircraft, trailers, mobile homes, or salvage items?
    _____ yes   _X_ no
If you answer "yes," how many items do you estimate you will sell each month?
_____

10 Do you sell tires at retail? (see instructions)
    _____ yes   _X_ no
If you answer "yes," do you pay the Tire User Fee to your supplier?
    _____ yes   _X_ no

11 Do you sell soft drinks (in closed or sealed containers) at retail? (See instructions for definition of soft drinks.)
    _X_ yes   _____ no

12 How much sales or use tax do you estimate you will pay each month as a retailer?
    _____ $200 or more
    _X_ less than $200
    _____ none

13 When did you (or will you) make your first inventory purchase or taxable sale?
    _01_/_29_/_00_
    month   day   year

14 By law, someone representing your business must complete the following information or we cannot process this form.

I accept personal responsibility for the filing of returns and the payment of taxes due.

Sidney Bones   01/29/00
Signature (in ink)   Date

Sidney Bones   owner
Printed name   Title

3251 Ulna Lane
Home address · number and street

Chicago   IL   60602
City   State   ZIP

123-45-6789   312 960-1211
Social Security number   Phone number

Do not write below this line. For official use only.

Filing req. _____ Tax distr. _____ Municipal ver._____

Loc. code _____

Loc. type _____ Cert. req. _____ No. of locations _____

ROT _____ **UT** _____ **RES** _____ **RR2** _____ **PST** _____

NUC-1 (R-11/93)

Section 3: Business Income and Replacement Tax Registration

If you are a sole proprietor, **do not** complete this section. Go to Section 4.

You must complete this section if you are a partnership, corporation, trust, estate, small business corporation, exempt organization, or any other type of business **except** a sole proprietorship.

1 What date is the end of your taxable year for filing your federal taxes?
(The date for the end of your Illinios tax year must be the same as the date for your federal tax year.)

_____ December 31 (calendar year)

_____ Other _____/_____
(list month and day)

2 **Out of state businesses only**
What date did you begin doing business in Illinois? (see instructions)

_____/_____/_____
Month   Day   Year

3 **Corporations and small business corporations only**
What is your corporation's file number (issued by the Illinois Office of the Secretary of State)?

_____

4 What date did you incorporate?

_____/_____/_____
Month   Day   Year

5 In what state did you incorporate?

_____
State

Do not write in this space. For official use only.

Filing requirement _____ Status _____

Effective date _____ Reason _____

Section 4: Withholding Agent Registration

If you do not (or will not) have employees, **do not** complete this section. Go to Section 5.

You must complete this section if you have employees who are subject to Illinois Withholding Tax. (For more information, see booklet IL-700, Withholding Tax Guide.)

1 What is your Illinois Employment Security account number (unemployment compensation)?

_____

2 What date did you (or will you) issue your first payroll check?

_____/_____/_____
Month   Day   Year

3 What is the total amout of Illinois Withholding Tax that you expect to withhold? (Check one item below.)

_____ less than $500 for the year

_____ less than $500 for the quarter, but more than $500 for the year

_____ more than $500, but no more than $1,000 at at any time during the quarter

_____ more than $1,000 at any time during the quarter*

If you withhold more than $1,000 at any time during the quarter, we will require you to file weekly. However, if your payroll is twice a month rather than weekly, we will allow you to file twice a month. Do you want this option?
_____ yes _____ no

Do not write in this space. For official use only.

Filing requirement _____ Status _____

Effective date _____ Reason _____

Section 5: Mailing Address for Forms

If you want your tax forms mailed to an address other than the address listed in Section 1, complete this section. If not, go to Section 6.

If you want all of your tax forms sent to **one** mailing address, complete the first address area below. If you want your tax forms sent to **different** mailing addresses, please complete the additional address areas on the following page.

Attention:_____

Number and street _____

_____

City, state, ZIP_____

Daytime phone no._____ Ext_____

Which forms do you want mailed to the above address?

_____ all tax forms

_____ sales tax

_____ business income tax

_____ withholding tax

continued on next page

Section 5 continued

Attention:_____

Number and street:_____

_____

City, state, ZIP:_____

Daytime phone no.:__(____)_____Ext_____

Which forms do you want mailed to the above address?

_____ sales tax

_____ business income tax

_____ withholding tax

Attention:_____

Number and street:_____

_____

City, state, ZIP:_____

Daytime phone no.:_____Ext_____

Which forms do you want mailed to the above address?

_____ sales tax

_____ business income tax

_____ withholding tax

Section 6: Registration for Other Taxes and Compliance Information

Depending on your type of business you may have to complete additional registration forms for other taxes. See Section 6 in the NUC-1 Instructions.

Department of Revenue Tax Enforcement - If you do not collect and remit any and all taxes due us, one or more of the following actions could occur:

- referral to a collection agency
- filing of a tax lien against your property
- garnishment of wages and bank accounts
- recommendation of professional license revocation
- civil judgements
- revocation of business certificates of registration
- withholding of state warrants
- seizure and sale of your assets
- nonrenewal of your corporate charter
- criminal prosecution

Section 7: Signature Affidavit

The signture below must be the signature of one of the owners, general partners, executive officers, executors, or trustees listed in Section 1, Item 9. Be sure to sign in ink and print the same name on the bottom line. If the person signing this form has power of attorney, complete and attach Form IL-2848, Power of Attorney.

Under penalties of perjury, I state that I have examined this application and, to the best of my knowledge, it is true, correct, and complete.

Sidney Bones
Signature of owner, partner, or officer

owner   01/29/00
Title   Date

Sidney Bones
Print the name of the above signature.

Mail this application to:

ILLINOIS DEPARTMENT OF REVENUE
CENTRAL REGISTRATION DIVISION
PO BOX 19030
SPRINGFIELD IL 62794-9030

If you have any questions, call 217 785-3707.

UI-1
Stock No. 4229 (Rev. 11/93)
IL 427-00015

STATE OF ILLINOIS
DEPARTMENT OF EMPLOYMENT SECURITY
401 SOUTH STATE STREET
CHICAGO, ILLINOIS 60605-2280

REPORT TO DETERMINE LIABILITY
UNDER THE UNEMPLOYMENT INSURANCE ACT

IMPORTANT: Every newly created employing unit shall file this report within 30 days of the date upon which it commences business

1. a. Employer name __Bones Enterprises__
   Doing Business As __Sid's Bones__
   b. What is your primary business activity in Illinois? __retail sales__
   c. What is your principal product or service? (Read instructions) _____ % Sales or receipts __novelties__
   _____ % Sales or receipts _____
   d. Business Address __6789 Graves Avenue__
   (Actual physical location / Number & Street or Rural Route)
   __Chicago   Illinois   60601   Cook   U.S.A.__
   (City/Town)   (State)   (Zip)   (County)   (Country)   Telephone No.
   e. If you want any correspondence sent to another address (other than the business address indicated above), please refer to the UI-1 Mailing form included in this packet.

2. Enter any employer's account number previously assigned to you by the Illinois Department of Employment Security
   _____

3. Identification number under which you file Federal Social Security Returns (Form 941) __345-67-8900__

4. a. Type of Organization (Check One): ____X____ Sole Proprietor _____Partnership _____Corporation
   Other (This includes: Trusts, Associations, Receiverships.)
   _____
   b. If a corporation, date incorporated _____ State in which incorporated _____

5. Enter the required information for owner or each partner or officer:

Name	Title	Social Security No.	Residence Address	Residence Telephone No.
Sidney Bones	owner	123-45-6789	3215 Ulna Lane, Chicago, IL 60602	312-960-1211

6. a. Date you first began employing workers in Illinois __01/29/00__ Date you ceased employing workers in Illinois _____
   b. Date of your first payroll in Illinois __02/13/00__

7. Did you acquire your Illinois business, or any portion of it, by purchase, reorganization, a change in entity, for example a change from sole proprietor to corporation? _____ YES __X__ NO. If yes, complete the form UI-1 S & P, REPORT TO DETERMINE SUCCESSION which is included in this packet. Please complete the remainder of the questions on this form as well.
   NOTE: If you acquired your business by purchase, reorganization, merger, etc., you must complete the form titled **REPORT TO DETERMINE SUCCESSION.** Responses to the questions on this form should reflect information relative to the operation of your business AFTER the date of acquisition. Failure to notify this Department in writing within 120 days of the date of acquisition, may result in a higher rate of contribution (820 ILCS 405/1507).

QUESTIONS NUMBER 8 AND 9 APPLY TO DOMESTIC, AGRICULTURAL, OR NONPROFIT EMPLOYERS. IF YOU ARE NOT ENGAGED IN ANY OF THESE TYPES OF ACTIVITIES, YOU MAY SKIP THIS SECTION AND PROCEED TO QUESTION 10.

8. a. Indicate if you employed workers engaged only in _____ DOMESTIC OR _____ AGRICULTURAL WORK.
   Check whether you paid wages in any calendar quarter of the current year or preceding four years
   _____ $1,000 for domestic workers _____ $20,000 for agricultural workers
   Circle the quarter and indicate the year when these wages were paid: Jan.-Mar._____ (year), April-June_____ (year), July - Sept._____ (year), Oct. - Dec. _____ (year).
   b. If you are an agricultural employer, indicate the earliest quarter and year in which you employed 10 or more workers in each of 20 weeks (weeks need not be consecutive) _____

9. Are you a nonprofit organization that is exempt from Federal income taxes under Section 501(c)(3) of the Internal Revenue Code? _____YES _____NO. If YES, attach the federal exemption letter and check here _____ if you employed 4 or more paid workers in Illinois within each of 20 or more calendar weeks during the current or preceding four years. If checked, indicate the earliest quarter and year in which that 20th week occurred _____. Do you wish to be a reimbursable employer? _____YES _____NO. If YES, a REIMBURSE BENEFITS IN LIEU OF PAYING CONTRIBUTIONS (UI-5(NP)) form will be mailed to you. You must complete this form and return it to this Department.

If you answered question 8 or answered yes to question 9, proceed to question 13. Otherwise proceed to question 10.

10. a. Have you had an ILLINOIS payroll totaling $1500 or more in any calendar quarter during the current or preceding four years?
    _____YES   X NO.
    If YES, indicate the first year with a quarterly payroll of $1500 or more _____
    b. Circle the quarter and enter the total wages paid in that quarter: January - March $_____ April-June $_____ July-Sept $_____ October-December $_____ .

11. a. Have you employed 1 or more workers in ILLINOIS within each of 20 or more calendar weeks during the current or preceding four years (weeks need not be consecutive)? _____YES X NO.
    b. If YES, indicate the first year with 20 or more calendar weeks of employment _____ .
    Circle the quarter in which that 20th week occurred: April-June   July-Sept.   Oct.-Dec.

12. Have you incurred liability under the Federal Unemployment Tax Act for any of the last 5 years? _____YES X NO.
    If YES, indicate the year(s) of such liability _____

13. Are there any persons not included in questions 11 or 12 who performed services for you, as an independent contractor or otherwise, or received compensation of any kind from you or operated within your business establishment? _____YES X NO. If YES, attach a sheet stating the number of such persons and give details as to the type of service and the date such services were performed.

14. Complete the following section only if you have multiple worksites in Illinois.
    The following information is required for reporting of statistical data to the federal government. Please complete the information as completely and accurately as possible.

    Enter below the required information for each place of business (worksite) in Illinois (use additional sheets if necessary). Read instructions carefully. If any worksite is engaged in performing support services for other units of the company, please indicate the nature of the activity in "section c-Primary Activity". Examples of Support Services are: Central Administrative Office, Research, Development or Testing, Storage (warehouse). See instructions for additional examples.

a) Physical Location of Each Establishment (Street, city, zip code)	b) County	c) Primary Activity	d) Average No. of Employees

15. If you are determined not liable, based upon the provisions of the Unemployment Insurance Act, you may voluntarily elect coverage under Section 205(h). Please indicate whether you want voluntary coverage X YES. If checked, we will mail you form UI-1B, VOLUNTARY ELECTION OF COVERAGE. Please complete that form and return it to this Department.

CERTIFICATION: I hereby certify that the information contained in this report and any sheets attached hereto is true and correct. This report must be signed by owner, partner, or officer. If signed by any other person, a power of attorney giving such individual authority to sign must be attached. A Power of Attorney form is included in this packet.

Employer Name _____
Signed by ___*Sidney Bones*_____ Date __01/29/00_____
Title ___owner_____

Area		INDUSTRY		SOURCE_____REC'D DATE_____
				A/C_____NL_____
				LIAB. DATE_____QTR_____SEC
				AUDITOR_____DATE_____

Illinois Withholding Allowance Worksheet

General Information

Complete this worksheet to figure your total withholding allowances.

Everyone must complete Part 1.

Complete Part 2 if you (or your spouse) are
• age 65 or older or legally blind, or
• you wrote an amount on Line 4 of the Deductions and Adjustments Worksheet for federal Form W-4.

If you have more than one job or if your spouse works, you may claim all of your allowances on one job or you may claim some on each job, but you may **not** claim the same allowances more than once. Your withholding will usually be more accurate if you claim all your allowances on the Form IL-W-4 for the job with the largest wages and claim zero on all other Forms IL-W-4. If you have a working spouse, you may choose not to claim your spouse as a dependent (this may help avoid having too little withheld).

Part 1: Figure your basic personal allowances (including allowances for dependents)

Check all that apply:

☒ no one else can claim you as a dependent
☐ you can claim your spouse as a dependent

1 Write the total number of boxes you checked.　　　　　1 ___1___

2 Write the number of dependents (other than you or your spouse) who you will claim on your tax return.　　　　　2 ___0___

3 Add Lines 1 and 2. Write the result. This is the total number of basic personal allowances to which you are **entitled**.　　　　　3 ___0___

4 If you want to have additional Illinois Income Tax withheld from your pay, you must reduce the number of basic personal allowances you wrote on Line 3. Write the total number of basic personal allowances you elect to claim on Line 4 and on Form IL-W-4, Line 1.　　　　　4 ___1___

Part 2: Figure your additional allowances

Check all that apply:

☐ you are 65 or over　　　　☐ you are legally blind
☐ your spouse is 65 or over　　☐ your spouse is legally blind

5 Write the total number of boxes you checked.　　　　　5 ___0___

6 Write any amount that you reported on Line 4 of the Deductions and Adjustments Worksheet for federal Form W-4.　　　6 ___0___　　　6 ___0___

7 Divide Line 6 by 1,000. Round to the nearest whole number. Write the result on Line 7.　　　　　7 ___0___

8 Add Lines 5 and 7. Write the result. This is the total number of additional allowances to which you are **entitled**.　　　　　8 ___0___

9 If you want to have additional Illinois Income Tax withheld from your pay, you must reduce the number of additional allowances you wrote on Line 8. Write the total number of additional allowances you elect to claim on Line 9 and on Form IL-W-4, Line 2.　　　　　9 ___0___

Note: If you have non-wage income and you expect to owe Illinois Income Tax on that income, you may choose to have an additional amount withheld from your pay. On Line 3 of Form IL-W-4, write the additional amount you want your employer to withhold.

--------------------------- Cut here and give the certificate to your employer. Keep the top portion for your records. --------------------------- ✂

Illinois Department of Revenue
IL-W-4 **Employee's Illinois Withholding Allowance Certificate**

0 2 0 . 1 1 . 3 4 5 6
Social Security number

Jonathan Marrow
Name

101 Fossil Drive
Street address

Chicago　　　　　　　IL 60606
City　　　　　　　State　　ZIP

This form is authorized as outlined by the Illinois Income Tax Act. Disclosure of this information is REQUIRED. Failure to provide information could result in a penalty. This form has been approved by the Forms Management Center.　　　IL-492-0039

1 Write the total number of basic allowances that you are claiming (From worksheet, Part 1, Line 4).　　1 ___1___

2 Write the total number of additional allowances that you are claiming (From worksheet, Part 2, Line 9). 2 ___0___

3 Write the additional amount you want withheld (deducted) from each pay.　　3 ___0___

I certify that I am entitled to the number of withholding allowances claimed on this certificate.

Jonathan Marrow　　　　01/29/00
Your signature　　　　　　Date

Employer: Keep this certificate with your records. If you have referred the employee's federal certificate to IRS and the IRS has notified you to disregard it, you may also be required to disregard this certificate. Furthermore, even if you are not required to refer the employee's federal certificate to IRS, you may still be required to refer this certificate to the Illinois Department of Revenue for inspection. See Illinois Income Tax Regulations 86 Ill. Adm. Code 100.7110.

IL-W-4 (R-12/98)

Illinois Department of Revenue
CRT-61 Certificate of Resale

Step 1: Identify the seller

1 Name Harry's Wholesale Novelties

2 Business address 6699 Wahoo Drive

Chicago   IL   60606
City   State   Zip

Step 2: Identify the purchaser

3 Name Sid's Bones

4 Business address 6789 Graves Avenue

Chicago   IL   60601
City   State   Zip

5 Complete the information below. Check only one box.

☒ The purchaser is registered as a retailer with the Illinois
Department of Revenue. 3 4 7 8 - 9 2 0 1
Registration number

☐ The purchaser is registered as a reseller with the Illinois
Department of Revenue. _ _ _ _ - _ _ _ _ .
Resale number

☐ The purchaser is authorized to do business out-of-state and
will resell and deliver property only to purchasers located
outside the state of Illinois. See Line 5 instructions.

Step 3: Describe the property

6 Describe the property that is being purchased for resale or
list the invoice number and the date of purchase.
 Boxes of novelty toys, e.g. alien
 keychains, mini card deck, etc.

Step 4: Complete for blanket certificates

7 Complete the information below. Check only one box.

☒ I am the identified purchaser, and I certify that all of the
purchases that I make from this seller are for resale.

☐ I am the identified purchaser, and I certify that the following
percentage, _____ %, of all of the purchases that I make
from this seller are for resale.

Step 5: Purchaser's signature

I certify that I am purchasing the property described in Step 3
from the stated seller for the purpose of resale.

Sidney Bones   01 29 00
Purchaser's signature   Date

**Note: It is the seller's responsibility to verify that the
purchaser's registration or resale number is valid and active.**

General information

When is a Certificate of Resale required?
Generally, a Certificate of Resale is required for proof that no tax
is due on any sale that is made tax-free as a sale for resale. The
purchaser, at the seller's request, must provide the information
that is needed to complete this certificate.

Who keeps the Certificate of Resale?
The seller must keep the certificate. We may request it as proof
that no tax was due on the sale of the specified property.
Do not mail the certificate to us.

Can other forms be used?
Yes. You can use other forms or statements in place of this
certificate but whatever you use as proof that a sale was made
for resale must contain
* the seller's name and address;
* the purchaser's name and address;
* a description of the property being purchased;
* a statement that the property is being purchased for resale;
* the purchaser's signature and date of signing; and
* either a registration number, a resale number, or a certification
of resale to an out-of-state purchaser.
Note: A purchase order signed by the purchaser may be used as
a Certificate of Resale if it contains all of the above required
information.

CRT-61 (N-1/98)
IL-492-3850

When is a blanket certificate of resale used?
The purchaser may provide a blanket certificate of resale to any
seller from whom all purchases made are sales for resale. A blanket
certificate can also specify that a percentage of the purchases made
from the identified seller will be for resale. In either instance, blanket
certificates should be kept up-to-date. If a specified percentage
changes, a new certificate should be provided. Otherwise, all
certificates should be updated at least every three years.

Specific instructions

Step 1: Identify the seller
Lines 1 and 2 Write the seller's name and mailing address.

Step 2: Identify the purchaser
Lines 3 and 4 Write the purchaser's name and mailing address.

Line 5 Check the statement that applies to the purchaser's
business, and provide any additional requested information.
Note: A statement by the purchaser that property will be sold for
resale will not be accepted by the department without supporting
evidence (*e.g.*, proof of out-of-state registration).

Step 3: Describe the property
Line 6 On the lines provided, briefly describe the tangible
personal property that was purchased for resale or list the invoice
number and date of purchase.

Step 4: Complete for blanket certificates
Line 7 The purchaser must check the statement that applies,
and provide any additional requested information.

Step 5: Purchaser's signature
The purchaser must sign and date the form.

SAMPLE FORM 8109-B: FEDERAL TAX DEPOSIT COUPONS

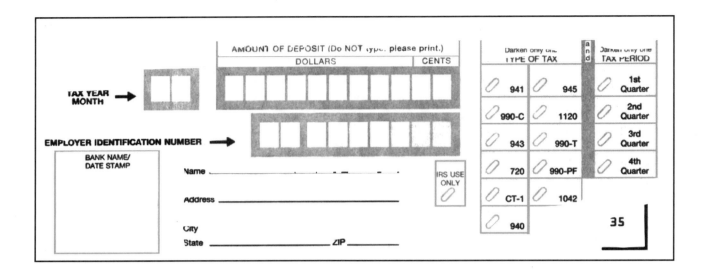

1040-ES: Estimated Tax Payment Voucher

Cat. No. 61900V

OMB No. 1545-0087

Form 1040-ES (OCR)

Department of the Treasury
Internal Revenue Service

2000

Estimated Tax

Payment Voucher **4**

Calendar year—
Due Jan. 15, 2000

Cross out any errors and print the correct information. Get **Form 8822** to report a new address (see instructions). For Paperwork Reduction Act Notice, see instructions.

0746497

234-56-7890   DC   9712

234-56-7890   DC WARD 30 0 9712 430 07

2001

JOHN DOE
123 ANYWHERE STREET
CHICAGO, IL 60601

CHICAGO, IL 60601-0001

Enter the amount of your payment. File this voucher only if you are making a payment of **estimated** tax.	$	▸ Make your check or money order payable to **"Internal Revenue Service."** ▸ Write your social security number and "1997 Form 1040-ES" on your payment. ▸ Send your payment and payment voucher to the address above. ▸ Do not send cash. Do not staple your payment to the voucher.

form 17

SAMPLE FORM W-2: WAGE AND TAX STATEMENT

a Control number 59-1234567	22222	Void ☐	For Official Use Only ▶ OMB No. 1545-0008 25,650.00 5,050.00	

b Employer's identification number Sid's Bones	1 Wages, tips, other compensation 25,650.00	2 Federal income tax withheld 1,590.30

c Employer's name, address, and ZIP code 6789 Graves Avenue Chicago, IL 60601 321-54-6879	3 Social security wages 25,650.00	4 Social security tax withheld 371.93
	5 Medicare wages and tips 0	6 Medicare tax withheld 0
	7 Social security tips 0	8 Allocated tips 0

d Employee's social security number John A. Smith	9 Advance EIC payment 0	10 Dependent care benefits 0

e Employee's name (first, middle initial, last) 567 Wharf Boulevard Chicago, IL 60601	11 Nonqualified plans	12 Benefits included in box 1
	13 See Instrs. for box 13	14 Other

15 Statutory employee ☐	Deceased ☐	Pension plan ☐	Legal rep. ☐	Hshld. emp. ☐	Subtotal ☐	Deferred compensation ☐

f Employee's address and ZIP code

16 State	Employer's state I.D. No.	17 State wages, tips, etc.	18 State income tax	19 Locality name	20 Local wages, tips, etc.	21 Local income tax
IL	234567	26,500.00	1,010.00			

Cat. No. 10134D   Department of the Treasury—Internal Revenue Service

Form **W-2** Wage and Tax Statement **2000**

For Paperwork Reduction Act Notice, see separate instructions.

Copy A For Social Security Administration

FORM 1099: MISCELLANEOUS INCOME

9595	☐ VOID	☐ CORRECTED		
PAYER'S name. street address, city, state, and ZIP code Bones Enterprises 6789 Graves Avenue Chicago, IL 60601	1 Rents $	OMB No. 1545-0115		
	2 Royalties $	**1996**	**Miscellaneous Income**	
	3 Other income $	Form **1099-MISC**		
PAYER'S Federal identification number 59-1234567	RECIPIENT'S identification number 678-90-1234	4 Federal income tax withheld $	5 Fishing boat proceeds $ 2000	Copy A For Internal Revenue Service Center
RECIPIENT'S name John A. Smith	6 Medical and health care payments $	7 Nonemployee compensation $ 21,000	File with Form 1096.	
	8 Substitute payments in lieu of dividends or interest $	9 Payer made direct sales of $5,000 or more of consumer products to a buyer (recipient) for resale ▶ ☐	For Paperwork Reduction Act Notice and instructions for	
Street address (including apt. no.) 567 Wharf Boulevard				
City, state. and ZIP code Chicago, IL 60601	10 Crop insurance proceeds $	11 State income tax withheld $ 00.00	completing this form, see **Instructions for Forms 1099, 1098, 5498, and W-2G.**	
Account number (optional)	2nd TIN Not. ☐	12 State/Payer's state number 8884444		

Form **1099-MISC**   Cat. No. 14425J   Department of the Treasury - Internal Revenue Service

Do NOT Cut or Separate Forms on This Page

FORM 1096: MISCELLANEOUS INCOME

DO NOT STAPLE 6969

Form **1096**	Annual Summary and Transmittal of	OMB No. 1545-0108
Department of the Treasury Internal Revenue Service	U.S. Information Returns	20**00**

A T T A C H   I R S   L A B E L   H E R E

FILER'S name

Bones Enterprises

Street address (including room or suite number)

6789 Graves Avenue

City, state, and ZIP code
Chicago, IL 60601

If you are not using a preprinted label, enter in box 1 or 2 below the identification number you used as the filer on the information returns being transmitted. Do not fill in both boxes 1 and 2.

Name of person to contact if the IRS needs more information
Sidney Bones
Telephone number
(630) 962-0000

For Official Use Only

1 Employer identification number	2 Social security number	3 Total number of forms	4 Federal income tax withheld	5 Total amount reported with this Form 1096
59-123456		3	$ 0	$ $63,000

Enter an "X" in only one box below to indicate the type of form being filed.   If this is your FINAL return, enter an "X" here . . ▶ ☐

W-2G 32	1098 81	1099-A 80	1099-B 79	1099-C 85	1099-DIV 91	1099-G 86	1099-INT 92	1099-MISC 95	1099-OID 96	1099-PATR 97	1099-R 98	1099-S 75	5498 28
☐	☐	☐	☐	☐	☐	☐	☐	☐	☒	☐	☐	☐	☐

X

APPENDIX D: READY-TO-USE FORMS & TAX TIMETABLE

The following forms may be photocopied or removed from this book and used immediately. Some of the tax forms explained in this book are not included here because you should use original returns provided by the IRS (940, 941) or the Illinois Department of Revenue (quarterly unemployment compensation form).

These forms are included on the following pages:

TAX TIMETABLE

	Illinois				Federal			
	Sales	Unem- ployment	IL-W-4 Withholding	Income Tax	Est. Payment	Annual Return	Form 941*	Misc.
JAN.	20th	31st			15th		31st	31st 940 W-2 508 1099
FEB.	20th		28th					28th W-3
MAR.	20th			Corporate 15th		15th Corp. & Partnership		
APR.	20th	30th	30th	Individual 15th	15th	15th Personal	30th	30th 508
MAY	20th							
JUN.	20th				15th			
JUL.	20th	31st	31st				31st	31st 508
AUG.	20th							
SEP.	20th				15th			
OCT.	20th	31st	31st				31st	31st 508
NOV.	20th							
DEC.	20th							

* In addition to form 941, deposits must be made regularly if withholding exceeds $1,000 in any month

STATE OF ILLINOIS)   File No._____

COUNTY OF _____)SS.   Filing Fee $5.00

CERTIFICATE

It is hereby certified that the undersigned is/are conducting or transacting business under the Assumed Name of:

_____;

(List the Business Name)

The Business is being conducted at the following locations: _____

_____;

(List all Business Addresses located in the County)

The nature of the Business being conducted or transacted is _____

_____;

(Declare the Type of Business)

The true and real full name or names of the person or persons owning, conducting, or transacting the business are as follows:

PRINT NAME   PRINT RESIDENCE ADDRESS

_____   _____

_____   _____

_____   _____

_____   _____

Dated this _____ day of _____, 20_____.

SIGNATURE _____

SIGNATURE _____

SIGNATURE _____

SIGNATURE _____

(All persons must sign)

STATE OF ILLINOIS)
COUNTY OF _____)SS.

I, _____, a Notary Public in and for said County and State, do hereby certify that _____

_____

is/are the same person(s) whose name(s) is/are subscribed to the foregoing instrument, and that

_____

_____

appeared before me this day in person and acknowledged that he/she/they has/have read and signed said instrument, and that each of the statement contained therein are true.

_____

Notary Public

Form AB2   My commission expires on the _____
FILE ONE COPY ONLY   day of _____, 20 ___

ASSUMED BUSINESS NAME REGISTRATION

PLEASE READ ALL INSTRUCTIONS CAREFULLY BEFORE COMPLETING APPLICATION

HOW TO COMPLETE THE APPLICATION FOR CERTIFICATE UNDER THE "ASSUMED BUSINESS NAME" ACT

805 Illinois Compiled Statutes 405/0.01 et seq.

1. The County Clerk provides a form for filing under the Assumed Business Name Act to persons conducting business as a sole proprietorship or a general partnership.

2. Any person(s) conducting or transacting business in Illinois under an assumed name, or any name other than the real name(s) of the persons conducting or transacting the business, are required to file an application for certificate. (This does not include businesses operated under the actual name of the owner).

3. The certificate must be filed in each county where the person(s) conduct or transact, or intend to transact, business under an assumed name.

4. The filing fee for the initial application is $5.00; however, if the business is conducted at more than one location, then an additional fee of $2.00 per additional location is charged. All addresses where the person(s) conduct or transact business, must be listed on the application. All addresses must include: **CITY, STATE AND ZIP CODE.**

5. The nature of the business must be disclosed at the time of application.

6. The full name(s) of the person(s) owning, conducting, or transacting the business must be shown along with the full and complete residence address(es) of each person(s). All addresses must include: **CITY, STATE AND ZIP CODE.**

7. The certificate must be signed by each person(s) conducting, or transacting, or intending to conduct or transact business. Each person(s) signature must be verified by a Notary Public.

8. The legal notice form must be completed and returned with your certificate form.

9. After filing the application for a certificate, a notice of the filing of the certificate must be published in a newspaper of general circulation in the county in which the business is, or will be, conducted.

10. The first publication must be made within **15 calendar days** after the initial filing of the certificate.

11. You must publish once a week for three (3) consecutive weeks.

12. Proof of publication must be filed within **50 days** of filing the certificate. A photocopy of the notice is not sufficient; the applicant must provide a signed and notarized affidavit with a clipping of the ad attached. Failure to file the proof of publication renders the registration **VOID.** After the third week of publication you will receive the notarized affidavit from the newspaper in which you published.

13. If any person on the certificate changes his or her legal name, or residence address, or if the address of the business is changed, or if another person or persons are added to the business, or if a person or persons wish to withdraw his or her name and have no further connection with or financial interest in the business, then an additional or supplementary certificate must be filed with the County Clerk, and a new notice must be published as set forth in items 9 to 12, above.

14. Checks or money orders should be made payable to your County Clerk.

form 3

TRADEMARK OR SERVICEMARK APPLICATION
Complete and Return with $10 Fee and Three Specimens
<u>Must be typewritten</u>

1. Name of Registrant _____

2. Business Address _____
    Street

    _____

    City   State   ZIP Code

3. Is registrant a (**check one**)

    ❑ Corporation   ❑ Union   ❑ General Partnership   ❑ Limited Liability Partnership (LLP)

    ❑ Individual   ❑ Association   ❑ Limited Partnership (LP)   ❑ Limited Liability Company (LLC)

    ❑ Other (specify) _____

4. A. If a **Corporation**, **LP**, **LLP**, or **LLC**, in what state is it organized? _____

    B. If an **LP** or **LLP**, what is the name of one of the general partners? _____

    _____

5. Name of mark _____

    _____

6. Describe the specific goods or services in connection with which mark is used _____

    _____

    _____

7. *Class No. _____ **(One classification number only; classes are listed on the back.)**

8. A. If a **Trademark**, check how the mark is used. (**check as many as apply**) By applying it: directly to the goods _____ , directly to the containers for the goods _____ , to tags or labels affixed to the goods _____ , to tags or labels affixed to the containers for the goods _____ , or by displaying it in physical association with the goods in the sale or distribution thereof _____ .

    OR

    B. If a **Servicemark**, check how the mark is used. (**check as many as apply**) By displaying it: in advertisements of the service _____ , on documents, wrappers, or articles delivered in connection with the service rendered _____ , in other fashion _____ , if so, **(specify)**: _____

9. Date of the first use of mark by applicant or predecessor. Mark must be used in Illinois prior to registration. **(If first use of mark was in Illinois, use same date in both A and B.)**

    A. Anywhere _____ **(month, day, and year)**

    B. In Illinois _____ **(month, day, and year)**

10. If either of the above first uses was by a predecessor of applicant, state which use or uses were by a predecessor and identify predecessor _____

    The applicant hereby appoints the Secretary of State of Illinois as agent for service of process in an action relating only to the registration which may be issued pursuant to this application if the registrant be, or shall become, a non-resident individual, or foreign partnership, limited liability company, association, or corporation not licensed to do business in this State, or cannot be found in this State.

The undersigned hereby declares, under penalty of perjury, that the statements made in the foregoing application are true and that to his/her knowledge no other person has registered the mark, either federally or in this State, or has the right to use the mark either in the identical form thereof or in such near resemblance thereto as to be likely, when applied to the goods or services of such other person, to cause confusion or to cause mistake, or to deceive.

X _____
_____
Signature of Applicant

_____
Type or Print Name of Applicant

_____
Official Capacity

NOTE

The application must be accompanied by three specimens or facsimiles of the mark and by a filing fee of $10.00 payable to the Secretary of State. Clip specimens or facsimiles to application. DO NOT GLUE OR STAPLE.

Specimens larger than 3" x 3" will not be accepted. If the specimens are larger than that, send facsimiles such as photostats reduced in size of the actual specimens.

Send a separate check for each application. This will prevent return of multiple applications for correction.

The following general classes of goods and services are established for convenience of administration of this Act but not to limit or extend the applicant's or registrant's rights. A single application for registration of a mark may include any or all goods or services upon which the mark is actually being used and which are comprised in a single class. In no event shall a single application include goods or services upon which the mark is being used and which fall within different classes.

CLASSIFICATION OF GOODS FOR TRADEMARKS

(1) Chemicals
(2) Paints
(3) Cosmetics and cleaning preparations
(4) Lubricants and fuels
(5) Pharmaceuticals
(6) Metal goods
(7) Machinery
(8) Hand tools
(9) Electrical and scientific apparatus
(10) Medical apparatus
(11) Environmental control apparatus

(12) Vehicles
(13) Firearms
(14) Jewelry
(15) Musical instruments
(16) Paper goods and printed matter
(17} Rubber goods
(18) Leather goods
(19) Non-metallic building materials
(20) Furniture and articles not otherwise classified
(21) Housewares and glass
(22) Cordage and fibers

(23) Yarns and threads
(24) Fabrics
(25) Clothing
(26) Fancy goods
(27) Floor coverings
(28) Toys and sporting goods
(29) Meals and processed foods
(30) Staple foods
(31) Natural agricultural products
(32) Light beverages
(33) Wine and spirits
(34) Smoker's articles

CLASSIFICATION OF SERVICES FOR SERVICEMARKS

(35) Advertising and business
(36) Insurance and financial
(37) Building construction and repair

(38) Telecommunications
(39) Transportation and storage
(40) Treatment of materials

(41) Education and entertainment
(42) Miscellaneous

*The Secretary of State will fill in the answer to question #7 if no answer is given and has the right to change the classification if that furnished by applicant is not correct. *Each classification requires a separate application, set of three specimens, and fee.*

> **RETURN TO:**
> Secretary of State's Office
> Department of Business Services
> Trademark Division
> 3rd Floor, Howlett Building
> Springfield, IL 62756
>
> (217) 524-0400
> http://www.sos.state.il.us

C-246.3

form 4

U.S. Department of Justice
Immigration and Naturalization Service

OMB No. 1115-0136
Employment Eligibility Verification

Please read instructions carefully before completing this form. The instructions must be available during completion of this form. **ANTI-DISCRIMINATION NOTICE.** It is illegal to discriminate against work eligible individuals. Employers **CANNOT** specify which document(s) they will accept from an employee. The refusal to hire an individual because of a future expiration date may also constitute illegal discrimination.

Section 1. Employee Information and Verification. To be completed and signed by employee at the time employment begins

Print Name: Last	First	Middle Initial	Maiden Name

Address *(Street Name and Number)*		Apt. #	Date of Birth *(month/day/year)*

City	State	Zip Code	Social Security #

I am aware that federal law provides for imprisonment and/or fines for false statements or *use of false documents in connection with the* completion of this form.

I attest, under penalty of perjury, that I am (check one of the following):
- ☐ A citizen or national of the United States
- ☐ A Lawful Permanent Resident (Alien # A _____)
- ☐ An alien authorized to work until _____ / _____ / _____
  (Alien # or Admission # _____)

Employee's Signature	Date *(month/day/year)*

Preparer and/or Translator Certification. *(To be completed and signed if Section 1 is prepared by a person other than the employee.) I attest, under penalty of perjury, that I have assisted in the completion of this form and that to the best of my knowledge the information is true and correct.*

Preparer's/Translator's Signature	Print Name

Address *(Street Name and Number, City, State, Zip Code)*	Date *(month/day/year)*

Section 2. Employer Review and Verification. To be completed and signed by employer. **Examine one document from List A OR examine one document from List B and one from List C** as listed on the reverse of this form and record the title, number and expiration date, if any, of the document(s)

List A	OR	List B	AND	List C
Document title: _____		_____		_____
Issuing authority: _____		_____		_____
Document #: _____		_____		_____
Expiration Date *(if any)*: ___/___/___		___/___/___		___/___/___
Document #: _____				
Expiration Date *(if any)*: ___/___/___				

CERTIFICATION - I attest, under penalty of perjury, that I have examined the document(s) presented by the above-named employee, that the above-listed document(s) appear to be genuine and to relate to the employee named, that the employee began employment on *(month/day/year)* ___/___/___ and that to the best of my knowledge the employee is eligible to work in the United States. (State employment agencies may omit the date the employee began employment).

Signature of Employer or Authorized Representative	Print Name	Title

Business or Organization Name	Address *(Street Name and Number, City, State, Zip Code)*	Date *(month/day/year)*

Section 3. Updating and Reverification. To be completed and signed by employer

A. New Name *(if applicable)*	B. Date of rehire *(month/day/year)* *(if applicable)*

C. If employee's previous grant of work authorization has expired, provide the information below for the document that establishes current employment eligibility.

Document Title: _____ Document #: _____ Expiration Date (if any): ___/___/___

I attest, under penalty of perjury, that to the best of my knowledge, this employee is eligible to work in the United States, and if the employee presented document(s), the document(s) I have examined appear to be genuine and to relate to the individual.

Signature of Employer or Authorized Representative	Date *(month/day/year)*

Form I-9 (Rev. 11-21-91) N

INSTRUCTIONS
PLEASE READ ALL INSTRUCTIONS CAREFULLY BEFORE COMPLETING THIS FORM.

Anti-Discrimination Notice. It is illegal to discriminate against any individual (other than an alien not authorized to work in the U.S.) in hiring, discharging, or recruiting or referring for a fee because of that individual's national origin or citizenship status. It is illegal to discriminate against work eligible individuals. Employers **CANNOT** specify which document(s) they will accept from an employee. The refusal to hire an individual because of a future expiration date may also constitute illegal discrimination.

Section 1 - Employee. All employees, citizens and noncitizens, hired after November 6, 1986, must complete Section 1 of this form at the time of hire, which is the actual beginning of employment. **The employer is responsible for ensuring that Section 1 is timely and properly completed.**

Preparer/Translator Certification. The Preparer/Translator Certification must be completed if Section 1 is prepared by a person other than the employee. A preparer/translator may be used only when the employee is unable to complete Section 1 on his/her own. However, the employee must still sign Section 1 personally.

Section 2 - Employer. For the purpose of completing this form, the term "employer" includes those recruiters and referrers for a fee who are agricultural associations, agricultural employers, or farm labor contractors.

Employers must complete Section 2 by examining evidence of identity and employment eligibility within three (3) business days of the date employment begins. If employees are authorized to work, but are unable to present the required document(s) within three business days, they must present a receipt for the application of the document(s) within three business days and the actual document(s) within ninety (90) days. However, if employers hire individuals for a duration of less than three business days, Section 2 must be completed at the time employment begins. **Employers must record: 1)** document title; **2)** issuing authority; **3)** document number, **4)** expiration date, if any; and **5)** the date employment begins. Employers must sign and date the certification. Employees must present original documents. Employers may, but are not required to, photocopy the document(s) presented. These photocopies may only be used for the verification process and must be retained with the I-9. **However, employers are still responsible for completing the I-9.**

Section 3 - Updating and Reverification. Employers must complete Section 3 when updating and/or reverifying the I-9. Employers must reverify employment eligibility of their employees on or before the expiration date recorded in Section 1. Employers **CANNOT** specify which document(s) they will accept from an employee.

- If an employee's name has changed at the time this form is being updated/ reverified, complete Block A.

- If an employee is rehired within three (3) years of the date this form was originally completed and the employee is still eligible to be employed on the same basis as previously indicated on this form (updating), complete Block B and the signature block.

- If an employee is rehired within three (3) years of the date this form was originally completed and the employee's work authorization has expired **or** if a current employee's work authorization is about to expire (reverification), complete Block B and:
  - examine any document that reflects that the employee is authorized to work in the U.S. (see List A **or** C),
  - record the document title, document number and expiration date (if any) in Block C, and
  - complete the signature block.

Photocopying and Retaining Form I-9. A blank I-9 may be reproduced provided both sides are copied. The Instructions must be available to all employees completing this form. Employers must retain completed I-9s for three (3) years after the date of hire **or** one (1) year after the date employment ends, whichever is later.

For more detailed information, you may refer to the INS Handbook for Employers, (Form M-274). You may obtain the handbook at your local INS office.

Privacy Act Notice. The authority for collecting this information is the Immigration Reform and Control Act of 1986, Pub. L. 99-603 (8 U.S.C. 1324a).

This information is for employers to verify the eligibility of individuals for employment to preclude the unlawful hiring, or recruiting or referring for a fee, of aliens who are not authorized to work in the United States.

This information will be used by employers as a record of their basis for determining eligibility of an employee to work in the United States. The form will be kept by the employer and made available for inspection by officials of the U.S. Immigration and Naturalization Service, the Department of Labor, and the Office of Special Counsel for Immigration Related Unfair Employment Practices.

Submission of the information required in this form is voluntary. However, an individual may not begin employment unless this form is completed since employers are subject to civil or criminal penalties if they do not comply with the Immigration Reform and Control Act of 1986.

Reporting Burden. We try to create forms and instructions that are accurate, can be easily understood, and which impose the least possible burden on you to provide us with information. Often this is difficult because some immigration laws are very complex. Accordingly, the reporting burden for this collection of information is computed as follows: **1)** learning about this form, 5 minutes; **2)** completing the form, 5 minutes; and **3)** assembling and filing (recordkeeping) the form, 5 minutes, for an average of 15 minutes per response. If you have comments regarding the accuracy of this burden estimate, or suggestions for making this form simpler, you can write to both the Immigration and Naturalization Service, 425 I Street, N.W., Room 5304, Washington, D. C. 20536; and the Office of Management and Budget, Paperwork Reduction Project, OMB No. 1115-0136, Washington, D.C. 20503.

Instructions for Form SS-4

(Rev. December 2001)

**Department of the Treasury
Internal Revenue Service**

Application for Employer Identification Number

Section references are to the Internal Revenue Code unless otherwise noted.

General Instructions

Use these instructions to complete **Form SS-4,** Application for Employer Identification Number. Also see **Do I Need an EIN?** on page 2 of Form SS-4.

Purpose of Form

Use Form SS-4 to apply for an employer identification number (EIN). An EIN is a nine-digit number (for example, 12-3456789) assigned to sole proprietors, corporations, partnerships, estates, trusts, and other entities for tax filing and reporting purposes. The information you provide on this form will establish your business tax account.

 *An EIN is for use in connection with your business activities only. Do **not** use your EIN in place of your social security number (SSN).*

File only one Form SS-4. Generally, a sole proprietor should file only one Form SS-4 and needs only one EIN, regardless of the number of businesses operated as a sole proprietorship or trade names under which a business operates. However, if the proprietorship incorporates or enters into a partnership, a new EIN is required. Also, each corporation in an affiliated group must have its own EIN.

EIN applied for, but not received. If you do not have an EIN by the time a **return** is due, write "Applied For" and the date you applied in the space shown for the number. **Do not** show your social security number (SSN) as an EIN on returns.

If you do not have an EIN by the time a **tax deposit** is due, send your payment to the Internal Revenue Service Center for your filing area as shown in the instructions for the form that you are are filing. Make your check or money order payable to the **"United States Treasury"** and show your name (as shown on Form SS-4), address, type of tax, period covered, and date you applied for an EIN.

Related Forms and Publications

The following **forms** and **instructions** may be useful to filers of Form SS-4:
- **Form 990-T,** Exempt Organization Business Income Tax Return
- **Instructions for Form 990-T**
- **Schedule C (Form 1040),** Profit or Loss From Business
- **Schedule F (Form 1040),** Profit or Loss From Farming
- **Instructions for Form 1041 and Schedules A, B, D, G, I, J, and K-1,** U.S. Income Tax Return for Estates and Trusts

- **Form 1042,** Annual Withholding Tax Return for U.S. Source Income of Foreign Persons
- **Instructions for Form 1065,** U.S. Return of Partnership Income
- **Instructions for Form 1066,** U.S. Real Estate Mortgage Investment Conduit (REMIC) Income Tax Return
- **Instructions for Forms 1120 and 1120-A**
- **Form 2553,** Election by a Small Business Corporation
- **Form 2848,** Power of Attorney and Declaration of Representative
- **Form 8821,** Tax Information Authorization
- **Form 8832,** Entity Classification Election

For more **information** about filing Form SS-4 and related issues, see:
- **Circular A,** Agricultural Employer's Tax Guide (Pub. 51)
- **Circular E,** Employer's Tax Guide (Pub. 15)
- **Pub. 538,** Accounting Periods and Methods
- **Pub. 542,** Corporations
- **Pub. 557,** Exempt Status for Your Organization
- **Pub. 583,** Starting a Business and Keeping Records
- **Pub. 966,** EFTPS: Now a Full Range of Electronic Choices to Pay All Your Federal Taxes
- **Pub. 1635,** Understanding Your EIN
- **Package 1023,** Application for Recognition of Exemption
- **Package 1024,** Application for Recognition of Exemption Under Section 501(a)

How To Get Forms and Publications

Phone. You can order forms, instructions, and publications by phone 24 hours a day, 7 days a week. Just call 1-800-TAX-FORM (1-800-829-3676). You should receive your order or notification of its status within 10 workdays.

Personal computer. With your personal computer and modem, you can get the forms and information you need using the IRS Web Site at **www.irs.gov** or File Transfer Protocol at **ftp.irs.gov.**

CD-ROM. For small businesses, return preparers, or others who may frequently need tax forms or publications, a CD-ROM containing over 2,000 tax products (including many prior year forms) can be purchased from the National Technical Information Service (NTIS).

To order **Pub. 1796,** Federal Tax Products on CD-ROM, call **1-877-CDFORMS** (1-877-233-6767) toll free or connect to **www.irs.gov/cdorders.**

Tax Help for Your Business

IRS-sponsored Small Business Workshops provide information about your Federal and state tax obligations. For information about workshops in your area, call 1-800-829-1040 and ask for your Taxpayer Education Coordinator.

How To Apply

You can apply for an EIN by telephone, fax, or mail depending on how soon you need to use the EIN.

Application by Tele-TIN. Under the Tele-TIN program, you can receive your EIN by telephone and use it immediately to file a return or make a payment. To receive an EIN by telephone, IRS suggests that you complete Form SS-4 so that you will have all relevant information available. Then call the Tele-TIN number at 1-866-816-2065. (International applicants must call 215-516-6999.) Tele-TIN hours of operation are 7:30 a.m. to 5:30 p.m. The person making the call must be authorized to sign the form or be an authorized designee. See **Signature** and **Third Party Designee** on page 6. Also see the **TIP** below.

An IRS representative will use the information from the Form SS-4 to establish your account and assign you an EIN. Write the number you are given on the upper right corner of the form and sign and date it. Keep this copy for your records.

If requested by an IRS representative, mail or fax (facsimile) the signed Form SS-4 (including any Third Party Designee authorization) **within 24 hours** to the Tele-TIN Unit at the service center address provided by the IRS representative.

 *Taxpayer representatives can use Tele-TIN to apply for an EIN on behalf of their client and request that the EIN be faxed to their **client** on the same day. (**Note:** By utilizing this procedure, you are authorizing the IRS to fax the EIN without a cover sheet.)*

Application by Fax-TIN. Under the Fax-TIN program, you can receive your EIN by fax within 4 business days. Complete and fax Form SS-4 to the IRS using the Fax-TIN number listed below for your state. A long-distance charge to callers outside of the local calling area will apply. Fax-TIN numbers can only be used to apply for an EIN. **The numbers may change without notice.** Fax-TIN is available 24 hours a day, 7 days a week.

Be sure to provide your fax number so that IRS can fax the EIN back to you. (**Note:** By utilizing this procedure, you are authorizing the IRS to fax the EIN without a cover sheet.)

Do not call Tele-TIN for the same entity because duplicate EINs may be issued. See **Third Party Designee** on page 6.

Application by mail. Complete Form SS-4 at least 4 to 5 weeks before you will need an EIN. Sign and date the application and mail it to the service center address for your state. You will receive your EIN in the mail in approximately 4 weeks. See also **Third Party Designee** on page 6.

Call 1-800-829-1040 to verify a number or to ask about the status of an application by mail.

If your principal business, office or agency, or legal residence in the case of an individual, is located in:	Call the Tele-TIN or Fax-TIN number shown or file with the "Internal Revenue Service Center" at:
Connecticut, Delaware, District of Columbia, Florida, Georgia, Maine, Maryland, Massachusetts, New Hampshire, New Jersey, New York, North Carolina, Ohio, Pennsylvania, Rhode Island, South Carolina, Vermont, Virginia, West Virginia	Attn: EIN Operation Holtsville, NY 00501 Tele-TIN 866-816-2065 Fax-TIN 631-447-8960
Illinois, Indiana, Kentucky, Michigan	Attn: EIN Operation Cincinnati, OH 45999 Tele-TIN 866-816-2065 Fax-TIN 859-669-5760
Alabama, Alaska, Arizona, Arkansas, California, Colorado, Hawaii, Idaho, Iowa, Kansas, Louisiana, Minnesota, Mississippi, Missouri, Montana, Nebraska, Nevada, New Mexico, North Dakota, Oklahoma, Oregon, Puerto Rico, South Dakota, Tennessee, Texas, Utah, Washington, Wisconsin, Wyoming	Attn: EIN Operation Philadelphia, PA 19255 Tele-TIN 866-816-2065 Fax-TIN 215-516-3990
If you have no legal residence, principal place of business, or principal office or agency in any state:	Attn: EIN Operation Philadelphia, PA 19255 Tele-TIN 215-516-6999 Fax-TIN 215-516-3990

Specific Instructions

Print or type all entries on Form SS-4. Follow the instructions for each line to expedite processing and to avoid unnecessary IRS requests for additional information. Enter "N/A" (nonapplicable) on the lines that do not apply.

Line 1—Legal name of entity (or individual) for whom the EIN is being requested. Enter the legal name of the entity (or individual) applying for the EIN exactly as it appears on the social security card, charter, or other applicable legal document.

Individuals. Enter your first name, middle initial, and last name. If you are a sole proprietor, enter your individual name, not your business name. Enter your business name on line 2. Do not use abbreviations or nicknames on line 1.

Trusts. Enter the name of the trust.

Estate of a decedent. Enter the name of the estate.

Partnerships. Enter the legal name of the partnership as it appears in the partnership agreement.

Corporations. Enter the corporate name as it appears in the corporation charter or other legal document creating it.

Plan administrators. Enter the name of the plan administrator. A plan administrator who already has an EIN should use that number.

Line 2—Trade name of business. Enter the trade name of the business if different from the legal name. The trade name is the "doing business as " (DBA) name.

 *Use the full legal name shown on line 1 on all tax returns filed for the entity. (However, if you enter a trade name on line 2 and choose to use the trade name instead of the legal name, enter the trade name on **all returns** you file.) To prevent processing delays and errors, **always** use the legal name only (or the trade name only) on **all** tax returns.*

Line 3—Executor, trustee, "care of" name. Trusts enter the name of the trustee. Estates enter the name of the executor, administrator, or other fiduciary. If the entity applying has a designated person to receive tax information, enter that person's name as the "care of" person. Enter the individual's first name, middle initial, and last name.

Lines 4a-b—Mailing address. Enter the mailing address for the entity's correspondence. If line 3 is completed, enter the address for the executor, trustee or "care of" person. Generally, this address will be used on all tax returns.

 *File **Form 8822**, Change of Address, to report any subsequent changes to the entity's mailing address.*

Lines 5a-b—Street address. Provide the entity's physical address **only** if different from its mailing address shown in lines 4a-b. **Do not** enter a P.O. box number here.

Line 6—County and state where principal business is located. Enter the entity's primary **physical** location.

Lines 7a-b—Name of principal officer, general partner, grantor, owner, or trustor. Enter the first name, middle initial, last name, and SSN of **(a)** the principal officer if the business is a corporation, **(b)** a general partner if a partnership, **(c)** the owner of an entity that is disregarded as separate from its owner (disregarded entities owned by a corporation enter the corporation's name and EIN), or **(d)** a grantor, owner, or trustor if a trust.

If the person in question is an **alien individual** with a previously assigned individual taxpayer identification number (ITIN), enter the ITIN in the space provided and submit a copy of an official identifying document. If necessary, complete **Form W-7,** Application for IRS Individual Taxpayer Identification Number, to obtain an ITIN.

You are **required** to enter an SSN, ITIN, or EIN unless the only reason you are applying for an EIN is to make an entity classification election (see Regulations section 301.7701-1 through 301.7701-3) and you are a nonresident alien with no effectively connected income from sources within the United States.

Line 8a—Type of entity. Check the box that best describes the type of entity applying for the EIN. If you are an alien individual with an ITIN previously assigned to you, enter the ITIN in place of a requested SSN.

 *This is not an election for a tax classification of an entity. See **"Limited liability company (LLC)"** on page 4.*

Other. If not specifically mentioned, check the "Other" box, enter the type of entity and the type of return, if any, that will be filed (for example, "Common Trust Fund, Form 1065" or "Created a Pension Plan"). Do not enter "N/A." If you are an alien individual applying for an EIN, see the **Lines 7a-b** instructions above.

- **Household employer.** If you are an individual, check the "Other" box and enter "Household Employer" and your SSN. If you are a state or local agency serving as a tax reporting agent for public assistance recipients who become household employers, check the "Other" box and enter "Household Employer Agent." If you are a trust that qualifies as a household employer, you do not need a separate EIN for reporting tax information relating to household employees; use the EIN of the trust.
- **QSub.** For a qualified subchapter S subsidiary (QSub) check the "Other" box and specify "QSub."
- **Withholding agent.** If you are a withholding agent required to file Form 1042, check the "Other" box and enter "Withholding Agent."

Sole proprietor. Check this box if you file Schedule C, C-EZ, or F (Form 1040) and have a qualified plan, or are required to file excise, employment, or alcohol, tobacco, or firearms returns, or are a payer of gambling winnings. Enter your SSN (or ITIN) in the space provided. If you are a nonresident alien with no effectively connected income from sources within the United States, you do not need to enter an SSN or ITIN.

Corporation. This box is for any corporation **other than a personal service corporation.** If you check this box, enter the income tax form number to be filed by the entity in the space provided.

 *If you entered **"1120S"** after the "Corporation" checkbox, the corporation **must** file Form 2553 **no later than the 15th day of the 3rd month of the tax year the election is to take effect.** Until Form 2553 has been received and approved, you will be considered a Form 1120 filer. See the Instructions for Form 2553.*

Personal service corp. Check this box if the entity is a personal service corporation. An entity is a personal service corporation for a tax year only if:
- The principal activity of the entity during the testing period (prior tax year) for the tax year is the performance of personal services substantially by employee-owners, and
- The employee-owners own at least 10% of the fair market value of the outstanding stock in the entity on the last day of the testing period.

Personal services include performance of services in such fields as health, law, accounting, or consulting. For more information about personal service corporations, see the Instructions for Forms 1120 and 1120-A and Pub. 542.

Other nonprofit organization. Check this box if the nonprofit organization is other than a church or church-controlled organization and specify the type of nonprofit organization (for example, an educational organization).

 *If the organization also seeks tax-exempt status, you **must** file either Package 1023 or Package 1024. See Pub. 557 for more information.*

If the organization is covered by a group exemption letter, enter the four-digit **group exemption number (GEN).** (Do not confuse the GEN with the nine-digit EIN.) If you do not know the GEN, contact the parent organization. Get Pub. 557 for more information about group exemption numbers.

Plan administrator. If the plan administrator is an individual, enter the plan administrator's SSN in the space provided.

REMIC. Check this box if the entity has elected to be treated as a real estate mortgage investment conduit (REMIC). See the Instructions for Form 1066 for more information.

Limited liability company (LLC). An LLC is an entity organized under the laws of a state or foreign country as a limited liability company. For Federal tax purposes, an LLC may be treated as a partnership or corporation or be disregarded as an entity separate from its owner.

By **default,** a domestic LLC with only one member is **disregarded** as an entity separate from its owner and must include all of its income and expenses on the owner's tax return (e.g., **Schedule C (Form 1040)**). Also by default, a domestic LLC with two or more members is treated as a partnership. A domestic LLC may file Form 8832 to avoid either default classification and elect to be classified as an association taxable as a corporation. For more information on entity classifications (including the rules for foreign entities), see the instructions for Form 8832.

 Do not *file Form 8832 if the LLC accepts the default classifications above.* ***However, if the LLC will be electing S Corporation status, it must timely file both Form 8832 and Form 2553.***

Complete Form SS-4 for LLCs as follows:
• A single-member, domestic LLC that accepts the default classification (above) does not need an EIN and generally should not file Form SS-4. Generally, the LLC should use the name and EIN of its **owner** for all Federal tax purposes. However, the reporting and payment of employment taxes for employees of the LLC may be made using the name and EIN or **either** the owner or the LLC as explained in Notice 99-6, 1999-1 C.B. 321. You can find Notice 99-6 on page 12 of Internal Revenue Bulletin 1999-3 at **www.irs.gov. (Note:** If the LLC-applicant indicates in box 13 that it has employees or expects to have employees, the owner (whether an individual or other entity) of a single-member domestic LLC will also be assigned its own EIN (if it does not

already have one) even if the LLC will be filing the employment tax returns.)
• A single-member, domestic LLC that accepts the default classification (above) and wants an EIN for filing employment tax returns (see above) or non-Federal purposes, such as a state requirement, must check the "Other" box and write "Disregarded Entity" or, when applicable, "Disregarded Entity—Sole Proprietorship" in the space provided.
• A multi-member, domestic LLC that accepts the default classification (above) must check the "Partnership" box.
• A domestic LLC that will be filing Form 8832 to elect corporate status must check the "Corporation" box and write in "Single-Member" or "Multi-Member" immediately below the "form number" entry line.

Line 9—Reason for applying. Check only **one** box. Do not enter "N/A."

Started new business. Check this box if you are starting a new business that requires an EIN. If you check this box, enter the type of business being started. **Do not** apply if you already have an EIN and are only adding another place of business.

Hired employees. Check this box if the existing business is requesting an EIN because it has hired or is hiring employees and is therefore required to file employment tax returns. **Do not** apply if you already have an EIN and are only hiring employees. For information on employment taxes (e.g., for family members), see Circular E.

 You may be required to make electronic deposits of all depository taxes (such as employment tax, excise tax, and corporate income tax) using the Electronic Federal Tax Payment System (EFTPS). See section 11, Depositing Taxes, of Circular E and Pub. 966.

Created a pension plan. Check this box if you have created a pension plan and need an EIN for reporting purposes. Also, enter the type of plan in the space provided.

 Check this box if you are applying for a trust EIN when a new pension plan is established. In addition, check the "Other" box in line 8a and write "Created a Pension Plan" in the space provided.

Banking purpose. Check this box if you are requesting an EIN for banking purposes only, and enter the banking purpose (for example, a bowling league for depositing dues or an investment club for dividend and interest reporting).

Changed type of organization. Check this box if the business is changing its type of organization for example, the business was a sole proprietorship and has been incorporated or has become a partnership. If you check this box, specify in the space provided (including available space immediately below) the type of change made. For example, "From Sole Proprietorship to Partnership."

Purchased going business. Check this box if you purchased an existing business. **Do not** use the former owner's EIN unless you became the "owner" of a corporation by acquiring its stock.

Created a trust. Check this box if you created a trust, and enter the type of trust created. For example, indicate if the trust is a nonexempt charitable trust or a split-interest trust.

Exception. Do **not** file this form for certain grantor-type trusts. The trustee does not need an EIN for the trust if the trustee furnishes the name and TIN of the grantor/owner and the address of the trust to all payors. See the Instructions for Form 1041 for more information.

 Do not check this box if you are applying for a trust EIN when a new pension plan is established. Check "Created a pension plan."

Other. Check this box if you are requesting an EIN for any other reason; and enter the reason. For example, a newly-formed state government entity should enter "Newly-Formed State Government Entity" in the space provided.

Line 10—Date business started or acquired. If you are starting a new business, enter the starting date of the business. If the business you acquired is already operating, enter the date you acquired the business. Trusts should enter the date the trust was legally created. Estates should enter the date of death of the decedent whose name appears on line 1 or the date when the estate was legally funded.

Line 11—Closing month of accounting year. Enter the last month of your accounting year or tax year. An accounting or tax year is usually 12 consecutive months, either a calendar year or a fiscal year (including a period of 52 or 53 weeks). A calendar year is 12 consecutive months ending on December 31. A fiscal year is either 12 consecutive months ending on the last day of any month other than December or a 52-53 week year. For more information on accounting periods, see Pub. 538.

Individuals. Your tax year generally will be a calendar year.

Partnerships. Partnerships must adopt one of the following tax years:
- The tax year of the majority of its partners,
- The tax year common to all of its principal partners,
- The tax year that results in the least aggregate deferral of income, or
- In certain cases, some other tax year.
  See the Instructions for Form 1065 for more information.

REMICs. REMICs must have a calendar year as their tax year.

Personal service corporations. A personal service corporation generally must adopt a calendar year unless:
- It can establish a business purpose for having a different tax year, or
- It elects under section 444 to have a tax year other than a calendar year.

Trusts. Generally, a trust must adopt a calendar year except for the following:
- Tax-exempt trusts,
- Charitable trusts, and
- Grantor-owned trusts.

200

Line 12—First date wages or annuities were paid or will be paid. If the business has or will have employees, enter the date on which the business began or will begin to pay wages. If the business does not plan to have employees, enter "N/A."

Withholding agent. Enter the date you began or will begin to pay income (including annuities) to a nonresident alien. This also applies to individuals who are required to file Form 1042 to report alimony paid to a nonresident alien.

Line 13—Highest number of employees expected in the next 12 months. Complete each box by entering the number (including zero ("-0-")) of "Agricultural," "Household," or "Other" employees expected by the applicant in the next 12 months. For a definition of agricultural labor (farmwork), see Circular A.

Lines 14 and 15. Check the **one** box in line 14 that best describes the principal activity of the applicant's business. Check the "Other" box (and specify the applicant's principal activity) if none of the listed boxes applies.

Use line 15 to describe the applicant's principal line of business in more detail. For example, if you checked the "Construction" box in line 14, enter additional detail such as "General contractor for residential buildings" in line 15.

 Do not complete lines 14 and 15 if you entered zero "(-0-)" in line 13.

Construction. Check this box if the applicant is engaged in erecting buildings or other structures, (e.g., streets, highways, bridges, tunnels). The term "Construction" also includes special trade contractors, (e.g., plumbing, HVAC, electrical, carpentry, concrete, excavation, etc. contractors).

Real estate. Check this box if the applicant is engaged in renting or leasing real estate to others; managing, selling, buying or renting real estate for others; or providing related real estate services (e.g., appraisal services).

Rental and leasing. Check this box if the applicant is engaged in providing tangible goods such as autos, computers, consumer goods, or industrial machinery and equipment to customers in return for a periodic rental or lease payment.

Manufacturing. Check this box if the applicant is engaged in the mechanical, physical, or chemical transformation of materials, substances, or components into new products. The assembling of component parts of manufactured products is also considered to be manufacturing.

Transportation & warehousing. Check this box if the applicant provides transportation of passengers or cargo; warehousing or storage of goods; scenic or sight-seeing transportation; or support activities related to these modes of transportation.

Finance & insurance. Check this box if the applicant is engaged in transactions involving the creation, liquidation, or change of ownership of financial assets and/or facilitating such financial transactions;

underwriting annuities/insurance policies; facilitating such underwriting by selling insurance policies; or by providing other insurance or employee-benefit related services.

Health care and social assistance. Check this box if the applicant is engaged in providing physical, medical, or psychiatric care using licensed health care professionals or providing social assistance activities such as youth centers, adoption agencies, individual/family services, temporary shelters, etc.

Accommodation & food services. Check this box if the applicant is engaged in providing customers with lodging, meal preparation, snacks, or beverages for immediate consumption.

Wholesale–agent/broker. Check this box if the applicant is engaged in arranging for the purchase or sale of goods owned by others or purchasing goods on a commission basis for goods traded in the wholesale market, usually between businesses.

Wholesale–other. Check this box if the applicant is engaged in selling goods in the wholesale market generally to other businesses for resale on their own account.

Retail. Check this box if the applicant is engaged in selling merchandise to the general public from a fixed store; by direct, mail-order, or electronic sales; or by using vending machines.

Other. Check this box if the applicant is engaged in an activity not described above. Describe the applicant's principal business activity in the space provided.

Lines 16a-c. Check the applicable box in line 16a to indicate whether or not the entity (or individual) applying for an EIN was issued one previously. Complete lines 16b and 16c **only** if the "Yes" box in line 16a is checked. If the applicant previously applied for **more than one** EIN, write "See Attached" in the empty space in line 16a and attach a separate sheet providing the line 16b and 16c information for each EIN previously requested.

Third Party Designee. Complete this section **only** if you want to authorize the named individual to receive the entity's EIN and answer questions about the completion of Form SS-4. The designee's authority terminates at the time the EIN is assigned and released to the designee. **You must complete the signature area for the authorization to be valid.**

Signature. When required, the application must be signed by **(a)** the individual, if the applicant is an individual, **(b)** the president, vice president, or other principal officer, if the applicant is a corporation, **(c)** a responsible and duly authorized member or officer having knowledge of its affairs, if the applicant is a partnership, government entity, or other unincorporated organization, or **(d)** the fiduciary, if the applicant is a trust or an estate. Foreign applicants may have any duly-authorized person, (e.g., division manager), sign Form SS-4.

Privacy Act and Paperwork Reduction Act Notice. We ask for the information on this form to carry out the Internal Revenue laws of the United States. We need it to comply with section 6109 and the regulations thereunder which generally require the inclusion of an employer identification number (EIN) on certain returns, statements, or other documents filed with the Internal Revenue Service. If your entity is required to obtain an EIN, you are required to provide all of the information requested on this form. Information on this form may be used to determine which Federal tax returns you are required to file and to provide you with related forms and publications.

We disclose this form to the Social Security Administration for their use in determining compliance with applicable laws. We may give this information to the Department of Justice for use in civil and criminal litigation, and to the cities, states, and the District of Columbia for use in administering their tax laws. We may also disclose this information to Federal, state, or local agencies that investigate or respond to acts or threats of terrorism or participate in intelligence or counterintelligence activities concerning terrorism.

We will be unable to issue an EIN to you unless you provide all of the requested information which applies to your entity. Providing false information could subject you to penalties.

You are not required to provide the information requested on a form that is subject to the Paperwork Reduction Act unless the form displays a valid OMB control number. Books or records relating to a form or its instructions must be retained as long as their contents may become material in the administration of any Internal Revenue law. Generally, tax returns and return information are confidential, as required by section 6103.

The time needed to complete and file this form will vary depending on individual circumstances. The estimated average time is:

Recordkeeping	6 min.
Learning about the law or the form	22 min.
Preparing the form	46 min.
Copying, assembling, and sending the form to the IRS	20 min.

If you have comments concerning the accuracy of these time estimates or suggestions for making this form simpler, we would be happy to hear from you. You can write to the Tax Forms Committee, Western Area Distribution Center, Rancho Cordova, CA 95743-0001. **Do not** send the form to this address. Instead, see **How To Apply** on page 2.

Do I Need an EIN?

File Form SS-4 if the applicant entity does not already have an EIN but is required to show an EIN on any return, statement, or other document.[1] **See also the separate instructions for each line on Form SS-4.**

IF the applicant...	AND...	THEN...
Started a new business	Does not currently have (nor expect to have) employees	Complete lines 1, 2, 4a- 6, 8a, and 9- 16c.
Hired (or will hire) employees, including household employees	Does not already have an EIN	Complete lines 1, 2, 4a- 6, 7a- b (if applicable), 8a, 8b (if applicable), and 9- 16c.
Opened a bank account	Needs an EIN for banking purposes only	Complete lines 1- 5b, 7a- b (if applicable), 8a, 9, and 16a- c.
Changed type of organization	Either the legal character of the organization or its ownership changed (e.g., you incorporate a sole proprietorship or form a partnership)[2]	Complete lines 1- 16c (as applicable).
Purchased a going business[3]	Does not already have an EIN	Complete lines 1- 16c (as applicable).
Created a trust	The trust is other than a grantor trust or an IRA trust[4]	Complete lines 1- 16c (as applicable).
Created a pension plan as a plan administrator[5]	Needs an EIN for reporting purposes	Complete lines 1, 2, 4a- 6, 8a, 9, and 16a- c.
Is a foreign person needing an EIN to comply with IRS withholding regulations	Needs an EIN to complete a Form W-8 (other than Form W-8ECI), avoid withholding on portfolio assets, or claim tax treaty benefits[6]	Complete lines 1- 5b, 7a- b (SSN or ITIN optional), 8a- 9, and 16a- c.
Is administering an estate	Needs an EIN to report estate income on Form 1041	Complete lines 1, 3, 4a- b, 8a, 9, and 16a- c.
Is a withholding agent for taxes on non-wage income paid to an alien (i.e., individual, corporation, or partnership, etc.)	Is an agent, broker, fiduciary, manager, tenant, or spouse who is required to file **Form 1042,** Annual Withholding Tax Return for U.S. Source Income of Foreign Persons	Complete lines 1, 2, 3 (if applicable), 4a- 5b, 7a- b (if applicable), 8a, 9, and 16a- c.
Is a state or local agency	Serves as a tax reporting agent for public assistance recipients under Rev. Proc. 80-4, 1980-1 C.B. 581[7]	Complete lines 1, 2, 4a- 5b, 8a, 9, and 16a- c.
Is a single-member LLC	Needs an EIN to file **Form 8832,** Classification Election, for filing employment tax returns, **or** for state reporting purposes[8]	Complete lines 1- 16c (as applicable).
Is an S corporation	Needs an EIN to file **Form 2553,** Election by a Small Business Corporation[9]	Complete lines 1- 16c (as applicable).

[1] For example, a sole proprietorship or self-employed farmer who establishes a qualified retirement plan, or is required to file excise, employment, alcohol, tobacco, or firearms returns, must have an EIN. **A partnership, corporation, REMIC (real estate mortgage investment conduit), nonprofit organization (church, club, etc.), or farmers' cooperative must use an EIN for any tax-related purpose even if the entity does not have employees.**

[2] However, **do not** apply for a new EIN if the existing entity only **(a)** changed its business name, **(b)** elected on Form 8832 to change the way it is taxed (or is covered by the default rules), or **(c)** terminated its partnership status because at least 50% of the total interests in partnership capital and profits were sold or exchanged within a 12-month period. (The EIN of the terminated partnership should continue to be used. See Regulations section 301.6109-1(d)(2)(iii).)

[3] Do not use the EIN of the prior business unless you became the "owner" of a corporation by acquiring its stock.

[4] However, IRA trusts that are required to file **Form 990-T,** Exempt Organization Business Income Tax Return, must have an EIN.

[5] A plan administrator is the person or group of persons specified as the administrator by the instrument under which the plan is operated.

[6] Entities applying to be a Qualified Intermediary (QI) need a QI-EIN even if they already have an EIN. **See Rev. Proc. 2000-12.**

[7] See also *Household employer* on page 4. (**Note:** State or local agencies may need an EIN for other reasons, e.g., hired employees.)

[8] Most LLCs **do not** need to file Form 8832. See **Limited liability company (LLC)** on page 4 for details on completing Form SS-4 for an LLC.

[9] An existing corporation that is electing or revoking S corporation status should use its previously-assigned EIN.

Form **SS-4**

(Rev. December 2001)

Department of the Treasury
Internal Revenue Service

Application for Employer Identification Number

(For use by employers, corporations, partnerships, trusts, estates, churches, government agencies, Indian tribal entities, certain individuals, and others.)

· See separate instructions for each line. · Keep a copy for your records.

EIN

OMB No. 1545-0003

Type or print clearly.

1 Legal name of entity (or individual) for whom the EIN is being requested

2 Trade name of business (if different from name on line 1)

3 Executor, trustee, "care of" name

4a Mailing address (room, apt., suite no. and street, or P.O. box)

5a Street address (if different) (Do not enter a P.O. box.)

4b City, state, and ZIP code

5b City, state, and ZIP code

6 County and state where principal business is located

7a Name of principal officer, general partner, grantor, owner, or trustor

7b SSN, ITIN, or EIN

8a **Type of entity** (check only one box)

☐ Sole proprietor (SSN) _____

☐ Partnership

☐ Corporation (enter form number to be filed) · _____

☐ Personal service corp.

☐ Church or church-controlled organization

☐ Other nonprofit organization (specify) · _____

☐ Other (specify) · _____

☐ Estate (SSN of decedent) _____

☐ Plan administrator (SSN) _____

☐ Trust (SSN of grantor) _____

☐ National Guard   ☐ State/local government

☐ Farmers' cooperative   ☐ Federal government/military

☐ REMIC   ☐ Indian tribal governments/enterprises

Group Exemption Number (GEN) · _____

8b If a corporation, name the state or foreign country (if applicable) where incorporated

State

Foreign country

9 **Reason for applying** (check only one box)

☐ Started new business (specify type) · _____

☐ Hired employees (Check the box and see line 12.)

☐ Compliance with IRS withholding regulations

☐ Other (specify) · _____

☐ Banking purpose (specify purpose) · _____

☐ Changed type of organization (specify new type) · _____

☐ Purchased going business

☐ Created a trust (specify type) · _____

☐ Created a pension plan (specify type) · _____

10 Date business started or acquired (month, day, year)

11 Closing month of accounting year

12 First date wages or annuities were paid or will be paid (month, day, year). **Note:** *If applicant is a withholding agent, enter date income will first be paid to nonresident alien. (month, day, year)* · . . . .

13 Highest number of employees expected in the next 12 months. **Note:** *If the applicant does not expect to have any employees during the period, enter "-0-."* . . . .

Agricultural	Household	Other

14 Check **one** box that best describes the principal activity of your business.

☐ Construction   ☐ Rental & leasing   ☐ Transportation & warehousing

☐ Real estate   ☐ Manufacturing   ☐ Finance & insurance

☐ Health care & social assistance   ☐ Wholesale–agent/broker

☐ Accommodation & food service   ☐ Wholesale–other   ☐ Retail

☐ Other (specify)

15 Indicate principal line of merchandise sold; specific construction work done; products produced; or services provided.

16a Has the applicant ever applied for an employer identification number for this or any other business? . . . . . ☐ **Yes**   ☐ **No**

Note: *If "Yes," please complete lines 16b and 16c.*

16b If you checked "Yes" on line 16a, give applicant's legal name and trade name shown on prior application if different from line 1 or 2 above.

Legal name ·

Trade name ·

16c Approximate date when, and city and state where, the application was filed. Enter previous employer identification number if known.

Approximate date when filed (mo., day, year)

City and state where filed

Previous EIN

Third Party Designee

Complete this section **only** if you want to authorize the named individual to receive the entity's EIN and answer questions about the completion of this form.

Designee's name

Address and ZIP code

Designee's telephone number (include area code)

( )

Designee's fax number (include area code)

( )

Under penalties of perjury, I declare that I have examined this application, and to the best of my knowledge and belief, it is true, correct, and complete.

Name and title (type or print clearly) ·

Signature ·

Date ·

Applicant's telephone number (include area code)

( )

Applicant's fax number (include area code)

( )

For Privacy Act and Paperwork Reduction Act Notice, see separate instructions.

Cat. No. 16055N

Form **SS-4** (Rev. 12-2001)

Form **SS-8**

(Rev. June 1997)

Department of the Treasury
Internal Revenue Service

Determination of Employee Work Status
for Purposes of Federal Employment Taxes
and Income Tax Withholding

OMB No. 1545-0004

Paperwork Reduction Act Notice

We ask for the information on this form to carry out the Internal Revenue laws of the United States. You are required to give us the information. We need it to ensure that you are complying with these laws and to allow us to figure and collect the right amount of tax.

You are not required to provide the information requested on a form that is subject to the Paperwork Reduction Act unless the form displays a valid OMB control number. Books or records relating to a form or its instructions must be retained as long as their contents may become material in the administration of any Internal Revenue law. Generally, tax returns and return information are confidential, as required by Code section 6103.

The time needed to complete and file this form will vary depending on individual circumstances. The estimated average time is: **Recordkeeping,** 34 hr., 55 min.; **Learning about the law or the form,** 12 min.; and **Preparing and sending the form to the IRS,** 46 min. If you have comments concerning the accuracy of these time estimates or suggestions for making this form simpler, we would be happy to hear from you. You can write to the Tax Forms Committee, Western Area Distribution Center, Rancho Cordova, CA 95743-0001. **DO NOT** send the tax form to this address. Instead, see **General Information** for where to file.

Purpose

Employers and workers file Form SS-8 to get a determination as to whether a worker is an employee for purposes of Federal employment taxes and income tax withholding.

General Information

Complete this form carefully. If the firm is completing the form, complete it for **ONE** individual who is representative of the class of workers whose status is in question. If you want a written determination for more than one class of workers, complete a separate Form SS-8 for one worker

from each class whose status is typical of that class. A written determination for any worker will apply to other workers of the same class if the facts are not materially different from those of the worker whose status was ruled upon.

Caution: Form SS-8 is **not** a claim for refund of social security and Medicare taxes or Federal income tax withholding. Also, a determination that an individual is an employee does not necessarily reduce any current or prior tax liability. A worker must file his or her income tax return even if a determination has not been made by the due date of the return.

Where to file.—In the list below, find the state where your legal residence, principal place of business, office, or agency is located. Send Form SS-8 to the address listed for your location.

Location:	Send to:
Alaska, Arizona, Arkansas, California, Colorado, Hawaii, Idaho, Illinois, Iowa, Kansas, Minnesota, Missouri, Montana, Nebraska, Nevada, New Mexico, North Dakota, Oklahoma, Oregon, South Dakota, Texas, Utah, Washington, Wisconsin, Wyoming	Internal Revenue Service SS-8 Determinations P.O. Box 1231, Stop 4106 AUSC Austin, TX 78767
Alabama, Connecticut, Delaware, District of Columbia, Florida, Georgia, Indiana, Kentucky, Louisiana, Maine, Maryland, Massachusetts, Michigan, Mississippi, New Hampshire, New Jersey, New York, North Carolina, Ohio, Pennsylvania, Rhode Island, South Carolina, Tennessee, Vermont, Virginia, West Virginia, All other locations not listed	Internal Revenue Service SS-8 Determinations Two Lakemont Road Newport, VT 05855-1555
American Samoa, Guam, Puerto Rico, U.S. Virgin Islands	Internal Revenue Service Mercantile Plaza 2 Avenue Ponce de Leon San Juan, Puerto Rico 00918

Name of firm (or person) for whom the worker performed services	Name of worker

Address of firm (include street address, apt. or suite no., city, state, and ZIP code)	Address of worker (include street address, apt. or suite no., city, state, and ZIP code)

Trade name	Telephone number (include area code) ( )	Worker's social security number

Telephone number (include area code) ( )	Firm's employer identification number	

Check type of firm for which the work relationship is in question:

☐ **Individual**   ☐ **Partnership**   ☐ **Corporation**   ☐ **Other** (specify) ▶ ....

Important Information Needed To Process Your Request

This form is being completed by: ☐ Firm   ☐ Worker

If this form is being completed by the worker, the IRS **must** have your permission to disclose your name to the firm.

Do you object to disclosing your name and the information on this form to the firm? . . . .   ☐ Yes   ☐ No

If you answer "Yes," the IRS cannot act on your request. **Do not complete the rest of this form unless the IRS asks for it.**

Under section 6110 of the Internal Revenue Code, the information on this form and related file documents will be open to the public if any ruling or determination is made. However, names, addresses, and taxpayer identification numbers will be removed before the information is made public.

Is there any other information you want removed? . . . .   ☐ Yes   ☐ No

If you check "Yes," we cannot process your request unless you submit a copy of this form and copies of all supporting documents showing, in brackets, the information you want removed. Attach a separate statement showing which specific exemption of section 6110(c) applies to each bracketed part.

Cat. No. 16106T

Form **SS-8** (Rev. 6-97)

*This form is designed to cover many work activities, so some of the questions may not apply to you. **You must answer ALL items or mark them "Unknown" or "Does not apply."** If you need more space, attach another sheet.*

Total number of workers in this class. (Attach names and addresses. If more than 10 workers, list only 10.) ▶ _____

This information is about services performed by the worker from _____ to _____
                                                                                          (month, day, year)   (month, day, year)

Is the worker still performing services for the firm? . . . . ☐ **Yes** ☐ **No**

● If "No," what was the date of termination? ▶ _____
                                                                    (month, day, year)

1a Describe the firm's business ....

  b Describe the work done by the worker ....
....

2a If the work is done under a written agreement between the firm and the worker, attach a copy.

  b If the agreement is not in writing, describe the terms and conditions of the work arrangement ....
....
....

  c If the actual working arrangement differs in any way from the agreement, explain the differences and why they occur ....
....
....

3a Is the worker given training by the firm? . . . . ☐ **Yes** ☐ **No**
  ● If "Yes," what kind? ....
  ● How often? ....

  b Is the worker given instructions in the way the work is to be done (exclusive of actual training in 3a)? . ☐ **Yes** ☐ **No**
  ● If "Yes," give specific examples ....

  c Attach samples of any written instructions or procedures.

  d Does the firm have the right to change the methods used by the worker or direct that person on how to
  do the work? . . . . ☐ **Yes** ☐ **No**
  ● Explain your answer ....
....

  e Does the operation of the firm's business require that the worker be supervised or controlled in the
  performance of the service? . . . . ☐ **Yes** ☐ **No**
  ● Explain your answer ....
....

4a The firm engages the worker:
  ☐ To perform and complete a particular job only
  ☐ To work at a job for an indefinite period of time
  ☐ Other (explain) ....

  b Is the worker required to follow a routine or a schedule established by the firm? . . . . ☐ **Yes** ☐ **No**
  ● If "Yes," what is the routine or schedule? ....
....
....

  c Does the worker report to the firm or its representative?. . . . . ☐ **Yes** ☐ **No**
  ● If "Yes," how often? ....
  ● For what purpose? ....
  ● In what manner (in person, in writing, by telephone, etc.)? ....
  ● Attach copies of any report forms used in reporting to the firm.

  d Does the worker furnish a time record to the firm? . . . . ☐ **Yes** ☐ **No**
  ● If "Yes," attach copies of time records.

5a State the kind and value of tools, equipment, supplies, and materials furnished by:
  ● The firm ....
....
  ● The worker ....
....

  b What expenses are incurred by the worker in the performance of services for the firm? ....

  c Does the firm reimburse the worker for any expenses? . . . . ☐ **Yes** ☐ **No**
  ● If "Yes," specify the reimbursed expenses ....

205

6a Will the worker perform the services personally? . . . . □ **Yes** □ **No**

b Does the worker have helpers? . . . . □ **Yes** □ **No**

  • If "Yes," who hires the helpers? □ Firm □ Worker

  • If the helpers are hired by the worker, is the firm's approval necessary? . . . . □ **Yes** □ **No**

  • Who pays the helpers?   □ Firm □ Worker

  • If the worker pays the helpers, does the firm repay the worker? . . . . □ **Yes** □ **No**

  • Are social security and Medicare taxes and Federal income tax withheld from the helpers' pay? . . □ **Yes** □ **No**

  • If "Yes," who reports and pays these taxes?   □ Firm   □ Worker

  • Who reports the helpers' earnings to the Internal Revenue Service? □ Firm □ Worker

  • What services do the helpers perform? ....

7 At what location are the services performed? □ Firm's □ Worker's □ Other (specify) ....

8a Type of pay worker receives:

  □ Salary   □ Commission □ Hourly wage   □ Piecework □ Lump sum □ Other (specify) ....

b Does the firm guarantee a minimum amount of pay to the worker? . . . . □ **Yes** □ **No**

c Does the firm allow the worker a drawing account or advances against pay? . . . . □ **Yes** □ **No**

  • If "Yes," is the worker paid such advances on a regular basis? . . . . □ **Yes** □ **No**

d How does the worker repay such advances? ....

9a Is the worker eligible for a pension, bonus, paid vacations, sick pay, etc.? . . . . □ **Yes** □ **No**

  • If "Yes," specify ....

b Does the firm carry worker's compensation insurance on the worker? . . . . □ **Yes** □ **No**

c Does the firm withhold social security and Medicare taxes from amounts paid the worker? . . . . . □ **Yes** □ **No**

d Does the firm withhold Federal income tax from amounts paid the worker? . . . . □ **Yes** □ **No**

e How does the firm report the worker's earnings to the Internal Revenue Service?

  □ Form W-2 □ Form 1099-MISC   □ Does not report □ Other (specify) ....

  • Attach a copy.

f Does the firm bond the worker?   . . . . □ **Yes** □ **No**

10a Approximately how many hours a day does the worker perform services for the firm? ....

b Does the firm set hours of work for the worker? . . . . □ **Yes** □ **No**

  • If "Yes," what are the worker's set hours? _____ a.m./p.m. to _____ a.m./p.m. (Circle whether a.m. or p.m.)

c Does the worker perform similar services for others? . . . . □ **Yes** □ **No** □ **Unknown**

  • If "Yes," are these services performed on a daily basis for other firms? . . . . . □ **Yes** □ **No** □ **Unknown**

  • Percentage of time spent in performing these services for:

    This firm .... % Other firms .... %   □ **Unknown**

  • Does the firm have priority on the worker's time? . . . . □ **Yes** □ **No**

  • If "No," explain

d Is the worker prohibited from competing with the firm either while performing services or during any later
period? . . . . □ **Yes** □ **No**

11a Can the firm discharge the worker at any time without incurring a liability? . . . . □ **Yes** □ **No**

  • If "No," explain ....

b Can the worker terminate the services at any time without incurring a liability? . . . . □ **Yes** □ **No**

  • If "No," explain ....

12a Does the worker perform services for the firm under:

  □ The firm's business name   □ The worker's own business name   □ Other (specify) ....

b Does the worker advertise or maintain a business listing in the telephone directory, a trade
journal, etc.? . . . . □ **Yes** □ **No** □ **Unknown**

  • If "Yes," specify ....

c Does the worker represent himself or herself to the public as being in business to perform
the same or similar services? . . . . □ **Yes** □ **No** □ **Unknown**

  • If "Yes," how? ....

d Does the worker have his or her own shop or office? . . . . □ **Yes** □ **No** □ **Unknown**

  • If "Yes," where? ....

e Does the firm represent the worker as an employee of the firm to its customers? . . . . □ **Yes** □ **No**

  • If "No," how is the worker represented? ....

f How did the firm learn of the worker's services? ....

13 Is a license necessary for the work? . . . . □ **Yes** □ **No** □ **Unknown**

  • If "Yes," what kind of license is required? ....

  • Who issues the license? ....

  • Who pays the license fee?

14 Does the worker have a financial investment in a business related to the services performed?. . . . . □ **Yes** □ **No** □ **Unknown**
   - If "Yes," specify and give amount of the investment ....

15 Can the worker incur a loss in the performance of the service for the firm? . . . . □ **Yes** □ **No**
   - If "Yes," how? ....

16a Has any other government agency ruled on the status of the firm's workers? . . . . □ **Yes** □ **No**
   - If "Yes," attach a copy of the ruling.

   b Is the same issue being considered by any IRS office in connection with the audit of the worker's tax return or the firm's tax return, or has it been considered recently? . . . . □ **Yes** □ **No**
   - If "Yes," for which year(s)? ....

17 Does the worker assemble or process a product at home or away from the firm's place of business? □ **Yes** □ **No**
   - If "Yes," who furnishes materials or goods used by the worker? □ **Firm**   □ **Worker**   □ **Other**
   - Is the worker furnished a pattern or given instructions to follow in making the product? . . . . . □ **Yes** □ **No**
   - Is the worker required to return the finished product to the firm or to someone designated by the firm? □ **Yes** □ **No**

18 Attach a detailed explanation of any other reason why you believe the worker is an employee or an independent contractor.

Answer items 19a through o only if the worker is a salesperson or provides a service directly to customers.

19a Are leads to prospective customers furnished by the firm?. . . . . □ **Yes** □ **No** □ **Does not apply**
   b Is the worker required to pursue or report on leads? . . . . □ **Yes** □ **No** □ **Does not apply**
   c Is the worker required to adhere to prices, terms, and conditions of sale established by the firm? . . □ **Yes** □ **No**
   d Are orders submitted to and subject to approval by the firm? . . . . □ **Yes** □ **No**
   e Is the worker expected to attend sales meetings?. . . . . □ **Yes** □ **No**
   - If "Yes," is the worker subject to any kind of penalty for failing to attend? . . . . □ **Yes** □ **No**
   f Does the firm assign a specific territory to the worker? . . . . □ **Yes** □ **No**
   g Whom does the customer pay?   □ **Firm**   □ **Worker**
   - If worker, does the worker remit the total amount to the firm? . . . . □ **Yes** □ **No**
   h Does the worker sell a consumer product in a home or establishment other than a permanent retail establishment? . . . . □ **Yes** □ **No**
   i List the products and/or services distributed by the worker, such as meat, vegetables, fruit, bakery products, beverages (other than milk), or laundry or dry cleaning services. If more than one type of product and/or service is distributed, specify the principal one ....
   j Did the firm or another person assign the route or territory and a list of customers to the worker? . . □ **Yes** □ **No**
   - If "Yes," enter the name and job title of the person who made the assignment ....
   k Did the worker pay the firm or person for the privilege of serving customers on the route or in the territory? □ **Yes** □ **No**
   - If "Yes," how much did the worker pay (not including any amount paid for a truck or racks, etc.)? $ ....
   - What factors were considered in determining the value of the route or territory? ....
   l How are new customers obtained by the worker? Explain fully, showing whether the new customers called the firm for service, were solicited by the worker, or both ....
   m Does the worker sell life insurance? . . . . □ **Yes** □ **No**
   - If "Yes," is the selling of life insurance or annuity contracts for the firm the worker's entire business activity? . . . . □ **Yes** □ **No**
   - If "No," list the other business activities and the amount of time spent on them ....
   n Does the worker sell other types of insurance for the firm? . . . . □ **Yes** □ **No**
   - If "Yes," state the percentage of the worker's total working time spent in selling other types of insurance................ %
   - At the time the contract was entered into between the firm and the worker, was it their intention that the worker sell life insurance for the firm: □ on a full-time basis   □ on a part-time basis
   - State the manner in which the intention was expressed ....
   o Is the worker a traveling or city salesperson? . . . . □ **Yes** □ **No**
   - If "Yes," from whom does the worker principally solicit orders for the firm? ....
   - If the worker solicits orders from wholesalers, retailers, contractors, or operators of hotels, restaurants, or other similar establishments, specify the percentage of the worker's time spent in the solicitation .... %
   - Is the merchandise purchased by the customers for resale or for use in their business operations? If used by the customers in their business operations, describe the merchandise and state whether it is equipment installed on their premises or a consumable supply

Under penalties of perjury, I declare that I have examined this request, including accompanying documents, and to the best of my knowledge and belief, the facts presented are true, correct, and complete.

Signature ▶   Title ▶   Date ▶

If the firm is completing this form, an officer or member of the firm must sign it. If the worker is completing this form, the worker must sign it. If the worker wants a written determination about services performed for two or more firms, a separate form must be completed and signed for each firm. Additional copies of this form may be obtained by calling 1-800-TAX-FORM (1-800-829-3676).

Form W-4 (2002)

Purpose. Complete Form W-4 so your employer can withhold the correct Federal income tax from your pay. Because your tax situation may change, you may want to refigure your withholding each year.

Exemption from withholding. If you are exempt, complete only lines 1, 2, 3, 4, and 7 and sign the form to validate it. Your exemption for 2002 expires February 16, 2003. See **Pub. 505**, Tax Withholding and Estimated Tax.

Note: *You cannot claim exemption from withholding if (a) your income exceeds $750 and includes more than $250 of unearned income (e.g., interest and dividends) and (b) another person can claim you as a dependent on their tax return.*

Basic instructions. If you are not exempt, complete the **Personal Allowances Worksheet** below. The worksheets on page 2 adjust your withholding allowances based on itemized deductions, certain credits, adjustments to

income, or two-earner/two-job situations. Complete all worksheets that apply. **However, you may claim fewer (or zero) allowances.**

Head of household. Generally, you may claim head of household filing status on your tax return only if you are unmarried and pay more than 50% of the costs of keeping up a home for yourself and your dependent(s) or other qualifying individuals. See line **E** below.

Tax credits. You can take projected tax credits into account in figuring your allowable number of withholding allowances. Credits for child or dependent care expenses and the child tax credit may be claimed using the **Personal Allowances Worksheet** below. See **Pub. 919,** How Do I Adjust My Tax Withholding? for information on converting your other credits into withholding allowances.

Nonwage income. If you have a large amount of nonwage income, such as interest or dividends, consider making estimated tax payments using **Form 1040-ES**, Estimated Tax for Individuals. Otherwise, you may owe additional tax.

Two earners/two jobs. If you have a working spouse or more than one job, figure the total number of allowances you are entitled to claim on all jobs using worksheets from only one Form W-4. Your withholding usually will be most accurate when all allowances are claimed on the Form W-4 for the highest paying job and zero allowances are claimed on the others.

Nonresident alien. If you are a nonresident alien, see the **Instructions for Form 8233** before completing this Form W-4.

Check your withholding. After your Form W-4 takes effect, use Pub. 919 to see how the dollar amount you are having withheld compares to your projected total tax for 2002. See Pub. 919, especially if you used the **Two-Earner/Two-Job Worksheet** on page 2 and your earnings exceed $125,000 (Single) or $175,000 (Married).

Recent name change? If your name on line 1 differs from that shown on your social security card, call 1-800-772-1213 for a new social security card.

Personal Allowances Worksheet (Keep for your records.)

A Enter "1" for **yourself** if no one else can claim you as a dependent . . . . **A** _____

B Enter "1" if:
- You are single and have only one job; or
- You are married, have only one job, and your spouse does not work; or
- Your wages from a second job or your spouse's wages (or the total of both) are $1,000 or less.

. . **B** _____

C Enter "1" for your **spouse**. But, you may choose to enter "-0-" if you are married and have either a working spouse or more than one job. (Entering "-0-" may help you avoid having too little tax withheld.). . . . . **C** _____

D Enter number of **dependents** (other than your spouse or yourself) you will claim on your tax return . . . . **D** _____

E Enter "1" if you will file as **head of household** on your tax return (see conditions under **Head of household** above) . **E** _____

F Enter "1" if you have at least $1,500 of **child or dependent care expenses** for which you plan to claim a credit . . **F** _____

(**Note:** *Do **not** include child support payments. See **Pub. 503**, Child and Dependent Care Expenses, for details.*)

G **Child Tax Credit** (including additional child tax credit):
- If your total income will be between $15,000 and $42,000 ($20,000 and $65,000 if married), enter "1" for each eligible child plus **1 additional** if you have three to five eligible children or **2 additional** if you have six or more eligible children.
- If your total income will be between $42,000 and $80,000 ($65,000 and $115,000 if married), enter "1" if you have one or two eligible children, "2" if you have three eligible children, "3" if you have four eligible children, or "4" if you have five or more eligible children. **G** _____

H Add lines A through G and enter total here. **Note:** *This may be different from the number of exemptions you claim on your tax return.* ▶ **H** _____

For accuracy, complete all worksheets that apply.
- If you plan to **itemize or claim adjustments to income** and want to reduce your withholding, see the **Deductions and Adjustments Worksheet** on page 2.
- If you have **more than one job** or are **married and you and your spouse both work** and the combined earnings from all jobs exceed $35,000, see the **Two-Earner/Two-Job Worksheet** on page 2 to avoid having too little tax withheld.
- If **neither** of the above situations applies, **stop here** and enter the number from line H on line 5 of Form W-4 below.

- Cut here and give Form W-4 to your employer. Keep the top part for your records. - - - - - - - - - - - - - - - - - -

Form **W-4**
Department of the Treasury
Internal Revenue Service

Employee's Withholding Allowance Certificate

▶ **For Privacy Act and Paperwork Reduction Act Notice, see page 2.**

OMB No. 1545-0010

2002

1 Type or print your first name and middle initial	Last name	2 Your social security number
Home address (number and street or rural route)	3 ☐ Single ☐ Married ☐ Married, but withhold at higher Single rate. Note: If married, but legally separated, or spouse is a nonresident alien, check the "Single" box.	
City or town, state, and ZIP code	4 If your last name differs from that on your social security card, check here. You must call 1-800-772-1213 for a new card. ▶ ☐	

5 Total number of allowances you are claiming (from line **H** above **or** from the applicable worksheet on page 2) . . . **5** _____

6 Additional amount, if any, you want withheld from each paycheck . . . . **6** $ _____

7 I claim exemption from withholding for 2002, and I certify that I meet **both** of the following conditions for exemption:
- Last year I had a right to a refund of **all** Federal income tax withheld because I had **no** tax liability **and**
- This year I expect a refund of **all** Federal income tax withheld because I expect to have **no** tax liability.

If you meet both conditions, write "Exempt" here . . . . ▶ **7** _____

Under penalties of perjury, I certify that I am entitled to the number of withholding allowances claimed on this certificate, or I am entitled to claim exempt status.

Employee's signature
(Form is not valid unless you sign it.) ▶ _____ Date ▶ _____

8 Employer's name and address (Employer: Complete lines 8 and 10 only if sending to the IRS.)	9 Office code (optional)	10 Employer identification number

Cat. No. 10220Q

Deductions and Adjustments Worksheet

Note: *Use this worksheet only if you plan to itemize deductions, claim certain credits, or claim adjustments to income on your 2002 tax return.*

1   Enter an estimate of your 2002 itemized deductions. These include qualifying home mortgage interest, charitable contributions, state and local taxes, medical expenses in excess of 7.5% of your income, and miscellaneous deductions. (For 2002, you may have to reduce your itemized deductions if your income is over $137,300 ($68,650 if married filing separately). See **Worksheet 3** in Pub. 919 for details.) . . .   **1** $ _____

2   Enter: { $7,850 if married filing jointly or qualifying widow(er)
              $6,900 if head of household
              $4,700 if single
              $3,925 if married filing separately }   . . . . .   **2** $ _____

3   **Subtract** line 2 from line 1. If line 2 is greater than line 1, enter "-0-" . . . . . .   **3** $ _____
4   Enter an estimate of your 2002 adjustments to income, including alimony, deductible IRA contributions, and student loan interest   **4** $ _____
5   **Add** lines 3 and 4 and enter the total. Include any amount for credits from **Worksheet 7** in Pub. 919. ..   **5** $ _____
6   Enter an estimate of your 2002 nonwage income (such as dividends or interest) . . . .   **6** $ _____
7   **Subtract** line 6 from line 5. Enter the result, but not less than "-0-" . . . .   **7** $ _____
8   **Divide** the amount on line 7 by $3,000 and enter the result here. Drop any fraction . . . . . .   **8**   _____
9   Enter the number from the **Personal Allowances Worksheet,** line H, page 1 . . . . . .   **9**   _____
10 **Add** lines 8 and 9 and enter the total here. If you plan to use the **Two-Earner/Two-Job Worksheet,** also enter this total on line 1 below. Otherwise, **stop here** and enter this total on Form W-4, line 5, page 1   **10**   _____

Two-Earner/Two-Job Worksheet

Note: *Use this worksheet only if the instructions under line H on page 1 direct you here.*

1   Enter the number from line H, page 1 (or from line 10 above if you used the **Deductions and Adjustments Worksheet**)   **1**   _____
2   Find the number in **Table 1** below that applies to the **lowest** paying job and enter it here . . . . .   **2**   _____
3   If line 1 is **more than or equal to** line 2, subtract line 2 from line 1. Enter the result here (if zero, enter "-0-") and on Form W-4, line 5, page 1. **Do not** use the rest of this worksheet . . . .   **3**   _____

Note: *If line 1 is **less than** line 2, enter "-0-" on Form W-4, line 5, page 1. Complete lines 4-9 below to calculate the additional withholding amount necessary to avoid a year end tax bill.*

4   Enter the number from line 2 of this worksheet . . . .   **4**   _____
5   Enter the number from line 1 of this worksheet . . . .   **5**   _____
6   **Subtract** line 5 from line 4 . . . .   **6**   _____
7   Find the amount in **Table 2** below that applies to the **highest** paying job and enter it here . . . . .   **7** $ _____
8   **Multiply** line 7 by line 6 and enter the result here. This is the additional annual withholding needed . .   **8** $ _____
9   Divide line 8 by the number of pay periods remaining in 2002. For example, divide by 26 if you are paid every two weeks and you complete this form in December 2001. Enter the result here and on Form W-4, line 6, page 1. This is the additional amount to be withheld from each paycheck . . . .   **9** $ _____

Table 1: Two-Earner/Two-Job Worksheet

Married Filing Jointly				All Others			
If wages from **LOWEST** paying job are-	Enter on line 2 above	If wages from **LOWEST** paying job are-	Enter on line 2 above	If wages from **LOWEST** paying job are-	Enter on line 2 above	If wages from **LOWEST** paying job are-	Enter on line 2 above
$0 - $4,000	0	44,001 - 50,000	8	$0 - $6,000	0	75,001 - 95,000	8
4,001 - 9,000	1	50,001 - 55,000	9	6,001 - 11,000	1	95,001 - 110,000	9
9,001 - 15,000	2	55,001 - 65,000	10	11,001 - 17,000	2	110,001 and over	10
15,001 - 20,000	3	65,001 - 80,000	11	17,001 - 23,000	3		
20,001 - 25,000	4	80,001 - 95,000	12	23,001 - 28,000	4		
25,001 - 32,000	5	95,001 - 110,000	13	28,001 - 38,000	5		
32,001 - 38,000	6	110,001 - 125,000	14	38,001 - 55,000	6		
38,001 - 44,000	7	125,001 and over	15	55,001 - 75,000	7		

Table 2: Two-Earner/Two-Job Worksheet

Married Filing Jointly		All Others	
If wages from **HIGHEST** paying job are-	Enter on line 7 above	If wages from **HIGHEST** paying job are-	Enter on line 7 above
$0 - $50,000	$450	$0 - $30,000	$450
50,001 - 100,000	800	30,001 - 70,000	800
100,001 - 150,000	900	70,001 - 140,000	900
150,001 - 270,000	1,050	140,001 - 300,000	1,050
270,001 and over	1,150	300,001 and over	1,150

Illinois Department of Revenue
NUC-1 Illinois Business Registration

Read this information first

You must read the instructions before completing this form. Be sure to complete all of the information that relates to your business. If you omit any required information, we cannot properly register your business.

You may need the following information:
- a federal employer identification number (FEIN)
- an Employment Security account number
- a corporation number (corporate file no.)

If you photocopy this form, be sure to mail us the original.

Section 1: Identify your business

1 Business trade name: _____

   _____

   Corporate or partnership name if other than above:

   _____

   Principal business address: (Do not use a p.o. box number.)

   _____
   Number and street

   _____
   City   State   ZIP

2 Daytime phone no.:__(_____)_____Ext._____

3 FEIN: ___ ___ - ___ ___ ___ ___ ___ ___ ___

4 Check one of the following categories which best describes your type of business:
   _____ Agricultural, forestry, or animal products services
   _____ Construction   _____ Retail
   _____ Wholesale   _____ Service
   _____ Manufacturing

5 Describe your principal business activity:
   _____

6 Date business started in Illinois under your current ownership?
   _____/_____/_____
   Month   Day   Year

7 The above business is located (check one and complete):

   _____ inside the city, village, or town limits of
          _____

   _____ outside the city, village or town limits in the county of
          _____

8 Check your type of business ownership:

   _____ A1 Individual (sole proprietor)
   _____ B0 Husband/wife (sole proprietors)
   _____ C2 Partnership (no. of general partners: _____)
   _____ D3 Corporation
   _____ E4 Trust
   _____ F5 Estate
   _____ G6 Small business corporation (IRC 1361)
   _____ H7 Exempt organization (IRC 501)
   _____ I9 Government

9 You **must** complete the following information for all owners, general partners, executive officers, executors, and trustees. If your business ownership is a corporation, you must **at least** provide the information for the president, secretary, and treasurer. If a person holds more than one title, the name must appear separately with each title held. Attach additional sheets if necessary.

Legal name (last, first, middle)	SSN/FEIN
Title	Home address
Legal name (last, first, middle)	SSN/FEIN
Title	Home address
Legal name (last, first, middle)	SSN/FEIN
Title	Home address
Legal name (last, first, middle)	SSN/FEIN
Title	Home address

10 Did you buy this business from someone? _____ yes _____ no
    If you answer "yes," complete the following information about the previous ownership:

    Name: _____

    Address: _____

    City, state, ZIP: _____

    Phone no.: ___(_____)_____

    FEIN: _____ IBT:_____

Note: You must complete Form NUC-542-A, Notice of Sale/Purchase of Business Assets, if you bought the business from someone. If you do not complete Form NUC-542-A, you may have to pay any taxes, penalties, and interest owed to us by the former owner of the business.

This form is authorized by Section 2(a) of the Illinois Retailers' Occupation Tax Act and Section 501 of the Illinois Income Tax Act. Disclosure of this information is REQUIRED. Failure to provide information could result in this form's not being processed. This form has been approved by the Forms Management Center.

Section 2: Sales Tax and Reseller Registration

If you do not make any sales (retail or wholesale) or inventory purchases, **do not** complete this section. Go to Section 3.

You **must** complete this section if you
- sell merchandise from a site in Illinois
- are a serviceperson who sells merchandise while performing your service (see instructions)
- use merchandise in Illinois that you buy from out-of-state businesses that do not collect Illinois tax,
- are an out-of-state business that sells or leases merchandise to Illinois customers or solicits orders.

Answer ALL of the following questions:

1 Do you sell any merchandise at retail from a site in Illinois? (A site can be permanent, such as an office or warehouse, or can be changeable, such as a fair, flea market, art show, or trade show.)

_____ yes   _____ no

2 Do you conduct business at more than one site in Illinois?

_____ yes   _____ no

If you answer "yes," you must attach Schedule M.

3 Are you a serviceperson who sells merchandise while performing your service? (see instructions)

_____ yes   _____ no

4 Do you ever purchase merchandise (that you will personally use in your business) from out-of-state businesses that do not collect Illinois tax from you?

_____ yes   _____ no

5 Is your business located outside Illinois?

_____ yes   _____ no

If you answer "yes,"

A do you have an office, agent, salesperson, or representative in Illinois? (see instructions)

_____ yes   _____ no

B do you solicit orders for merchandise? (see instructions)

_____ yes   _____ no

C will any of the merchandise that you sell to Illinois customers be delivered in your own vehicles?

_____ yes   _____ no

D do you bring merchandise into Illinois that you will use or lease in Illinois? (see instuctions)

_____ yes   _____ no

6 Do you sell all merchandise in such a way that no sales tax is due?

_____ yes   _____ no

If you answer "yes," will you make any withdrawals from your sales inventory for your own use in Illinois?

_____ yes   _____ no

7 Are you a distributor, supplier, or reseller of motor fuels? (see instructions)

_____ yes   _____ no

If you answer "yes" and you are a distributor or supplier, what is your Illinois motor fuel license number?

_____

8 Do you own vending machines through which merchandise is sold?

_____ yes   _____ no

If you answer "yes," how many machines do you own?

_____

9 Do you sell new or used cars, trucks, motorcycles, watercraft, aircraft, trailers, mobile homes, or salvage items?

_____ yes   _____ no

If you answer "yes," how many items do you estimate you will sell each month?

_____

10 Do you sell tires at retail? (see instructions)

_____ yes   _____ no

If you answer "yes," do you pay the Tire User Fee to your supplier?

_____ yes   _____ no

11 Do you sell soft drinks (in closed or sealed containers) at retail? (See instructions for definition of soft drinks.)

_____ yes   _____ no

12 How much sales or use tax do you estimate you will pay each month as a retailer?

_____ $200 or more
_____ less than $200
_____ none

13 When did you (or will you) make your first inventory purchase or taxable sale?

_____ / _____ / _____
month   day   year

14 By law, someone representing your business must complete the following information or we cannot process this form.

I accept personal responsibility for the filing of returns and the payment of taxes due.

Signature (in ink)	Date
Printed name	Title
Home address - number and street	
City	State · ZIP
Social Security number	( ) Phone number

Do not write below this line. For official use only.

Filing req. _____ Tax distr. _____ Municipal ver. _____

Loc. code _____

Loc. type _____ Cert. req. _____ No. of locations _____

ROT _____ UT _____ RES _____ RR2 _____ PST _____

NUC-1 (R-11/93)

Section 3: Business Income and Replacement Tax Registration

If you are a sole proprietor, **do not** complete this section. Go to Section 4.

You must complete this section if you are a partnership, corporation, trust, estate, small business corporation, exempt organization, or any other type of business **except** a sole proprietorship.

1 What date is the end of your taxable year for filing your federal taxes?
(The date for the end of your Illinios tax year must be the same as the date for your federal tax year.)

_____ December 31 (calendar year)

_____ Other _____/_____
(list month and day)

2 Out of state businesses only
What date did you begin doing business in Illinois?
(see instructions)

_____/_____/_____
Month   Day   Year

3 Corporations and small business corporations only
What is your corporation's file number (issued by the Illinois Office of the Secretary of State)?

_____

4 What date did you incorporate?

_____/_____/_____
Month   Day   Year

5 In what state did you incorporate?

_____
State

Do not write in this space. For official use only.

Filing requirement _____ Status _____

Effective date _____ Reason _____

Section 4: Withholding Agent Registration

If you do not (or will not) have employees, **do not** complete this section. Go to Section 5.

You must complete this section if you have employees who are subject to Illinois Withholding Tax. (For more information, see booklet IL-700, Withholding Tax Guide.)

1 What is your Illinois Employment Security account number (unemployment compensation)?

_____

2 What date did you (or will you) issue your first payroll check?

_____/_____/_____
Month   Day   Year

3 What is the total amout of Illinois Withholding Tax that you expect to withhold? (Check one item below.)

_____ less than $500 for the year

_____ less than $500 for the quarter, but more than $500 for the year

_____ more than $500, but no more than $1,000 at at any time during the quarter

_____ more than $1,000 at any time during the quarter*

If you withhold more than $1,000 at any time during the quarter, we will require you to file weekly. However, if your payroll is twice a month rather than weekly, we will allow you to file twice a month. Do you want this option?
_____ yes _____ no

Do not write in this space. For official use only.

Filing requirement _____ Status _____

Effective date _____ Reason _____

Section 5: Mailing Address for Forms

If you want your tax forms mailed to an address other than the address listed in Section 1, complete this section. If not, go to Section 6.

If you want all of your tax forms sent to **one** mailing address, complete the first address area below. If you want your tax forms sent to **different** mailing addresses, please complete the additional address areas on the following page.

Attention:_____

Number and street _____

_____

City, state, ZIP_____

Daytime phone no._____ Ext_____

Which forms do you want mailed to the above address?

_____ all tax forms

_____ sales tax

_____ business income tax

_____ withholding tax

continued on next page

Section 5 continued

Attention:_____

Number and street:_____

_____

City, state, ZIP:_____

Daytime phone no.:__(____)_____Ext_____

Which forms do you want mailed to the above address?

_____ sales tax

_____ business income tax

_____ withholding tax

Attention:_____

Number and street:_____

_____

City, state, ZIP:_____

Daytime phone no.:_____Ext_____

Which forms do you want mailed to the above address?

_____ sales tax

_____ business income tax

_____ withholding tax

Section 6: Registration for Other Taxes and Compliance Information

Depending on your type of business you may have to complete additional registration forms for other taxes. See Section 6 in the NUC-1 Instructions.

Department of Revenue Tax Enforcement - If you do not collect and remit any and all taxes due us, one or more of the following actions could occur:

- referral to a collection agency
- filing of a tax lien against your property
- garnishment of wages and bank accounts
- recommendation of professional license revocation
- civil judgements
- revocation of business certificates of registration
- withholding of state warrants
- seizure and sale of your assets
- nonrenewal of your corporate charter
- criminal prosecution

Section 7: Signature Affidavit

The signature below must be the signature of one of the owners, general partners, executive officers, executors, or trustees listed in Section 1, Item 9. Be sure to sign in ink and print the same name on the bottom line. If the person signing this form has power of attorney, complete and attach Form IL-2848, Power of Attorney.

Under penalties of perjury, I state that I have examined this application and, to the best of my knowledge, it is true, correct, and complete.

_____
Signature of owner, partner, or officer

_____
Title   Date

_____
Print the name of the above signature.

Mail this application to:

ILLINOIS DEPARTMENT OF REVENUE
CENTRAL REGISTRATION DIVISION
PO BOX 19030
SPRINGFIELD IL 62794-9030

If you have any questions, call 217 785-3707.

NUC-1 (R-11/93)

UI-1
Stock No. 4229 (Rev. '01/01
IL 427-00015

STATE OF ILLINOIS
DEPARTMENT OF EMPLOYMENT SECURITY
401 SOUTH STATE STREET
CHICAGO, ILLINOIS 60605-2280

REPORT TO DETERMINE LIABILITY
UNDER THE UNEMPLOYMENT INSURANCE ACT

IMPORTANT: Every newly created employing unit shall file this report within 30 days of the date upon which it commences business

1. a. Employer name_____
      Doing Business As_____
   b. What is your primary business activity in Illinois? _____
   c. What is your principal product or service? (Read instructions) _____ % Sales or receipts_____
                                                          _____ % Sales or receipts_____
   d. Business Address_____
      (Actual physical location / Number & Street or Rural Route)

      _____
      (City/Town)   (State)   (Zip)   (County)   (Country)   Telephone No.
   e. If you want any correspondence sent to another address (other than the business address indicated above), please refer to the UI-1
      Mailing form included in this packet.

2.   Enter any employer's account number previously assigned to you by the Illinois Department of Employment Security
      _____

3.   Identification number under which you file Federal Social Security Returns (Form 941)_____

4. a. Type of Organization (Check One): _____Sole Proprietor _____Partnership _____Corporation
      Other (This includes: Trusts, Associations, Receiverships.)

      _____
   b. If a corporation, date incorporated _____ State in which incorporated _____

5.   Enter the required information for owner or each partner or officer:
   Name   **Title**   **Social Security No. Residence Address**   **Residence Telephone No.**
   _____
   _____
   _____

6. a. Date you first began employing workers in Illinois _____ Date you ceased employing workers in Illinois _____
   b. Date of your first payroll in Illinois _____

7. Did you acquire your Illinois business, or any portion of it, by purchase, reorganization, a change in entity, for example a change from sole
   proprietor to corporation? _____ YES _____ NO. If yes, complete the form UI-1 S & P, REPORT TO DETERMINE SUCCESSION which is
   included in this packet. Please complete the remainder of the questions on this form as well.
   NOTE: If you acquired your business by purchase, reorganization, merger, etc., you must complete the form titled REPORT TO DETERMINE
   SUCCESSION. Responses to the questions on this form should reflect information relative to the operation of your business AFTER the date of
   acquisition. Failure to notify this Department in writing within 120 days of the date of acquisition, may result in a higher rate of contribution (820
   ILCS 405/1507).

QUESTIONS NUMBER 8 AND 9 APPLY TO DOMESTIC, AGRICULTURAL, OR NONPROFIT EMPLOYERS. IF YOU ARE NOT
ENGAGED IN ANY OF THESE TYPES OF ACTIVITIES, YOU MAY SKIP THIS SECTION AND PROCEED TO QUESTION 10.

8. a. Indicate if you employed workers engaged only in _____ DOMESTIC   OR   _____ AGRICULTURAL WORK.
      Check whether you paid wages in any calendar quarter of the current year or preceding four years
      _____ $1,000 for domestic workers   _____ $20,000 for agricultural workers
      Circle the quarter and indicate the year when these wages were paid: Jan.-Mar._____ (year), April-June_____ (year),
      July - Sept._____ (year), Oct. - Dec. _____ (year).
   b. If you are an agricultural employer, indicate the earliest quarter and year in which you employed 10 or more workers in each of 20 weeks (weeks
      need not be consecutive) _____

9.   Are you a nonprofit organization that is exempt from Federal income taxes under Section 501(c)(3) of the Internal Revenue Code?
      _____YES _____NO. If YES, attach the federal exemption letter and check here _____ if you employed 4 or more paid workers in Illinois
      within each of 20 or more calendar weeks during the current or preceding four years. If checked, indicate the earliest quarter and year in which
      that 20th week occurred _____. Do you wish to be a reimbursable employer? _____YES
      _____NO. If YES, a REIMBURSE BENEFITS IN LIEU OF PAYING CONTRIBUTIONS (UI-5(NP)) form will be mailed to you. You must
      complete this form and return it to this Department.

If you answered question 8 or answered yes to question 9, proceed to question 13. Otherwise proceed to question 10.

10. a. Have you had an ILLINOIS payroll totaling $1500 or more in any calendar quarter during the current or preceding four years? _____YES _____NO.
    If YES, indicate the first year with a quarterly payroll of $1500 or more _____
    b. Circle the quarter and enter the total wages paid in that quarter: January - March $_____ April-June $_____ July-Sept $_____ October-December $_____.

11. a. Have you employed 1 or more workers in ILLINOIS within each of 20 or more calendar weeks during the current or preceding four years (weeks need not be consecutive)? _____YES _____NO.
    b. If YES, indicate the first year with 20 or more calendar weeks of employment _____.
    Circle the quarter in which that 20th week occurred: April-June   July-Sept.   Oct.-Dec.

12. Have you incurred liability under the Federal Unemployment Tax Act for any of the last 5 years? _____YES _____NO.
    If YES, indicate the year(s) of such liability _____

13. Are there any persons not included in questions 11 or 12 who performed services for you, as an independent contractor or otherwise, or received compensation of any kind from you or operated within your business establishment? _____YES _____NO. If YES, attach a sheet stating the number of such persons and give details as to the type of service and the date such services were performed.

. . . .

14. Complete the following section only if you have multiple worksites in Illinois.
    The following information is required for reporting of statistical data to the federal government. Please complete the information as completely and accurately as possible.

    Enter below the required information for each place of business (worksite) in Illinois (use additional sheets if necessary). Read instructions carefully. If any worksite is engaged in performing support services for other units of the company, please indicate the nature of the activity in "section c-Primary Activity". Examples of Support Services are: Central Administrative Office, Research, Development or Testing, Storage (warehouse). See instructions for additional examples.

a) Physical Location of Each Establishment (Street, city, zip code)	b) County	c) Primary Activity	d) Average No. of Employees

15. If you are determined not liable, based upon the provisions of the Unemployment Insurance Act, you may voluntarily elect coverage under Section 205(h). Please indicate whether you want voluntary coverage _____ YES. If checked, we will mail you form UI-1B, VOLUNTARY ELECTION OF COVERAGE. Please complete that form and return it to this Department.

CERTIFICATION: I hereby certify that the information contained in this report and any sheets attached hereto is true and correct. This report must be signed by owner, partner, or officer. If signed by any other person, a power of attorney giving such individual authority to sign must be attached. A Power of Attorney form is included in this packet.

Employer Name _____

Signed by _____ Date _____

Title _____

| This state agency is requesting information that is necessary to accomplish the statutory purpose as outlined under 820 ILCS 405/100-3200. Disclosure of this information is REQUIRED. Failure to disclose this information may result in statutorily prescribed liability and sanction, including penalties and/or interest. This form has been approved by the Forms Management Center. | Area | | INDUSTRY | SOURCE_____ REC'D DATE_____

 A/C_____ NL_____

 LIAB. DATE_____ QTR_____ SEC_____

 AUDITOR_____ DATE_____ |

Illinois Department of Revenue

Instructions for Form IL-W-4, Employee's Illinois Withholding Allowance Certificate

Who must complete this form?

If you are an employee, you must complete this form so your employer can withhold the correct amount of Illinois Income Tax from your pay. The amount withheld from your pay depends, in part, on the number of allowances you claim on this form.

Even if you claimed exemption from withholding on your federal Form W-4, U.S. Employee's Withholding Allowance Certificate, because you do not expect to owe any federal income tax, you may be required to have Illinois Income Tax withheld from your pay.

When must I file?

You must file Form W-4 when Illinois Income Tax is required to be withheld from compensation that you receive as an employee. You should complete this form and give it to your employer on or before the date you start working for your employer. You may file a new Form IL-W-4 any time your withholding allowances increase. If the number of your previously claimed allowances decrease, you **must** file a new Form IL-W-4 within 10 days. However, the death of a spouse or a dependent does not affect your withholding allowances until the next tax year.

What is an "exemption"?

An "exemption" is a dollar amount on which you do not have to pay Illinois Income tax. Therefore, your employer will withhold Illinois Income Tax based on your compensation minus the exemptions to which you are entitled.

What is an "allowance"?

The amount which is exempt from Illinois Income Tax is based on the number of allowances you claim on this form. As an employee, you receive one allowance unless you are claimed as a dependent on another person's tax return (e.g. your parents claim you as a dependent on their tax return). if you are married, you may claim additional allowances for your spouse and any dependent that you are entitled to claim for federal income tax purposes. You also will receive additional allowances if you or your spouse are legally blind.

How do I figure the correct number of allowances?

Complete the worksheet on the back of this page to figure the correct number of allowances you are entitled to claim. Give your competed Form IL-W-4 to your employer. Keep the worksheet for your records. If you claim over 14 allowances, you must ask us for our approval.

Note: If you have more than one job or if your spouse works, you may claim all of your allowances on one job or you may claim some on each job, but you may **not** claim the same allowances more than once. Your withholding will usually be more accurate if you claim all your allowances on the Form IL-W-4 for the job with the largest wages and claim zero on all other Forms IL-W-4.

What if I underpay my tax?

If the amount withheld from your compensation is not enough to cover your tax liability for the year, (e.g., you have non-wage income, such as interest or dividends), you may request that your employer withhold an additional amount from your pay. Otherwise, you may owe additional tax at the end of the year and may owe a penalty. If you do not have enough tax withheld from your pay, and owe more than $250 tax at the end of the year, you may owe a late-payment penalty. You should either increase the amount you have withheld from your pay, or you must make estimated payments. If you are required to make estimated tax payments and failed to do so, or you fail to make your payments on time, you may owe a late-payment penalty. This penalty is figured separately for each quarter. You may owe a late-payment penalty if

- your Illinois Income Tax exceeds the total tax withheld or credited for the tax year by more than $250 (even if your previous year's tax liability was less than $250), or
- your estimated tax is underpaid for any quarter. You may be penalized even though you are receiving a refund on your Form IL-1040.

Note: You may still owe this penalty for an earlier quarter, even if you pay enough tax later to make up the underpayment from a previous quarter.

For additional information on penalties, see Publication 103, Uniform Penalties and Interest. Call 1-800-356-6302 to receive a copy of this publication.

Where do I get help?

You can get help by

- calling our Taxpayer Assistance Division at 1 800-732-8866 or 217 782-3336
- calling our TDD (telecommunications device for the deaf) at 1-800-544-5304
- writing to

  ILLINOIS DEPARTMENT OF REVENUE
  PO BOX 19044
  SPRINGFIELD, IL 63794-9044
- visiting our Web site at www.revenue.state.il.us

Illinois Withholding Allowance Worksheet

General Information

Complete this worksheet to figure your total withholding allowances.

Everyone must complete Part 1.

Complete Part 2 if you (or your spouse) are
- age 65 or older or legally blind, or
- you wrote an amount on Line 4 of the Deductions and Adjustments Worksheet for federal Form W-4.

If you have more than one job or if your spouse works, you may claim all of your allowances on one job or you may claim some on each job, but you may **not** claim the same allowances more than once. Your withholding will usually be more accurate if you claim all your allowances on the Form IL-W-4 for the job with the largest wages and claim zero on all other Forms IL-W-4. If you have a working spouse, you may choose not to claim your spouse as a dependent (this may help avoid having too little withheld).

Part 1: Figure your basic personal allowances (including allowances for dependents)

Check all that apply:
- ☐ no one else can claim you as a dependent
- ☐ you can claim your spouse as a dependent

1 Write the total number of boxes you checked. 1 _____

2 Write the number of dependents (other than you or your spouse) who you will claim on your tax return. 2 _____

3 Add Lines 1 and 2. Write the result. This is the total number of basic personal allowances to which you are **entitled**. 3 _____

4 If you want to have additional Illinois Income Tax withheld from your pay, you must reduce the number of basic personal allowances you wrote on Line 3. Write the total number of basic personal allowances you elect to claim on Line 4 and on Form IL-W-4, Line 1. 4 _____

Part 2: Figure your additional allowances

Check all that apply:
- ☐ you are 65 or over
- ☐ your spouse is 65 or over
- ☐ you are legally blind
- ☐ your spouse is legally blind

5 Write the total number of boxes you checked. 5 _____

6 Write any amount that you reported on Line 4 of the Deductions and Adjustments Worksheet for federal Form W-4. 6 _____

7 Divide Line 6 by 1,000. Round to the nearest whole number. Write the result on Line 7. 7 _____

8 Add Lines 5 and 7. Write the result. This is the total number of additional allowances to which you are **entitled**. 8 _____

9 If you want to have additional Illinois Income Tax withheld from your pay, you must reduce the number of additional allowances you wrote on Line 8. Write the total number of additional allowances you elect to claim on Line 9 and on Form IL-W-4, Line 2. 9 _____

Note: If you have non-wage income and you expect to owe Illinois Income Tax on that income, you may choose to have an additional amount withheld from your pay. On Line 3 of Form IL-W-4, write the additional amount you want your employer to withhold.

✂ — — — — — — — — — Cut here and give the certificate to your employer. Keep the top portion for your records. — — — — — — — — — ✂

Illinois Department of Revenue

IL-W-4 Employee's Illinois Withholding Allowance Certificate

_ _ _ - _ _ - _ _ _ _
Social Security number

Name

Street address

City _____ State ___ ZIP ___

1 Write the total number of basic allowances that you are claiming (From worksheet, Part 1, Line 4). 1_____

2 Write the total number of additional allowances that you are claiming (From worksheet, Part 2, Line 9). **2**_____

3 Write the additional amount you want withheld (deducted) from each pay. 3_____

I certify that I am entitled to the number of withholding allowances claimed on this certificate.

Your signature _____ Date _____

Employer: Keep this certificate with your records. If you have referred the employee's federal certificate to IRS and the IRS has notified you to disregard it, you may also be required to disregard this certificate. Furthermore, even if you are not required to refer the employee's federal certificate to IRS, you may still be required to refer this certificate to the Illinois Department of Revenue for inspection. See Illinois Income Tax Regulations 86 Ill. Adm. Code 100.7110.

IL-W-4 (R-12/98)

This page intentionally left blank.

Illinois Department of Revenue

ST-44 Illinois Use Tax Return (R-8/98)

REV 01
FORM 019
E S ___/___/___
NS   DP   CA
RC   (UG)

0775-0005

Name _____

Address _____
   Number and street

_____   Phone (___)_____
City   State   ZIP

SSN ___ ___ ___ - ___ ___ - ___ ___ ___ ___   FEIN ___ ___ - ___ ___ ___ ___ ___ ___ ___
   Social Security number   Federal employer identification number

1   Write the date of your last purchase.*   ___/___/___
    (Please see the footnote in the instructions below.)   Month Day Year

1a Write the total cost of the general merchandise you purchased outside Illinois to use in Illinois. **1a** _____

1b Multiply Line 1a by 6.25% (.0625).   **1b** _____

2a Write the total cost of the food, drugs, and medical appliances you purchased outside
    Illinois to use in Illinois.   **2a** _____

2b Multiply Line 2a by 1% (.01).   **2b** _____

3   Add Lines 1b and 2b. This is your net tax on purchases.   **3** _____

4   Write the amount of tax you paid to another state (not to another country).   **4** _____

5   If Line 4 is greater than or equal to Line 3, you do not need to file this return. Otherwise,
    subtract Line 4 from Line 3. This is your total use tax due.   **5** _____

6   Penalty (See "What if I do not file or pay on time?")   **6** _____

7   Interest (See "What if I do not file or pay on time?")   **7** _____

8   Add Lines 5, 6, and 7. This is your total payment due.   **8** _____

STOP
- **DO NOT** attach your check or money order **OR** this form to any other return.
- **DO** make your check or money order payable to "**Illinois Department of Revenue.**"
- **DO** write your **SSN or FEIN** and "**ST-44**" on your check or money order and attach it to this form.
- **DO** mail all other returns separately.

Under penalties of perjury, I state that I have examined this return and, to the best of my knowledge, it is true, correct, and complete.

Sign here   _____   _____
          Taxpayer signature   Date

Mail this form and your payment to: Illinois Department of Revenue, Retailers' Occupation Tax, Springfield IL 62776-0001

Use Tax: Everyone's Responsibility

What is use tax?
Use tax is a type of sales tax designed to distribute the tax burden fairly among Illinois consumers and assure fair competition between Illinois and out-of-state businesses. Illinois law requires that when you buy an item from another state or country to use in Illinois, you pay tax at the Illinois rate. If you pay less than the Illinois rate to another state, you must pay Illinois the difference. If you purchase an item from another country, you must pay Illinois the full use tax rate.

Do I owe use tax?
You should complete this form and pay use tax if you
- purchased items outside Illinois that would be taxable in Illinois (including items from catalogs, TV advertisements, magazines, etc.);
- use these items in Illinois; and
- have not yet paid Illinois Sales Tax or an equivalent amount to another state.

How and when do I pay?
You must report use tax if the business from which you bought merchandise did not collect Illinois Sales Tax (this includes catalog order purchases). Some out-of-state businesses collect Illinois Sales Tax, and their customers pay the tax just as they would pay state sales tax to an Illinois business. **If you are a registered Illinois retailer or serviceperson** and currently file Form ST-1, Sales and Use Tax Return, you must report use tax on that form. **If you purchase a motor vehicle, boat, or aircraft** from an out-of-state dealer, you must report use tax on Form RUT-25, Motor Vehicle Use Tax Return. Otherwise, use this form (Form ST-44, Illinois Use Tax Return) to report your purchases.

* If you are filing on an annual basis, write the year only. Otherwise, you must write the entire date of your last purchase.

If your total tax liability for the year is
- $600 or less, you may pay the tax for the entire year (January 1 through December 31) by filing Form ST-44 on or before April 15 of the following year; or
- greater than $600, you must pay the tax by the last day of the month following the month in which the purchase was made.

What if I do not pay?
Illinois is increasing its efforts to collect this tax. Illinois shares sales information with other states and bills Illinois residents for unpaid tax, penalty, and interest. Illinois also gathers information on overseas purchases from the U.S. Customs Service. (Remember that use tax is due whether or not an item has to be declared or is subject to duty tax.) Illinois also encourages out-of-state businesses to register and collect the tax voluntarily as a convenience to their customers. If they do not, we can bill their Illinois customers directly.
Note: If you do not know or do not remember the cost of your purchase, you can contact the business where you purchased the merchandise for this information.

What if I do not file or pay on time?
You owe a **late filing penalty** if you do not file a processable return by the due date. You owe a **late payment penalty** if you do not pay the tax you owe by the original due date of the return. We will bill you for penalties and interest. See Publication 103, Uniform Penalties and Interest, if you prefer to figure these amounts. To receive a copy of this publication, call 1 800 356-6302.

What if I have questions?
If you have any questions, call our Springfield office weekdays between 8:00 a.m. and 5:00 p.m. at **1 800 732-8866** or **217 782-3336**; or call our TDD (telecommunications device for the deaf) at **1 800 544-5304**. You may also visit our Web site at **www.revenue.state.il.us**

This page intentionally left blank.

Illinois Department of Revenue
CRT-61 Certificate of Resale

Step 1: Identify the seller

1 Name _____

2 Business address _____

_____
City   State   Zip

Step 2: Identify the purchaser

3 Name _____

4 Business address _____

_____
City   State   Zip

5 Complete the information below. Check only one box.

☐ The purchaser is registered as a retailer with the Illinois Department of Revenue. _ _ _ _ - _ _ _ _ .
Registration number

☐ The purchaser is registered as a reseller with the Illinois Department of Revenue. _ _ _ _ - _ _ _ _ .
Resale number

☐ The purchaser is authorized to do business out-of-state and will resell and deliver property only to purchasers located outside the state of Illinois. See Line 5 instructions.

Step 3: Describe the property

6 Describe the property that is being purchased for resale or list the invoice number and the date of purchase.

_____

_____

_____

Step 4: Complete for blanket certificates

7 Complete the information below. Check only one box.

☐ I am the identified purchaser, and I certify that all of the purchases that I make from this seller are for resale.

☐ I am the identified purchaser, and I certify that the following percentage, _____ %, of all of the purchases that I make from this seller are for resale.

Step 5: Purchaser's signature

I certify that I am purchasing the property described in Step 3 from the stated seller for the purpose of resale.

_____   _ _/_ _/_ _ _ _
Purchaser's signature   Date

Note: It is the seller's responsibility to verify that the purchaser's registration or resale number is valid and active.

General information

When is a Certificate of Resale required?
Generally, a Certificate of Resale is required for proof that no tax is due on any sale that is made tax-free as a sale for resale. The purchaser, at the seller's request, must provide the information that is needed to complete this certificate.

Who keeps the Certificate of Resale?
The seller must keep the certificate. We may request it as proof that no tax was due on the sale of the specified property. **Do not** mail the certificate to us.

Can other forms be used?
Yes. You can use other forms or statements in place of this certificate but whatever you use as proof that a sale was made for resale must contain
- the seller's name and address;
- the purchaser's name and address;
- a description of the property being purchased;
- a statement that the property is being purchased for resale;
- the purchaser's signature and date of signing; and
- either a registration number, a resale number, or a certification of resale to an out-of-state purchaser.

Note: A purchase order signed by the purchaser may be used as a Certificate of Resale if it contains all of the above required information.

When is a blanket certificate of resale used?
The purchaser may provide a blanket certificate of resale to any seller from whom all purchases made are sales for resale. A blanket certificate can also specify that a percentage of the purchases made from the identified seller will be for resale. In either instance, blanket certificates should be kept up-to-date. If a specified percentage changes, a new certificate should be provided. Otherwise, all certificates should be updated at least every three years.

Specific instructions

Step 1: Identify the seller
Lines 1 and 2 Write the seller's name and mailing address.

Step 2: Identify the purchaser
Lines 3 and 4 Write the purchaser's name and mailing address.

Line 5 Check the statement that applies to the purchaser's business, and provide any additional requested information.
Note: A statement by the purchaser that property will be sold for resale will not be accepted by the department without supporting evidence (*e.g.*, proof of out-of-state registration).

Step 3: Describe the property
Line 6 On the lines provided, briefly describe the tangible personal property that was purchased for resale or list the invoice number and date of purchase.

Step 4: Complete for blanket certificates
Line 7 The purchaser must check the statement that applies, and provide any additional requested information.

Step 5: Purchaser's signature
The purchaser must sign and date the form.

CRT-61 (N- 01/00)
IL-492-3850

Form 8300

(Rev. August 1997)

Department of the Treasury
Internal Revenue Service

Report of Cash Payments Over $10,000
Received in a Trade or Business

▶ See instructions for definition of cash.
▶ Use this form for transactions occurring after July 31, 1997.
Please type or print.

OMB No. 1545-0892

1 Check appropriate box(es) if: **a** ☐ Amends prior report; **b** ☐ Suspicious transaction.

Part I Identity of Individual From Whom the Cash Was Received

2 If more than one individual is involved, check here and see instructions . . . . ▶ ☐

3 Last name	**4** First name	**5** M.I.	**6** Taxpayer identification number

7 Address (number, street, and apt. or suite no.)	**8** Date of birth . ▶ (see instructions) M M D D Y Y Y Y

9 City	**10** State	**11** ZIP code	**12** Country (if not U.S.)	**13** Occupation, profession, or business

14 Document used to verify identity: **a** Describe identification ▶ ....
b Issued by .... **c** Number ....

Part II Person on Whose Behalf This Transaction Was Conducted

15 If this transaction was conducted on behalf of more than one person, check here and see instructions . . . . . ▶ ☐

16 Individual's last name or Organization's name	**17** First name	**18** M.I.	**19** Taxpayer identification number

20 Doing business as (DBA) name (see instructions)	Employer identification number

21 Address (number, street, and apt. or suite no.)	**22** Occupation, profession, or business

23 City	**24** State	**25** ZIP code	**26** Country (if not U.S.)

27 Alien identification: **a** Describe identification ▶ ....
b Issued by .... **c** Number ....

Part III Description of Transaction and Method of Payment

28 Date cash received M M D D Y Y Y Y	**29** Total cash received $ .00	**30** If cash was received in more than one payment, check here . . . ▶ ☐	**31** Total price if different from item 29 $ .00

32 Amount of cash received (in U.S. dollar equivalent) (must equal item 29) (see instructions):

a U.S. currency $ _____ .00 (Amount in $100 bills or higher $ _____ .00)
b Foreign currency $ _____ .00 (Country ▶ _____)
c Cashier's check(s) $ _____ .00 ⎫ Issuer's name(s) and serial number(s) of the monetary instrument(s) ▶ ....
d Money order(s) $ _____ .00 ⎬
e Bank draft(s) $ _____ .00 ⎪ ....
f Traveler's check(s) $ _____ .00 ⎭ ....

33 Type of transaction

a ☐ Personal property purchased
b ☐ Real property purchased
c ☐ Personal services provided
d ☐ Business services provided
e ☐ Intangible property purchased
f ☐ Debt obligations paid
g ☐ Exchange of cash
h ☐ Escrow or trust funds
i ☐ Bail bond
j ☐ Other (specify) ▶

34 Specific description of property or service shown in 33. (Give serial or registration number, address, docket number, etc.) ▶ ....
....

Part IV Business That Received Cash

35 Name of business that received cash	**36** Employer identification number

37 Address (number, street, and apt. or suite no.)	Social security number

38 City	**39** State	**40** ZIP code	**41** Nature of your business

42 Under penalties of perjury, I declare that to the best of my knowledge the information I have furnished above is true, correct, and complete.

Signature of authorized official	Title of authorized official
43 Date of signature M M D D Y Y Y Y	**44** Type or print name of contact person	**45** Contact telephone number ( )

For Paperwork Reduction Act Notice, see page 4.   Cat. No. 62133S   Form **8300** (Rev. 8-97)

Multiple Parties
(Complete applicable parts below if box 2 or 15 on page 1 is checked)

Part I   Continued—Complete if box 2 on page 1 is checked

3 Last name	**4** First name	**5** M.I.	**6** Taxpayer identification number

7 Address (number, street, and apt. or suite no.)   **8** Date of birth . ▶ M M D D Y Y Y Y
                                                            (see instructions)

9 City	**10** State	**11** ZIP code	**12** Country (if not U.S.)	**13** Occupation, profession, or business

14 Document used to verify identity: **a** Describe identification ▶ ....
    b Issued by   **c** Number

3 Last name	**4** First name	**5** M.I.	**6** Taxpayer identification number

7 Address (number, street, and apt. or suite no.)   **8** Date of birth . ▶ M M D D Y Y Y Y
                                                            (see instructions)

9 City	**10** State	**11** ZIP code	**12** Country (if not U.S.)	**13** Occupation, profession, or business

14 Document used to verify identity: **a** Describe identification ▶ ....
    b Issued by   **c** Number

Part II   Continued—Complete if box 15 on page 1 is checked

16 Individual's last name or Organization's name	**17** First name	**18** M.I.	**19** Taxpayer identification number

20 Doing business as (DBA) name (see instructions)   Employer identification number

21 Address (number, street, and apt. or suite no.)	**22** Occupation, profession, or business

23 City	**24** State	**25** ZIP code	**26** Country (if not U.S.)

27 Alien identification: **a** Describe identification ▶ ....
    b Issued by   **c** Number

16 Individual's last name or Organization's name	**17** First name	**18** M.I.	**19** Taxpayer identification number

20 Doing business as (DBA) name (see instructions)   Employer identification number

21 Address (number, street, and apt. or suite no.)	**22** Occupation, profession, or business

23 City	**24** State	**25** ZIP code	**26** Country (if not U.S.)

27 Alien identification: **a** Describe identification ▶ ....
    b Issued by   **c** Number

Item You Should Note

Clerks of Federal or State courts must now file Form 8300 if more than $10,000 in cash is received as bail for an individual(s) charged with certain criminal offenses. For these purposes, a clerk includes the clerk's office or any other office, department, division, branch, or unit of the court that is authorized to receive bail. If a person receives bail on behalf of a clerk, the clerk is treated as receiving the bail.

If multiple payments are made in cash to satisfy bail and the initial payment does not exceed $10,000, the initial payment and subsequent payments must be aggregated and the information return must be filed by the 15th day after receipt of the payment that causes the aggregate amount to exceed $10,000 in cash. In such cases, the reporting requirement can be satisfied either by sending a single written statement with an aggregate amount listed or by furnishing a copy of each Form 8300 relating to that payer. Payments made to satisfy separate bail requirements are not required to be aggregated. See Treasury Regulations section 1.6050I-2.

Casinos must file Form 8300 for nongaming activities (restaurants, shops, etc.).

General Instructions

Who must file.—Each person engaged in a trade or business who, in the course of that trade or business, receives more than $10,000 in cash in one transaction or in two or more related transactions, must file Form 8300. Any transactions conducted between a payer (or its agent) and the recipient in a 24-hour period are related transactions. Transactions are considered related even if they occur over a period of more than 24 hours if the recipient knows, or has reason to know, that each transaction is one of a series of connected transactions.

Keep a copy of each Form 8300 for 5 years from the date you file it.

Voluntary use of Form 8300.—Form 8300 may be filed voluntarily for any suspicious transaction (see **Definitions**), even if the total amount does not exceed $10,000.

Exceptions.—Cash is not required to be reported if it is received:

● By a financial institution required to file **Form 4789,** Currency Transaction Report.

● By a casino required to file (or exempt from filing) **Form 8362,** Currency Transaction Report by Casinos, if the cash is received as part of its gaming business.

● By an agent who receives the cash from a principal, if the agent uses all of the cash within 15 days in a second transaction that is reportable on Form 8300 or on Form 4789, and discloses all the information necessary to complete Part II of Form 8300 or Form 4789 to the recipient of the cash in the second transaction.

● In a transaction occurring entirely outside the United States. See **Pub. 1544,** Reporting Cash Payments Over $10,000 (Received in a Trade or Business),

regarding transactions occurring in Puerto Rico, the Virgin Islands, and territories and possessions of the United States.

● In a transaction that is not in the course of a person's trade or business.

When to file.—File Form 8300 by the 15th day after the date the cash was received. If that date falls on a Saturday, Sunday, or legal holiday, file the form on the next business day.

Where to file.—File the form with the Internal Revenue Service, Detroit Computing Center, P.O. Box 32621, Detroit, MI 48232, or hand carry it to your local IRS office.

Statement to be provided.—You must give a written statement to each person named on a required Form 8300 on or before January 31 of the year following the calendar year in which the cash is received. The statement must show the name, telephone number, and address of the information contact for the business, the aggregate amount of reportable cash received, and that the information was furnished to the IRS. Keep a copy of the statement for your records.

Multiple payments.—If you receive more than one cash payment for a single transaction or for related transactions, you must report the multiple payments any time you receive a total amount that exceeds $10,000 within any 12-month period. Submit the report within 15 days of the date you receive the payment that causes the total amount to exceed $10,000. If more than one report is required within 15 days, you may file a combined report. File the combined report no later than the date the earliest report, if filed separately, would have to be filed.

Taxpayer identification number (TIN).—You must furnish the correct TIN of the person or persons from whom you receive the cash and, if applicable, the person or persons on whose behalf the transaction is being conducted. **You may be subject to penalties for an incorrect or missing TIN.**

The TIN for an individual (including a sole proprietorship) is the individual's social security number (SSN). For certain resident aliens who are not eligible to get an SSN and nonresident aliens who are required to file tax returns, it is an IRS Individual Taxpayer Identification Number (ITIN). For other persons, including corporations, partnerships, and estates, it is the employer identification number.

If you have requested but are not able to get a TIN for one or more of the parties to a transaction within 15 days following the transaction, file the report and attach a statement explaining why the TIN is not included.

Exception: *You are not required to provide the TIN of a person who is a nonresident alien individual or a foreign organization if that person does not have income effectively connected with the conduct of a U.S. trade or business and does not have an office or place of business, or fiscal or paying agent, in the United States. See Pub. 1544 for more information.*

Penalties.—You may be subject to penalties if you fail to file a correct and complete Form 8300 on time and you cannot show that the failure was due to reasonable cause. You may also be subject to penalties if you fail to furnish timely a correct and complete statement to each person named in a required report. A minimum penalty of $25,000 may be imposed if the failure is due to an intentional disregard of the cash reporting requirements.

Penalties may also be imposed for causing, or attempting to cause, a trade or business to fail to file a required report; for causing, or attempting to cause, a trade or business to file a required report containing a material omission or misstatement of fact; or for structuring, or attempting to structure, transactions to avoid the reporting requirements. These violations may also be subject to criminal prosecution which, upon conviction, may result in imprisonment of up to 5 years or fines of up to $250,000 for individuals and $500,000 for corporations or both.

Definitions

Cash.—The term "cash" means the following:

● U.S. and foreign coin and currency received in any transaction.

● A cashier's check, money order, bank draft, or traveler's check having a face amount of $10,000 or less that is received in a **designated reporting transaction** (defined below), or that is received in any transaction in which the recipient knows that the instrument is being used in an attempt to avoid the reporting of the transaction under section 6050I.

Note: *Cash does not include a check drawn on the payer's own account, such as a personal check, regardless of the amount.*

Designated reporting transaction.—A retail sale (or the receipt of funds by a broker or other intermediary in connection with a retail sale) of a consumer durable, a collectible, or a travel or entertainment activity.

*Retail sale.—*Any sale (whether or not the sale is for resale or for any other purpose) made in the course of a trade or business if that trade or business principally consists of making sales to ultimate consumers.

*Consumer durable.—*An item of tangible personal property of a type that, under ordinary usage, can reasonably be expected to remain useful for at least 1 year, and that has a sales price of more than $10,000.

*Collectible.—*Any work of art, rug, antique, metal, gem, stamp, coin, etc.

*Travel or entertainment activity.—*An item of travel or entertainment that pertains to a single trip or event if the combined sales price of the item and all other items relating to the same trip or event that are sold in the same transaction (or related transactions) exceeds $10,000.

*Exceptions.—*A cashier's check, money order, bank draft, or traveler's check is not considered received in a designated reporting transaction if it constitutes the proceeds of a bank loan or if it is received as a payment on certain promissory notes, installment sales contracts, or down payment plans. See Pub. 1544 for more information.

Person.—An individual, corporation, partnership, trust, estate, association, or company.

Recipient.—The person receiving the cash. Each branch or other unit of a person's trade or business is considered a separate recipient unless the branch receiving the cash (or a central office linking the branches), knows or has reason to know the identity of payers making cash payments to other branches.

Transaction.—Includes the purchase of property or services, the payment of debt, the exchange of a negotiable instrument for cash, and the receipt of cash to be held in escrow or trust. A single transaction may not be broken into multiple transactions to avoid reporting.

Suspicious transaction.—A transaction in which it appears that a person is attempting to cause Form 8300 not to be filed, or to file a false or incomplete form. The term also includes any transaction in which there is an indication of possible illegal activity.

Specific Instructions

You must complete all parts. However, you may skip Part II if the individual named in Part I is conducting the transaction on his or her behalf only.

Item 1.—If you are amending a prior report, check box 1a. Complete the appropriate items with the correct or amended information only. Complete all of Part IV. Staple a copy of the original report to the amended report.

To voluntarily report a suspicious transaction (see **Definitions**), check box 1b. You may also telephone your local IRS Criminal Investigation Division or call 1-800-800-2877.

Part I

Item 2.—If two or more individuals conducted the transaction you are reporting, check the box and complete Part I for any one of the individuals. Provide the same information for the other individual(s) on the back of the form. If more than three individuals are involved, provide the same information on additional sheets of paper and attach them to this form.

Item 6.—Enter the taxpayer identification number (TIN) of the individual named. See **Taxpayer identification number (TIN)** under **General Instructions** for more information.

Item 8.—Enter eight numerals for the date of birth of the individual named. For example, if the individual's birth date is July 6, 1960, enter 07 06 1960.

Item 13.—Fully describe the nature of the occupation, profession, or business (for example, "plumber," "attorney," or "automobile dealer"). Do not use general or nondescriptive terms such as "businessman" or "self-employed."

Item 14.—You must verify the name and address of the named individual(s). Verification must be made by examination of a document normally accepted as a means of identification when cashing checks (for example, a driver's license, passport, alien registration card, or other official document). In item 14a, enter the type of document examined. In item 14b, identify the issuer of the document. In item 14c, enter the document's number. For example, if the individual has a Utah driver's license, enter "driver's license" in item 14a, "Utah" in item 14b, and the number appearing on the license in item 14c.

Part II

Item 15.—If the transaction is being conducted on behalf of more than one person (including husband and wife or parent and child), check the box and complete Part II for any one of the persons. Provide the same information for the other person(s) on the back of the form. If more than three persons are involved, provide the same information on additional sheets of paper and attach them to this form.

Items 16 through 19.—If the person on whose behalf the transaction is being conducted is an individual, complete items 16, 17, and 18. Enter his or her TIN in item 19. If the individual is a sole proprietor and has an employer identification number (EIN), you must enter both the SSN and EIN in item 19. If the person is an organization, put its name as shown on required tax filings in item 16 and its EIN in item 19.

Item 20.—If a sole proprietor or organization named in items 16 through 18 is doing business under a name other than that entered in item 16 (e.g., a "trade" or "doing business as (DBA)" name), enter it here.

Item 27.—If the person is **NOT** required to furnish a TIN (see **Taxpayer identification number (TIN)** under **General Instructions**), complete this item. Enter a description of the type of official document issued to that person in item 27a (for example, "passport"), the country that issued the document in item 27b, and the document's number in item 27c.

Part III

Item 28.—Enter the date you received the cash. If you received the cash in more than one payment, enter the date you received the payment that caused the combined amount to exceed $10,000. See **Multiple payments** under **General Instructions** for more information.

Item 30.—Check this box if the amount shown in item 29 was received in more than one payment (for example, as installment payments or payments on related transactions).

Item 31.—Enter the total price of the property, services, amount of cash exchanged, etc. (for example, the total cost

of a vehicle purchased, cost of catering service, exchange of currency) if different from the amount shown in item 29.

Item 32.—Enter the dollar amount of each form of cash received. Show foreign currency amounts in U.S. dollar equivalent at a fair market rate of exchange available to the public. **The sum of the amounts must equal item 29.** For cashier's check, money order, bank draft, or traveler's check, provide the name of the issuer and the serial number of each instrument. Names of all issuers and all serial numbers involved must be provided. If necessary, provide this information on additional sheets of paper and attach them to this form.

Item 33.—Check the appropriate box(es) that describe the transaction. If the transaction is not specified in boxes a–i, check box j and briefly describe the transaction (for example, car lease, boat lease, house lease, aircraft rental).

Part IV

Item 36.—If you are a sole proprietorship, you must enter your SSN. If your business also has an EIN, you must provide the EIN as well. All other business entities must enter an EIN.

Item 41.—Fully describe the nature of your business, for example, "attorney," "jewelry dealer." Do not use general or nondescriptive terms such as "business" or "store."

Item 42.—This form must be signed by an individual who has been authorized to do so for the business that received the cash.

Paperwork Reduction Act Notice

The requested information is useful in criminal, tax, and regulatory investigations, for instance, by directing the Federal Government's attention to unusual or questionable transactions. Trades or businesses are required to provide the information under 26 U.S.C. 6050I.

You are not required to provide the information requested on a form that is subject to the Paperwork Reduction Act unless the form displays a valid OMB control number. Books or records relating to a form or its instructions must be retained as long as their contents may become material in the administration of any Internal Revenue law. Generally, tax returns and return information are confidential, as required by Code section 6103.

The time needed to complete this form will vary depending on individual circumstances. The estimated average time is 21 minutes. If you have comments concerning the accuracy of this time estimate or suggestions for making this form simpler, you can write to the Tax Forms Committee, Western Area Distribution Center, Rancho Cordova, CA 95743-0001. DO NOT send this form to this office. Instead, see **Where To File** on page 3.

Form **8850**	Pre-Screening Notice and Certification Request for	
(Rev. November 1998)	the Work Opportunity and Welfare-to-Work Credits	OMB No. 1545-1500
Department of the Treasury Internal Revenue Service	▶ See separate instructions.	

Job applicant: Fill in the lines below and check any boxes that apply. Complete only this side.

Your name _____ Social security number ▶ _____

Street address where you live _____

City or town, state, and ZIP code _____

Telephone no. ( ) - _____

If you are under age 25, enter your date of birth (month, day, year) ___ / ___ / ___

Work Opportunity Credit

1 ☐ Check here if you received a conditional certification from the state employment security agency (SESA) or a participating local agency for the work opportunity credit.

2 ☐ Check here if **any** of the following statements apply to you.

- I am a member of a family that has received assistance from Aid to Families with Dependent Children (AFDC) or its successor program, Temporary Assistance for Needy Families (TANF), for any 9 months during the last 18 months.

- I am a veteran and a member of a family that received food stamps for at least a 3-month period within the last 15 months.

- I was referred here by a rehabilitation agency approved by the state or the Department of Veterans Affairs.

- I am at least age 18 but **not** over age 24 and I am a member of a family that:
  a Received food stamps for the last 6 months, OR
  b Received food stamps for at least 3 of the last 5 months, BUT is no longer eligible to receive them.

- Within the past year, I was convicted of a felony or released from prison for a felony AND during the last 6 months I was a member of a low-income family.

- I received supplemental security income (SSI) benefits for any month ending within the last 60 days.

Welfare-to-Work Credit

3 ☐ Check here if you received a conditional certification from the SESA or a participating local agency for the welfare-to-work credit.

4 ☐ Check here if you are a member of a family that:
- Received AFDC or TANF payments for at least the last 18 months, OR
- Received AFDC or TANF payments for any 18 months beginning after August 5, 1997, OR
- Stopped being eligible for AFDC or TANF payments after August 5, 1997, because Federal or state law limited the maximum time those payments could be made.

All Applicants

Under penalties of perjury, I declare that I gave the above information to the employer on or before the day I was offered a job, and it is, to the best of my knowledge, true, correct, and complete.

Job applicant's signature ▶ _____ **Date** ___ / ___ / ___

For Privacy Act and Paperwork Reduction Act Notice, see page 2.   Cat. No. 22851L   Form **8850** (Rev. 11-98)

For Employer's Use Only

Employer's name _____ Telephone no. (___) - _____ EIN ▶ _____

Street address _____

City or town, state, and ZIP code _____

Person to contact, if different from above _____ Telephone no. (___) - _____

Street address _____

City or town, state, and ZIP code _____

If, based on the individual's age and home address, he or she is a member of group 4 or 6 (as described under **Members of Targeted Groups** in the separate instructions), enter that group number (4 or 6) . . . . ▶ _____

DATE APPLICANT: Gave information / /   Was offered job / /   Was hired / /   Started job / /

Under penalties of perjury, I declare that I completed this form on or before the day a job was offered to the applicant and that the information I have furnished is, to the best of my knowledge, true, correct, and complete. Based on the information the job applicant furnished on page 1, I believe the individual is a member of a targeted group or a long-term family assistance recipient. I hereby request a certification that the individual is a member of a targeted group or a long-term family assistance recipient.

Employer's signature ▶ _____ Title _____ Date / /

Privacy Act and Paperwork Reduction Act Notice

Section references are to the Internal Revenue Code.

Section 51(d)(12) permits a prospective employer to request the applicant to complete this form and give it to the prospective employer. The information will be used by the employer to complete the employer's Federal tax return. Completion of this form is voluntary and may assist members of targeted groups and long-term family assistance recipients in securing employment. Routine uses of this form include giving it to the state employment security agency (SESA), which will contact appropriate sources to confirm that the applicant is a member of a targeted group or a long-term family

assistance recipient. This form may also be given to the Internal Revenue Service for administration of the Internal Revenue laws, to the Department of Justice for civil and criminal litigation, to the Department of Labor for oversight of the certifications performed by the SESA, and to cities, states, and the District of Columbia for use in administering their tax laws.

You are not required to provide the information requested on a form that is subject to the Paperwork Reduction Act unless the form displays a valid OMB control number. Books or records relating to a form or its instructions must be retained as long as their contents may become material in the administration of any Internal Revenue law. Generally, tax returns and return information are confidential, as required by section 6103.

The time needed to complete and file this form will vary depending on individual circumstances. The estimated average time is:
Recordkeeping . . . . 2 hr., 47 min.
Learning about the law or the form . . . . 28 min.
Preparing and sending this form to the SESA . . . . 36 min.

If you have comments concerning the accuracy of these time estimates or suggestions for making this form simpler, we would be happy to hear from you. You can write to the Tax Forms Committee, Western Area Distribution Center, Rancho Cordova, CA 95743-0001.

DO NOT send this form to this address. Instead, see **When and Where To File** in the separate instructions.

Instructions for Form 8850

Department of the Treasury
Internal Revenue Service

(Revised November 1998)

**Pre-Screening Notice and Certification Request for the
Work Opportunity and Welfare-to-Work Credits**

Section references are to the Internal Revenue Code unless otherwise noted.

General Instructions

A Change To Note

The Tax and Trade Relief Extension Act of 1998 extended the work opportunity credit and the welfare-to-work credit to cover individuals who begin work for the employer before July 1, 1999.

Purpose of Form

Employers use Form 8850 to pre-screen and to make a written request to a state employment security agency (SESA) to certify an individual as:

● A member of a targeted group for purposes of qualifying for the work opportunity credit, or

● A long-term family assistance recipient for purposes of qualifying for the welfare-to-work credit.

Submitting Form 8850 to the SESA is but one step in the employer qualifying for the work opportunity credit or the welfare-to-work credit. The SESA must certify the job applicant is a member of a targeted group or is a long-term family assistance recipient. After starting work, the employee must meet the minimum number-of-hours-worked requirement for the work opportunity credit or the minimum number-of-hours, number-of-days requirement for the welfare-to-work credit. The employer may elect to take the applicable credit by filing **Form 5884,** Work Opportunity Credit, or **Form 8861,** Welfare-to-Work Credit.

Who Should Complete and Sign the Form

The job applicant gives information to the employer on or before the day a job offer is made. This information is entered on Form 8850. Based on the applicant's information, the employer determines whether or not he or she believes the applicant is a member of a targeted group (as defined under **Members of Targeted Groups** below) or a long-term family assistance recipient (as defined under **Welfare-to-Work Job Applicants** on page 2). If the employer believes the applicant is a member of a targeted group or a long-term family assistance recipient, the employer completes the rest of the form no later than the day the job offer is made. Both the job applicant and the employer must sign Form 8850 no later than the date for submitting the form to the SESA.

Instructions for Employer

When and Where To File

Do not file Form 8850 with the Internal Revenue Service. Instead, send it to the work opportunity tax credit (WOTC) coordinator for your SESA no later than the 21st day after the job applicant begins work for you.

To get the name, address, and phone and fax numbers of the WOTC coordinator for your SESA, visit the Department of Labor, Employment and Training Administration (ETA) web site at **www.ttrc.doleta.gov/common/directories**, or call **202-219-9092** (not a toll-free number).

Additional Requirements for Certification

In addition to filing Form 8850, you must complete and send to your state's WOTC coordinator **either:**

● **ETA Form 9062,** Conditional Certification Form, if the job applicant received this form from a participating agency (e.g., the Jobs Corps), **or**

● **ETA Form 9061,** Individual Characteristics Form, if the job applicant did not receive a conditional certification.

Using the Department of Labor's fax on demand service, you can get a directory of WOTC coordinators and ETA Form 9061 by calling **703-365-0768** (not a toll-free number) from the telephone connected to your fax machine and following the prompts. You can also get ETA Form 9061 from your local public employment service office, or you can download it from the ETA web site at **www.doleta.gov.**

Recordkeeping

Keep copies of Forms 8850, along with any transmittal letters that you submit to your SESA, as long as they may be needed for the administration of the Internal Revenue Code provisions relating to the work opportunity credit and the welfare-to-work credit. Records that support these credits usually must be kept for 3 years from the date any income tax return claiming the credits is due or filed, whichever is later.

Members of Targeted Groups

A job applicant may be certified as a member of a targeted group if he or she is:

1. A member of a family receiving assistance under a state plan approved under part A of title IV of the Social Security Act relating to Aid to Families with Dependent Children (AFDC) or its successor program, Temporary Assistance for Needy Families (TANF). The assistance must be received for any 9 months during the 18-month period that ends on the hiring date.

2. A veteran who is a member of a family receiving assistance under the Food Stamp program for generally at least a 3-month period during the 15-month period ending on the hiring date. See section 51(d)(3).

To be considered a **veteran,** the applicant must:

● Have served on active duty (not including training) in the Armed Forces of the United States for more than 180 days OR have been discharged for a service-connected disability, AND

● Not have a period of active duty (not including training) of more than 90 days that ended during the 60-day period ending on the hiring date.

3. An ex-felon who:

● Has been convicted of a felony under any Federal or state law,

● Is hired not more than 1 year after the conviction or release from prison for that felony, AND

● Is a member of a family that had income on an annual basis of 70% or less of the Bureau of Labor Statistics lower living standard during the 6 months preceding the earlier of the month the income determination occurs or the month in which the hiring date occurs.

Cat. No. 24833J

4. An individual who is at least age 18 but not yet age 25 on the hiring date and lives in an empowerment zone or enterprise community.

The Secretary of Housing and Urban Development (HUD) designated parts of the following cities as urban empowerment zones:

- Atlanta, GA (9.29 square miles)
- Baltimore, MD (6.8 square miles)
- Philadelphia, PA/Camden, NJ (4.4 square miles)
- Chicago, IL (14.33 square miles)
- Detroit, MI (18.3 square miles)
- New York City, NY (the Bronx and Manhattan) (7.6 square miles)

The Secretary of Agriculture (USDA) designated the following rural empowerment zones:

- The Kentucky Highlands (part of Wayne and all of Clinton and Jackson counties)
- Mid-Delta, Mississippi (parts of Bolivar, Holmes, Humphreys, Leflore, Sunflower, and Washington counties)
- Rio Grande Valley, Texas (parts of Cameron, Hidalgo, Starr, and Willacy counties)

Under section 1400, parts of Washington, DC, are treated as an empowerment zone. For more details, see Notice 98-57, 1998-47 I.R.B. 9.

There are 64 urban and 30 rural enterprise communities located in 35 states. There are no empowerment zones or enterprise communities in Puerto Rico, Guam, or any U.S. possession.

You may call HUD at **1-800-998-9999** for information on the six urban empowerment zones and Washington, DC. You may call the USDA at **1-800-645-4712** about the rural empowerment zones. On the Internet, you can visit the EZ/EC Home Page at **www.ezec.gov**. Your SESA has information on where the enterprise communities are located. Also, many enterprise communities have their own web sites.

5. An individual who has a physical or mental disability resulting in a substantial handicap to employment and who was referred to the employer upon completion of (or while receiving) rehabilitation services under a state plan of employment or a program approved by the Department of Veterans Affairs.

6. An individual who:

- Performs services for the employer between May 1 and September 15,
- Is age 16 but not yet age 18 on the hiring date (or if later, on May 1),
- Has never worked for the employer before, AND
- Lives in an empowerment zone or enterprise community.

7. An individual who:

- Is at least age 18 but not yet age 25 AND
- Is a member of a family that—

   a. Has received food stamps for the 6-month period ending on the hiring date OR

   b. Is no longer eligible for such assistance under section 6(o) of the Food Stamp Act of 1977 and the family received food stamps for at least 3 months of the 5-month period ending on the hiring date.

8. An individual who is receiving supplemental security income benefits under title XVI of the Social Security Act (including benefits of the type described in section 1616 of the Social Security Act or section 212 of Public Law 93-66) for any month ending within the 60-day period ending on the hiring date.

Welfare-to-Work Job Applicants

An individual may be certified as a long-term family assistance recipient if he or she is a member of a family that:

- Has received assistance payments from AFDC or TANF for at least 18 consecutive months ending on the hiring date, OR
- Receives assistance payments from AFDC or TANF for any 18 months (whether or not consecutive) beginning after August 5, 1997, OR
- After August 5, 1997, stops being eligible for assistance payments because Federal or state law limits the maximum period such assistance is payable, and the individual is hired not more than 2 years after such eligibility for assistance ends.

INDEX

C

D

E

W

Z

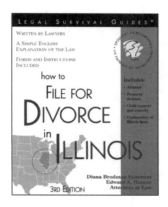

Sphinx® Publishing's National Titles
Valid in All 50 States

Legal Survival in Business

The Complete Book of Corporate Forms	$24.95
How to Form a Limited Liability Company	$22.95
Incorporate in Delaware from Any State	$24.95
Incorporate in Nevada from Any State	$24.95
How to Form a Nonprofit Corporation (2E)	$24.95
How to Form Your Own Corporation (3E)	$24.95
How to Form Your Own Partnership (2E)	$24.95
How to Register Your Own Copyright (4E)	$24.95
How to Register Your Own Trademark (3E)	$21.95
Most Valuable Business Legal Forms You'll Ever Need (3E)	$21.95

Legal Survival in Court

Crime Victim's Guide to Justice (2E)	$21.95
Grandparents' Rights (3E)	$24.95
Help Your Lawyer Win Your Case (2E)	$14.95
Jurors' Rights (2E)	$12.95
Legal Research Made Easy (3E)	$21.95
Winning Your Personal Injury Claim (2E)	$24.95
Your Rights When You Owe Too Much	$16.95

Legal Survival in Real Estate

Essential Guide to Real Estate Contracts	$18.95
Essential Guide to Real Estate Leases	$18.95
How to Buy a Condominium or Townhome (2E)	$19.95

Legal Survival in Personal Affairs

Cómo Hacer su Propio Testamento	$16.95
Cómo Solicitar su Propio Divorcio	$24.95
Cómo Restablecer su propio Crédito y Renegociar sus Deudas	$21.95
Guía de Inmigración a Estados Unidos (3E)	$24.95
Guía de Justicia para Víctimas del Crimen	$21.95
The 529 College Savings Plan	$16.95
How to File Your Own Bankruptcy (5E)	$21.95
How to File Your Own Divorce (4E)	$24.95
How to Make Your Own Simple Will (3E)	$18.95
How to Write Your Own Living Will (2E)	$16.95
How to Write Your Own Premarital Agreement (3E)	$24.95
Living Trusts and Other Ways to Avoid Probate (3E)	$24.95
Manual de Beneficios para el Seguro Social	$18.95
Mastering the MBE	$16.95
Most Valuable Personal Legal Forms You'll Ever Need	$24.95
Neighbor v. Neighbor (2E)	$16.95
The Nanny and Domestic Help Legal Kit	$22.95
The Power of Attorney Handbook (4E)	$19.95
Repair Your Own Credit and Deal with Debt	$18.95
The Social Security Benefits Handbook (3E)	$18.95
Social Security Q&A	$12.95
Sexual Harassment:Your Guide to Legal Action	$18.95
Unmarried Parents' Rights	$19.95
U.S.A. Immigration Guide (4E)	$24.95
The Visitation Handbook	$18.95
Win Your Unemployment Compensation Claim (2E)	$21.95
Your Right to Child Custody, Visitation and Support (2E)	$24.95

Legal Survival Guides are directly available from Sourcebooks, Inc., or from your local bookstores.
Prices are subject to change without notice.

For credit card orders call 1–800–432–7444, write P.O. Box 4410, Naperville, IL 60567-4410
or fax 630-961-2168

Find more legal information at: **www.SphinxLegal.com**

SPHINX® PUBLISHING ORDER FORM

BILL TO:		SHIP TO:	
Phone #	**Terms**	**F.O.B.** Chicago, IL	**Ship Date**

Charge my: ☐ VISA ☐ MasterCard ☐ American Express

☐ **Money Order or Personal Check**

Credit Card Number

Expiration Date

Qty	ISBN	Title	Retail	Ext.
		SPHINX PUBLISHING NATIONAL TITLES		
	1-57248-148-X	Cómo Hacer su Propio Testamento	$16.95	
	1-57248-147-1	Cómo Solicitar su Propio Divorcio	$24.95	
	1-57248-226-5	Cómo Restablecer su propio Crédito y Renegociar sus Deudas	$21.95	
	1-57248-238-9	The 529 College Savings Plan	$16.95	
	1-57248-166-8	The Complete Book of Corporate Forms	$24.95	
	1-57248-163-3	Crime Victim's Guide to Justice (2E)	$21.95	
	1-57248-159-5	Essential Guide to Real Estate Contracts	$18.95	
	1-57248-160-9	Essential Guide to Real Estate Leases	$18.95	
	1-57248-139-0	Grandparents' Rights (3E)	$24.95	
	1-57248-188-9	Guía de Inmigración a Estados Unidos (3E)	$24.95	
	1-57248-187-0	Guía de Justicia para Víctimas del Crimen	$21.95	
	1-57248-103-X	Help Your Lawyer Win Your Case (2E)	$14.95	
	1-57248-164-1	How to Buy a Condominium or Townhome (2E)	$19.95	
	1-57248-191-9	How to File Your Own Bankruptcy (5E)	$21.95	
	1-57248-132-3	How to File Your Own Divorce (4E)	$24.95	
	1-57248-083-1	How to Form a Limited Liability Company	$22.95	
	1-57248-231-1	How to Form a Nonprofit Corporation (2E)	$24.95	
	1-57248-133-1	How to Form Your Own Corporation (3E)	$24.95	
	1-57248-224-9	How to Form Your Own Partnership (2E)	$24.95	
	1-57248-232-X	How to Make Your Own Simple Will (3E)	$18.95	
	1-57248-200-1	How to Register Your Own Copyright (4E)	$24.95	
	1-57248-104-8	How to Register Your Own Trademark (3E)	$21.95	
	1-57248-118-8	How to Write Your Own Living Will (2E)	$16.95	
	1-57248-156-0	How to Write Your Own Premarital Agreement (3E)	$24.95	
	1-57248-230-3	Incorporate in Delaware from Any State	$24.95	
	1-57248-158-7	Incorporate in Nevada from Any State	$24.95	
	1-57071-333-2	Jurors' Rights (2E)	$12.95	
	1-57248-223-0	Legal Research Made Easy (3E)	$21.95	
	1-57248-165-X	Living Trusts and Other Ways to Avoid Probate (3E)	$24.95	
	1-57248-186-2	Manual de Beneficios para el Seguro Social	$18.95	

Qty	ISBN	Title	Retail	Ext.
	1-57248-220-6	Mastering the MBE	$16.95	
	1-57248-167-6	Most Valuable Bus. Legal Forms You'll Ever Need (3E)	$21.95	
	1-57248-130-7	Most Valuable Personal Legal Forms You'll Ever Need	$24.95	
	1-57248-098-X	The Nanny and Domestic Help Legal Kit	$22.95	
	1-57248-089-0	Neighbor v. Neighbor (2E)	$16.95	
	1-57248-169-2	The Power of Attorney Handbook (4E)	$19.95	
	1-57248-149-8	Repair Your Own Credit and Deal with Debt	$18.95	
	1-57248-217-6	Sexual Harassment: Your Guide to Legal Action	$18.95	
	1-57248-168-4	The Social Security Benefits Handbook (3E)	$18.95	
	1-57248-216-8	Social Security Q&A	$12.95	
	1-57071-399-5	Unmarried Parents' Rights	$19.95	
	1-57248-161-7	U.S.A. Immigration Guide (4E)	$24.95	
	1-57248-192-7	The Visitation Handbook	$18.95	
	1-57248-225-7	Win Your Unemployment Compensation Claim (2E)	$21.95	
	1-57248-138-2	Winning Your Personal Injury Claim (2E)	$24.95	
	1-57248-162-5	Your Right to Child Custody, Visitation and Support (2E)	$24.95	
	1-57248-157-9	Your Rights When You Owe Too Much	$16.95	
		CALIFORNIA TITLES		
	1-57248-150-1	CA Power of Attorney Handbook (2E)	$18.95	
	1-57248-151-X	How to File for Divorce in CA (3E)	$26.95	
	1-57071-356-1	How to Make a CA Will	$16.95	
	1-57248-145-5	How to Probate and Settle an Estate in California	$26.95	
	1-57248-146-3	How to Start a Business in CA	$18.95	
	1-57248-194-3	How to Win in Small Claims Court in CA (2E)	$18.95	
	1-57248-196-X	The Landlord's Legal Guide in CA	$24.95	
		FLORIDA TITLES		
	1-57071-363-4	Florida Power of Attorney Handbook (2E)	$16.95	
	1-57248-176-5	How to File for Divorce in FL (7E)	$26.95	
	1-57248-177-3	How to Form a Corporation in FL (5E)	$24.95	
	1-57248-203-6	How to Form a Limited Liability Co. in FL (2E)	$24.95	
	1-57071-401-0	How to Form a Partnership in FL	$22.95	

Form Continued on Following Page **SUBTOTAL**

SPHINX® PUBLISHING ORDER FORM

Qty	ISBN	Title	Retail	Ext.
_____	1-57248-113-7	How to Make a FL Will (6E)	$16.95	_____
_____	1-57248-088-2	How to Modify Your FL Divorce Judgment (4E)	$24.95	_____
_____	1-57248-144-7	How to Probate and Settle an Estate in FL (4E)	$26.95	_____
_____	1-57248-081-5	How to Start a Business in FL (5E)	$16.95	_____
_____	1-57248-204-4	How to Win in Small Claims Court in FL (7E)	$18.95	_____
_____	1-57248-202-8	Land Trusts in Florida (6E)	$29.95	_____
_____	1-57248-123-4	Landlords' Rights and Duties in FL (8E)	$21.95	_____

GEORGIA TITLES

Qty	ISBN	Title	Retail	Ext.
_____	1-57248-137-4	How to File for Divorce in GA (4E)	$21.95	_____
_____	1-57248-180-3	How to Make a GA Will (4E)	$21.95	_____
_____	1-57248-140-4	How to Start a Business in Georgia (2E)	$16.95	_____

ILLINOIS TITLES

Qty	ISBN	Title	Retail	Ext.
_____	1-57248-206-0	How to File for Divorce in IL (3E)	$24.95	_____
_____	1-57248-170-6	How to Make an IL Will (3E)	$16.95	_____
_____	1-57248-247-8	How to Start a Business in IL (3E)	$21.95	_____
_____	1-57248-078-5	Landlords' Rights & Duties in IL	$21.95	_____

MASSACHUSETTS TITLES

Qty	ISBN	Title	Retail	Ext.
_____	1-57248-128-5	How to File for Divorce in MA (3E)	$24.95	_____
_____	1-57248-115-3	How to Form a Corporation in MA	$24.95	_____
_____	1-57248-108-0	How to Make a MA Will (2E)	$16.95	_____
_____	1-57248-106-4	How to Start a Business in MA (2E)	$18.95	_____
_____	1-57248-209-5	The Landlord's Legal Guide in MA	$24.95	_____

MICHIGAN TITLES

Qty	ISBN	Title	Retail	Ext.
_____	1-57248-215-X	How to File for Divorce in MI (3E)	$24.95	_____
_____	1-57248-182-X	How to Make a MI Will (3E)	$16.95	_____
_____	1-57248-183-8	How to Start a Business in MI (3E)	$18.95	_____

MINNESOTA TITLES

Qty	ISBN	Title	Retail	Ext.
_____	1-57248-142-0	How to File for Divorce in MN	$21.95	_____
_____	1-57248-179-X	How to Form a Corporation in MN	$24.95	_____
_____	1-57248-178-1	How to Make a MN Will (2E)	$16.95	_____

NEW YORK TITLES

Qty	ISBN	Title	Retail	Ext.
_____	1-57248-193-5	Child Custody, Visitation and Support in NY	$26.95	_____
_____	1-57248-141-2	How to File for Divorce in NY (2E)	$26.95	_____
_____	1-57248-105-6	How to Form a Corporation in NY	$24.95	_____
_____	1-57248-095-5	How to Make a NY Will (2E)	$16.95	_____
_____	1-57248-199-4	How to Start a Business in NY (2E)	$18.95	_____

Qty	ISBN	Title	Retail	Ext.
_____	1-57248-198-6	How to Win in Small Claims Court in NY (2E)	$18.95	_____
_____	1-57248-197-8	Landlords' Legal Guide in NY	$24.95	_____
_____	1-57071-188-7	New York Power of Attorney Handbook	$19.95	_____
_____	1-57248-122-6	Tenants' Rights in NY	$21.95	_____

NORTH CAROLINA TITLES

Qty	ISBN	Title	Retail	Ext.
_____	1-57248-185-4	How to File for Divorce in NC (3E)	$22.95	_____
_____	1-57248-129-3	How to Make a NC Will (3E)	$16.95	_____
_____	1-57248-184-6	How to Start a Business in NC (3E)	$18.95	_____
_____	1-57248-091-2	Landlords' Rights & Duties in NC	$21.95	_____

OHIO TITLES

Qty	ISBN	Title	Retail	Ext.
_____	1-57248-190-0	How to File for Divorce in OH (2E)	$24.95	_____
_____	1-57248-174-9	How to Form a Corporation in OH	$24.95	_____
_____	1-57248-173-0	How to Make an OH Will	$16.95	_____

PENNSYLVANIA TITLES

Qty	ISBN	Title	Retail	Ext.
_____	1-57248-242-7	Child Custody, Visitation and Support in Pennsylvania	$26.95	_____
_____	1-57248-211-7	How to File for Divorce in PA (3E)	$26.95	_____
_____	1-57248-094-7	How to Make a PA Will (2E)	$16.95	_____
_____	1-57248-112-9	How to Start a Business in PA (2E)	$18.95	_____
_____	1-57071-179-8	Landlords' Rights and Duties in PA	$19.95	_____

TEXAS TITLES

Qty	ISBN	Title	Retail	Ext.
_____	1-57248-171-4	Child Custody, Visitation, and Support in TX	$22.95	_____
_____	1-57248-172-2	How to File for Divorce in TX (3E)	$24.95	_____
_____	1-57248-114-5	How to Form a Corporation in TX (2E)	$24.95	_____
_____	1-57071-417-7	How to Make a TX Will (2E)	$16.95	_____
_____	1-57248-214-1	How to Probate and Settle an Estate in TX (3E)	$26.95	_____
_____	1-57248-228-1	How to Start a Business in TX (3E)	$18.95	_____
_____	1-57248-111-0	How to Win in Small Claims Court in TX (2E)	$16.95	_____
_____	1-57248-110-2	Landlords' Rights and Duties in TX (2E)	$21.95	_____

SUBTOTAL THIS PAGE _____

SUBTOTAL PREVIOUS PAGE _____

Shipping — $5.00 for 1st book, $1.00 each additional _____

Illinois residents add 6.75% sales tax _____

Connecticut residents add 6.00% sales tax _____

TOTAL _____

To order, call Sourcebooks at 1-800-432-7444 or FAX (630) 961-2168 (Bookstores, libraries, wholesalers—please call for discount)
Prices are subject to change without notice.
Find more legal information at: **www.SphinxLegal.com**